Mission and Money

Theology and Mission in World Christianity

Edited by

Kirsteen Kim (*Leeds Trinity University, UK*)
Stephen B. Bevans (*Catholic Theological Union, Chicago, USA*)
Miikka Ruokanen (*University of Helsinki, Finland/*
Nanjing Union Theological Seminary, China)

VOLUME 1

The titles published in this series are listed at *brill.com/tmwc*

Mission and Money

Christian Mission in the Context of Global Inequalities

Edited by

Mari-Anna Auvinen-Pöntinen and Jonas Adelin Jørgensen

BRILL

LEIDEN | BOSTON

Library of Congress Cataloging-in-Publication Data

Names: Auvinen-Pöntinen, Mari-Anna, editor. | Jørgensen, Jonas Adelin, editor.
Title: Mission and money : Christian mission in the context of global inequalities / Edited by Mari-Anna Auvinen-Pöntinen and Jonas Adelin Jørgensen.
Description: Boston : Brill, 2016. | Series: Theology and mission in world Christianity ; volume 1 | Includes bibliographical references and index.
Identifiers: LCCN 2016008961 (print) | LCCN 2016009198 (ebook) | ISBN 9789004318304 (pbk. : alk. paper) | ISBN 9789004318496 (E-book)
Subjects: LCSH: Missions—Congresses. | Economics—Religious aspects—Christianity—Congresses. | Poverty—Religious aspects—Christianity—Congresses.
Classification: LCC BV2063.M558 2016 (print) | LCC BV2063 (ebook) | DDC 266—dc23
LC record available at http://lccn.loc.gov/2016008961

Typeface for the Latin, Greek, and Cyrillic scripts: "Brill". See and download: brill.com/brill-typeface.

ISSN 2452-2953
ISBN 978-90-04-31830-4 (paperback)
ISBN 978-90-04-31849-6 (e-book)

This book is printed on acid-free paper and produced in a sustainable manner.

Printed by Printforce, United Kingdom

Contents

Notes on Contributors

Dr. Mari-Anna Auvinen-Pöntinen
is General Secretary of the Finnish Ecumenical Council. Previously she worked as a missiologist in the Finnish Evangelical Lutheran Mission (FELM). She is a member of the Nordic Institute for Missiology and Ecumenism (NIME) board.

Prof. Stephen B. Bevans, SVD
is Professor of Mission and Culture at the Catholic Theological Union in Chicago. His profound work has concentrated on the theology of mission and contextual theology.

Prof. Jonathan J. Bonk
is serving as Research Professor of Mission at Boston University. He is also emeritus executive director at the Overseas Ministries Study Center in Winnipeg, Canada.

Prof. Ulrich Duchrow
is Professor of Systematic Theology at the University of Heidelberg in Germany. He is the co-founder and moderator of Kairos Europa, an ecumenical grass-roots network striving for economic justice.

Dr. Jonas Adelin Jørgensen
is Secretary General at the Danish Mission Council. He is also chairperson of the Nordic Institute for Missiology and Ecumenism (NIME) board.

Prof. Vesa Kanniainen
is Professor of Economics in the Department of Political and Economic Studies at the University of Helsinki. His research areas are ethics and economics, entrepreneurship, public finance, corporate finance, and evolutionary studies.

Prof. Veli-Matti Kärkkäinen
is Professor of Systematic Theology at Fuller Theological Seminary in Pasadena, California, USA. He is also a docent of ecumenics at the University of Helsinki.

Prof. Tinyiko Sam Maluleke
is Professor of Theology at the University of Pretoria in South Africa. He is a missiologist by training and has published widely in the areas of mission

history, postcolonial studies of Christianity, and the intersection between religion and politics.

Prof. Gerrie Ter Haar
is an emerita professor of Religion and Development at the International Institute of Social Studies (ISS) of Erasmus University, Rotterdam. She is a scholar of religion and development with 30 years of experience in African studies.

Dr. Evi Voulgaraki-Pissina
teaches Missiology, History of Religions, Homiletics and Scientific Methodology at the Ecclesial Academy of Athens. Her research areas are mission and interreligious studies, religion and politics, patristics, and late antiquity.

Prof. Mika Vähäkangas
is Professor of Mission Studies and Ecumenics at the Lund University, Sweden. He is the current president of the International Association for Mission Studies (IAMS).

Prof. Felix Wilfred
is an emeritus professor at the State University of Madras. He is also Director of the Asian Centre for Cross Cultural Studies in Tamilnadu, India.

Introduction

Jonas Adelin Jørgensen and Mari-Anna Auvinen-Pöntinen

Why "Mission and Money"?

From the 4th to the 7th of April 2014 scholars from all over the world gathered at the ecumenical Cultural Center Sofia in Helsinki for a three-day conference—IAMS Europe[1]—in order to discuss mission in the context of global inequalities. Most of the scholars were missiologists, anthropologists and development researchers, but the conference had also invited economists to talk about the ethics of the global economy.

The starting point for the Nordic Institute for Missiology and Ecumenism (NIME) and the Finnish organizing committee was the challenge that is raised by the World Council of Churches' new missiological document, *Together towards Life; Mission and Evangelism in Changing Landscapes* (TTL 2012), which criticizes the world economy and seems to demonize money.[2] However, rather than merely claiming that serving "mammon" and giving into greed runs counter to Christian values, this view is about acknowledging that there may be something further that Christian mission needs to take into account.

The document also contains a controversial idea of mission. It talks about the "mission from the margins"[3] that recognizes all such structures that preserve the status quo of those "in the centre": those who have access to resources and rights. However, the document states that mission is not something to take people from the margins to the center but rather to reveal all those structures that dehumanize people and push them to the margins in the first place. According to the document, these include, for example, paternalism, patriarchalism, racism, casteism, and the oppression of indigenous people. Moreover, it talks about "market ideology" as one of those systems that maintain people in positions of either wealth or poverty. For better understanding of this kind of mission there is an urgent need to start a debate that addresses those structures and values that construct injustice and poverty.

1 International Association for Mission Studies European Conference (IAMS Europe) 2014 Helsinki, Finland.

2 TTL 2012, § 1, 30–31, 108. See http://www.oikoumene.org/en/resources/documents/commissions/mission-and-evangelism/together-towards-life-mission-and-evangelism-in-changing-landscapes.

3 TTL 2012, § 38–43.

 | DOI 10.1163/9789004318496_002

With the conference, we as organizers wanted to build bridges between missiology and economic studies in order to discover whether there are structures in global economics that could be challenged for ethical or spiritual reasons and to see whether insights may be found by working together. In short, we felt that an interdisciplinary perspective would be more fruitful than one that merely reflects negative attitudes towards something that is unfamiliar for the vast majority of missiologists. As one of the economics students asked: "Why don't you recognize economics as a tool to assist in improving living conditions, for example in Africa? Why demonize the whole arena of global economy, when economic principles can also be seen as instruments to be used for doing good?" Thus the conference aimed to build a platform for discussion between different spheres whereby missiology could benefit from the knowledge of economists and perhaps also vice versa; obviously the underlying larger issue is to seek scholarly cooperation in preventing marginalization and poverty. However, the conference was just a starting point, a first step forward, in a discussion often marginalized in academic missiological studies.

To further the discussion, this book presents a collection of reworked keynote presentations from the conference that cast light on the nexus of mission, theology, politics and economics. Considering the individual chapters in this volume in terms of the challenge highlighted above, it is obvious that what we have in mind is not simply to draw attention to the economic dimension of mission, let alone fundraising. Rather we have been asking ourselves more fundamental questions about the relation between economic power, development and shifting economies, and Christian mission. In other words, with this book we intend to engage and contribute to current academic studies of mission and global Christianity from an intentionally critical perspective, drawing on a number of critical theories and analyzing the challenges that present themselves to Christian communities and churches in a world of inequality. We believe that this book maps out and qualifies our future understanding and missiological discussions of these questions.

Critical Thinking, Economics, and Mission Studies

Critical thinking in the broad sense—understood as the ability to evaluate, compare, analyze, critique, and synthesize information—is integral to modern academic studies. The aim has been to release humans from their self-incurred tutelage; that is, critical thinking comprises liberating and self-liberating thought. Critical thinking thus becomes an ongoing process, a task, and an obligation, which aims at liberating humans from their immaturity, that is, the certain state of our will that prompts us to accept someone else's authority in areas where our own reason is called for.

From our perspective, mission studies is in a state of "immaturity" in respect to current economic crises and shifting economic powers, in that it lacks critical thinking focused on the relation between Christian missions and the logic of capitalized economies. The immaturity displays itself in the apparent lack of critical assessment of the relationship both on the side of secular academic approaches and from a religious and committed practitioner's approach. However, this need not be so: in our view, a missiological perspective presupposes a set of values as a starting point and has the capacity to engage critically with any subject of study, including economics.

What, then, is the set of values that has caused us to focus on money, debt, and inequality? Economy and ecumenism share the same linguistic root, namely *oekumenia*, 'household': what binds us together—economically as well as theologically—is that we are part of a common household. The theoretical exploration of globalization—again, both economically as well as theologically—has produced a vast number of studies that demonstrate how we are interconnected. Spurred on by the financial crises since 2008, we ask how inequalities affect mission and our attempts at partnership.

In a recent ecumenical statement, the values are formulated as follows:

> Recalling Christ, the host at the banquet, and committed to that unity for which he lived and prayed, we are called to ongoing co-operation, to deal with controversial issues and to work towards a common vision. We are challenged to welcome one another in our diversity, affirm our membership through baptism in the One Body of Christ, and recognize our need for mutuality, partnership, collaboration and networking in mission, so that the world might believe.[4]

This quotation points out the challenges in researching and discussing mission and money: diversity versus oneness, mutuality versus independence, partnership versus autonomy. The Christian theological vision centers on oneness and common hope. Our reality consists of diversity and inequalities. The area of reality which is most remote from the theological vision of oneness and common hope is the economy—which also includes the economic structures in mission work. Mutuality and partnership do not extend to budgeting in mission organizations and churches! If this is so, what might it entail to be part of the same household, the same *oekumenia*?

4 Edinburgh 2010 Common Call, 8.

In more detail, the problematic relation between mission and money may be subdivided into a number of problematic areas with which the individual chapters engage: gender aspects and the critique of patriarchal societies, where private ownership, debt, and male supremacy seem to be interrelated; economic inequality and the lack of political will to redistribute resources in a just way; or ecological disasters following modern industrial production, where consumption and greed lead to over-exhaustion of natural resources.

The new reverse missions from Africa, South Asia, and South America to Europe also raise a number of questions: To what degree does the prosperity gospel shape the mission of migrant churches? Are the migrants economic winners or losers? Does the prosperity gospel prescribe effective economic behavior—even if it is counterfeit theology? We know too little about the ethos shaped by these forms of charismatic Christian theology; again, our expertise as researchers is needed in this area.

The role of mission and Christianity in global inequalities also raises serious questions about the ability of Christian missions to transform individuals and societies in ways that reduce poverty. Have Christian missions really been friends of the poor—or have they rather been friends to poverty, establishing it as a permanent condition for converts and descendants? Our intuition is that the latter is not so—but we need data and research that substantiates the claim that mission and conversion is good in all areas of life: in economic terms as well as in the broader development frame.[5]

Introducing Chapters

This book is divided into three different sections. In Part 1 Professor Veli-Matti Kärkkäinen starts the discussion by drawing attention to theological reflections on money and mobility within Christian thinking. His article, "A Theological-Missiological Reflection on Money and Mobility in the Globalizing World", is actually the key note speech of the preconference that took place in Sofia 3–4.4.2013. This speech begins the discussion and approaches the question of mission and money from the Trinitarian theological point of view, taking account of the changing phenomenon of mobility as an ethical question.

5 One valuable starting point in this regard is provided by sociologist of religion, Robert Woodberry, who in "Missionary Roots of Liberal Democracy" (published in American Political Science Review, Vol. 106, No. 2, May 2012), has demonstrated statistically and argued historically that Christian missions have led not only to individual and existential transformation but also to societal development and economic growth.

Part II introduces the actual plenary speeches of the conference. The first article is Professor Vesa Kanniainen's "Ethics and Global Economics", which focuses on poverty and the mechanisms behind its changes during the second phase of globalization. Furthermore he deals with questions of equity and economic efficiency and discusses the development of human morality. Professor Kanniainen is an economist, but he also draws examples and quotations from the Bible to enlighten his moral arguments. Professor Felix Wilfred, in his article "Asian Perspectives on Global Economic Inequality", postulates a phenomenal growth of inequalities in relation to the neoliberal economy, with particular references to Asian contexts. He studies ideas and strategies that might lead towards greater equality and justice in the world and finally evaluates how religions could contribute to this positive development. It is obvious that Professor Wilfred holds capitalism to be one of those economic structures that should be challenged.

Professor Tinyiko Sam Maluleke, for his part, examines the roots and implications of the fundamental contradictions of Christian mission in the world today, namely that although the Christian center of gravity has numerically shifted from the North to the South, the economic centre of gravity is still firmly located in the North. Using South Africa as a case study, he traces the pathology of Christian mission towards wealth to the legacy of 19th and 20th century Christian missionary teachings. He argues that this legacy coupled with current contradictions account, in part, for contemporary missiological impotence in the face of global inequality. His critical insights, offered from a postcolonial perspective, unlock questions regarding missions and money during the colonial era and also in its aftermath in the present, suggesting new approaches to the mission of the churches and their attitude towards human wellbeing. Professor Gerrie ter Haar offers a different perspective, namely that of African International Churches, in her chapter "Poverty and Power: African Challenges to Christian Mission". In her contribution she specifically focuses on their idea of mission, which differs from most Western approaches.

Moving on from this Dr. Evi Voulgaraki-Pissina examines the context of inequalities within Europe, especially the relatively new form of poverty in Southern Europe and more particularly in Greece, and the challenges they pose from an Orthodox theological point of view to traditional missiological awareness and understanding. In her article, "The Mission of the Church amidst European Social and Economic Crisis; The Case of Greece", she calls churches to a holistic mission that would combine *martyria* (witness), social *diaconia*, and grass roots justice. Professor Ulrich Duchrow for his part uses a liberation theological lens in his article "Interreligious Liberation Theologies, Money and Just Relations". He is critical towards the nexus of debt-economies, patriarchy, and warfare, proposing spiritual and inter-religious co-work as an alternative in liberating activities.

Professor Jonathan Bonk, in his article "Economic Development and Christian Mission: A Perspective from History of Mission", evaluates development and its underlying motifs in the light of historical missiological activities. He argues that development often derives from motives other than those of really helping the neighbor, advocating the importance of changed attitudes and grass roots action instead of massive projects.

Part III of this volume includes a panel speech that took place in the last session of the conference, "Mission and Money in Two Recent Mission Documents: The WCC's *Together towards Life* and Pope Francis's *Evangelii Gaudium*", in which Professor Stephen Bevans evaluates two important mission documents. Professor Bevans also takes into full account the originating impetus for the conference and therefore his speech is included in this book. His speech is followed by a response to the whole discussion by Professor Mika Vähäkangas that contains his reflections on the basic questions that arose during the conference. His discourse, "Mission and Money: Mapping the Field", concludes the book.

A Word of Thanks

The chapters of this book emerge from the keynote presentations at the 2014 European Missiological Conference (IAMS Europe) and three shorter reflections taking place during the conference, though numerous other papers and considerable fruitful discussion also took place which could not be included in this volume. However, we hope that the discussion will progress and that the present book will contribute to further debate. We want to conclude this introduction by thanking all those attending and taking active part in the gathering. At this point we also owe special thanks to the keynote speakers and their respondents for accepting our invitations to attend. Although based on the presentations made at the conference, each of the contributions included in this volume was further revised in light of comments and input received at the conference and subjected to the further process of a rigorous peer review system, which has led to the current versions published here. We therefore owe further gratitude to our keynote speakers for sparing valuable time and scholarly effort to rewrite their presentations into chapters for this volume. Similarly we owe gratitude to the writers of the shorter reflections in Parts I and III.

We also want to thank the rest of the Finnish committee who planned the conference with us, including Professor Mika Vähäkangas, Dr. Jyri Komulainen and Dr. Pekka Lund. Similarly we want to thank the other members of the NIME board, namely doctoral student Aron Engberg, who is the board's secretary, Dr. Kristin Norseth and doctoral student Niklas Holmefur. In addition, we want to give thanks to the other organizing bodies: the Federation of Finnish Learned Societies, the Centre for Theology and Religious Studies at Lund University, the Faculty of Theology at the University of Helsinki, the Danish Mission Council and the Finnish Evangelical Lutheran Mission. We owe gratitude to the special listeners group of Professor Stephen Bevans, Professor Jesse Mugambi, Dr. Cathy Ross and Mrs. Eleonora Hof who imparted their spirit of wisdom to the conference. Regarding this book we thank Editor Mirjam Elbers from Brill, for her support of our manuscript proposal for the Mission Studies Supplement Series, and our proofreader Dr. Marie-Louise Karttunen.

On behalf of NIME and the local Finnish committee

Jonas Adelin Jørgensen
Chair, NIME board

Mari-Anna Auvinen-Pöntinen
Organizer of the conference

PART 1

CHAPTER 1

A Theological-Missiological Reflection on Money and Mobility in the Globalizing World

Veli-Matti Kärkkäinen

Money, Mobility, and Global Economics as a Theological Task

Let me begin this reflection on "Mission and Money"[1]—a topic whose time has not only come but is past due—with a couple of observations, both of which are worth mentioning despite their apparent obviousness. Firstly, on the relationship between *mission* and money: although missionaries and mission agencies have always talked about money—and indeed love money quite passionately! —we all know that that talk has been limited and specific. It has had to do with how to finance missions. Of course that is an important issue but money matters so much more in this complex global environment of ours. Add to that the mobility of money, goods, services, and people—and a picture containing considerable space for controversy and multiple interpretations begins to emerge. Secondly, on the relationship between *theology* and money: that is a theme that has received even less study and reflection. Indeed, it is almost shocking how little theologians have pondered upon the meaning of money. What Miroslav Volf has said about the lack of theological reflection on work, equally applies to the theme of money: he wonders why it is that theologians have devoted such an inordinate amount of time to the topics which occupy us for an hour on Sunday morning (sacramental theology) but have almost totally ignored what happens during the rest of the week!

My aim in this short essay is to offer some theological reflections on the meaning of money to Christian theology and mission in the context of global economics. I seek to draw from two kinds of resources: firstly, I make an effort to tap into the most distinctive feature of Christian tradition, that of Trinitarian theology; secondly, I listen carefully to what scholars of globalization,

1 I have kept the documentation to minimum because the topics treated here are discussed in detail in the following publications (with detailed documentation): Kärkkäinen, *Trinity and Revelation*, ch. 13; idem, *Creation and Humanity*, ch. 16.

 | DOI 10.1163/9789004318496_003

international politics, economy, sociology, and other "secular" fields are telling about money and mobility. I am convinced that examing the meaning of money and economics is a deeply theological task. It is an essential aspect in the continuing Christian pursuit of justice, equality, and fairness. Each and every human person created in the image of God deserves that.

The remainder of this essay consists of two sections. In the first part, I seek to identify and clarify some key aspects of economic marginality in our complex global situation. Therein, I wish to help theologians and missiologists to join the ongoing interdisciplinary conversation about some key aspects of global economics. The second part offers a theological response and few broad guidelines based on Trinitarian theological resources.

The Complex Task of Identifying Economic Marginality in the "Hybrid" Global Community

The analysis of the implications of money and mobility is a complex and challenging task at the beginning of the third millennium, a complexity that post-colonialists often describe with the term "hybrid". Hybridity refers to the bewildering diversity of societies and communities in terms of cultures, nationalities, ethnicities, identities, economic systems, and other markers which used to be easily identifiable. It suffices to give an obvious example: even determining one's own ethnicity has become a difficult task for numerous humans, and a related issue is that of identifying of nationality: ethnicity and language can any longer do so unambiguously. Boundary lines are blurred. As a result, racism is currently a highly fluid and elusive phenomenon that goes far beyond skin color to comprise a network of effects related to ethnicity, religions, economy, power structures, location, and so forth. When coupled with colonialism and slavery, as has happened with African Americans and the First Nations, it means nothing less than transforming human beings into commodities. Just think of the *Dalit* in India. Correctly, the Korean American theologian Sang Hyun Lee speaks of marginality in terms of "liminality," which refers to "the situation of being in between two or more worlds, and includes the meaning of being located at the periphery or edge of a society."[2] Such is life to the masses in our hybrid global village.

One part of the complexity of identifying the role of money has to do with the fact that it is intertwined with so many other issues. Just think of unemployment and the loss of a sense of meaningfulness of many unemployed—

2 Lee, *From a Liminal Place*, x.

and, on the other hand, the fatigue of many overworked. Or think of the sense of alienation in current anonymous work environments whose sole aim is efficiency, and so forth. Add to these viewpoints the effects of the growing gulf between the haves and have-nots; increasing migration because of economic (and socio-political) reasons; and new forms of slavery, including sexual slavery.

Indeed, in our hybrid world, many forms of economic oppression are subtle and delicate. Marginalization is often coupled with forces of dehumanization which is not only about genocide or other crimes against humanity, but may also be related to ethnicity, race, and immigration. Dehumanization may take the form of a certain presentation of women (or children or even men) as merely sexual objects in pornography. The objectification of women (and girls) may also take place in the culture's presentation of what makes femininity—coupled with a wide use of sexual symbols in marketing. It is these and other kinds of subtle forms of marginalization which often go unnoticed and yet have far-reaching effects on the majority of the world's population. They are often invisible and hence continue their harmful effects "behind the scenes." I propose that theologians and missiologists badly need to begin to collaborate with scholars in the various fields which study these phenomena. Only a wide interdisciplinary investigation may properly inform theological and missiological reflection.

So far we have talked about globalization as if everyone meant the same when using the term, but this is far from the case: its meaning is highly contested. A notoriously complex topic, not only economists, sociologists, and politicians but also philosophers and some theologians seek a proper understanding. It can be seen as either a positive or negative force, and it certainly has element of both sides to it. An essential part of "hyper-modern" globalization has to do with "culture industries," perhaps the most subtle and most powerful influence worldwide, that aim to shape global consumption, backed by massive advertising and marketing. While a number of globalization theorists speak of the consequences of global economy in terms of "calculations of risk"[3] (of medical, social, ecological, and other side-effects), theologians should concentrate on the effects of global economy on human persons.

Unlike the agrarian societies of the past, currently we live in a world in which the "desire to live one's own life has become the guiding impulse for people in the Western world... The ethic of individual self-interest and self-fulfilment have been given free rein in economic globalization and have become the most

---

3 See Hutton and Giddens, *On the Edge*; see also the pamphlet (originally lectures) by Giddens, *The Consequences of Modernity*.

powerful currents affecting human beings."[4] At the same time, people suffer from what the British philosopher-theologian Graham Ward has named "social atomism," or isolation in the midst of masses of other people.

Globalizing trends are not merely modern phenomena but go much farther back in history. Just think of the massive occupation of not only land and resources in the Majority World by the Western powers beginning in the late eighteenth century but also of colonialism's ideological, cultural, and epistemological oppression, and other means of violence. Lest it be mistakenly assumed that this only happened from the West to the "rest," (as dominant as that was), the same hegemonic abuse of power was in play, for example, in the subjugation of Korea by Japan in the early twentieth century and in the expansion of China over some of its neighboring territories. Though old, colonialism is still alive and well—meanwhile adopting new forms such as "McDonaldization."[5] Indeed, what is happening is that globalization "often seems to replace the old dictatorships of national elites with the new dictatorships of international finance."[6]

Whatever the meaning of globalization may be, it is clear that a defining feature of the global village is not only the mobility of money and resources but also of people, with one of the most distinguishing features of the postmodern milieu being the return of the nomadic lifestyle. Migration, immigration, and displacement have become standard features. While displacement, including landlessness, is of course not a new phenomenon, the nature of migration now is vastly different from the past. The leading sociologist of globalization, Zygmunt Bauman, has famously made a distinction between "tourists" and "vagabonds." Whereas tourists travel because they can, vagabonds are on the move because they do not have a choice and are regarded as useless to global markets because, as outcasts, they do not make good consumers. Indeed, they are marginalized even though they comprise the majority of the world, and their numbers are growing rapidly.

In this mobile world, slavery has not been eradicated and seems to be doing well though an astonishing and horrific aspect of its contemporary forms is that the price paid per human is dramatically lower than it used to be. If in the past a human was valued at the equivalent of about $40,000 in today's money, the average price of a modern slave is currently less than $100![7] Part of the wider slavery problem is the increasing traffic in labor and sex, which

---

4 Botman, "Covenantal Anthropology," 77–78 (77), engaging the ideas of Waters, *Globalization*.

5 Ritzer, *The McDonaldization of Society*.

6 Siglitz, *Globalization and Its Discontents*, 7, cited in Meeks, "Economy of Grace," 199.

7 Freetheslaves.net, FAQ's, http://www.freetheslaves.net/Document.Doc?id=37 (10/16/2013).

also includes children, the under-aged, and a high number of female victims. Those subjected to (economically and politically) forced migration and all forms of slavery and trafficking not only lack human value but also even minimal living conditions—and almost all of them are landless. This last issue should be considered in light of the observation of the famed OT theologian Walter Brueggemann, namely that "land is a central, if not *the central theme of* biblical faith."[8]

Before attempting a theological response to global economics, let me add an observation which may sound counterproductive. I agree with the Catholic Douglas Meek, the leading theologian of economics:

> The modern market system undoubtedly should be extolled as the most successful human instrument in modernity. Even beyond its effect in the astonishing growth in living standards, its most winsome and weighty claim is that it coordinates and governs masses of human beings peacefully, without command or coercion.[9]

The implication here is that theology should be able to do something further than merely "bark" at global economics.

The "Economy of Grace": Towards a Theology of Global Economics

I wish to begin my theological response with the help of a deeply held Christian conviction, based on the theology of Trinity: the idea of divine hospitality. In classical theology, God is both the Giver and Gift. Hence, to speak of God is to speak of giving, gift, and hospitality. No one else in the history of theology has spoken of this theme as powerfully as Martin Luther. At the end of his programmatic *Heidelberg Disputation* (thesis # 28), the Reformer differentiates absolutely free divine love from self-centered, conditional human love. Whereas human love is always oriented towards something which the human person may enjoy, God's love is self-giving: "The love of God does not find, but creates, that which is pleasing to it... Rather than seeking its own good, the love of God flows forth and bestows good." God's love seeks that which is worthless in itself and donates not only gifts but one's self. At the cross, God's self-giving *kenosis*, the most profound act of hospitality, came to its fullest expression.

---

8 Brueggemann, *The Land*, 3.

9 Meeks, "The Economy of Grace," 197.

Along with hospitality and giving, the Christian symbol of the Trinity also speaks of community, belonging, and sharing. The Trinity speaks of the community of equal, yet distinct persons. In classical theology this truth was expressed with the term *perichoresis*, mutual indwelling, a vision of an eternal, divine round dance. The Trinitarian symbol is a profound expression of solidarity with the world.

Based on these widely held theological convictions, I wish to term the Christian response "economy of grace" or "economy of God."[10] Despite the many similarities between the market system and Christian ethics, such as the value placed work and industry, personal and communal responsibility, demand for fairness, and so forth, there are a number of deep differences. Competition, greed, and maximization of profit are foreign to the Christian vision of divine hospitality. Indeed, Christian theology and global market ideology contain directly opposing beliefs. As detailed in Douglas Meek's *God the Economist*, while both view human beings as a creature of desire, "Christian anthropology imagines the end of the human being as praise of God; the market system views the end of the human being as maximized utility." The market calls for unending pursuit of the satisfaction of needs while in the Christian vision, true "enjoyment" (Augustine's *fruit*) can only be had in God and "in participation in the abundance of God's communion through God's grace."[11] The vicious circle of the market system's constant creation of "artificial scarcity" which imposes constantly new needs and products to fulfill them, coupled with massive ubiquitous advertising, can be broken only by desiring God and the moderate fulfillments that God the Creator graciously grants to creatures.

Based on these theological resources, let us attempt to formulate a few broad guidelines with a view to helping Christians think about the use of resources, that is, a theology of global economics. Let me frame them in the following manner and then try to clarify and illustrate each point:

1) The inviolability of each human person as the image of God;
2) The human vocation of service and sharing, based on the Trinitarian theology of communion and divine hospitality;
3) The stewardship principle according to which, as vice-regents, human beings are to be caretakers not only of human communities but also the community of nature and the environment.

---

10 I am following here Meeks, "Economy of Grace." For a more detailed discussion, see his *God the Economist*.

11 Meeks, "Economy of Grace," 205.

Firstly, the inviolability of each human person supports the principle of freedom and dignity of all. Contributing substantially to human dignity is access to meeting basic needs such as hunger, thirst, rest, safety, belonging to community, and the opportunity to pursue meaningful life. The right to work similarly belongs to those values. Economic theorist Adam Smith's advocacy of the division of labor primarily on the basis of pursuit of self-interest and self-love, although probably true as an empirical statement, cannot be endorsed uncritically on the basis of gospel values. On the other hand, while working towards a system of economic sharing which would help all men and women meet these basic needs, theology should also critique the fundamental ideology of contemporary societies, both capitalist and socialist, which is based on the hegemony of desires. We are beings of desires—unlimited desires! Modern economic theory exploits that basic human orientation as it claims that in the midst of limited resources, everybody has to compete.

Contrary to global economics, Christian theology says that true good is given only by God and that desire is no "god." Theology speaks of "Sabbath Economics: The Theology of Enough."[12] That will also help us negotiate the "paradox of abundance" (Walter Brueggemann): for us humans, security in abundance depends upon the wisdom of knowing that we are dependent upon God and that in our well-being, we rely on the health of the created order.[13]

Secondly, integral communion theology is needed to help overcome the rampant individualism of much of the contemporary world, particularly in the Global North. Trinitarian communion theology interrupts and defeats the self-centered "need-based" lifestyle where every affluent individual has become an idol whose lifestyle is funded by a consumerist culture in which all others have to suffer from scarcity in order to support that demonic pursuit of "happiness."

Whereas Christian vision supports freedom and liberty rightly understood, the market system's notion of freedom—framed primarily in terms of freedom of choice in order to best serve one's individual needs—must be subjected to theological critique which takes into account that hospitality, concern for the well-being and flourishing of other human beings and communities are true Christian values. Instead of *exclusive* property rights, the Christian vision funds *inclusive* rights in which all we have is acknowledged as a gift from God, of which we are to be good and responsible stewards in order to find fulfillment

12 Browning, "Sabbath Reflections 5."

13 Brueggemann, "Liturgy of Abundance, Myth of Scarcity."

as God's servants and in service to others. Ultimately, in the Christian vision, "God's grace is the being of the human; the human is the gift of God."[14]

Whereas the market system depends exclusively on the logic of exchange (currently handled with the help of money), the Christian vision also knows the logic of gift-giving and altruistic sharing, echoing the triune God's free gift-giving; this observation is, of course, not a naive denial of the great value of a fair and moderate system of commodity exchange but rather a move to put it in perspective. Instead of being governed by an anonymous logic of exchange, flourishing life requires personal sharing and the giving of gifts that foster interdependence, friendship, and mutuality, rather than debt, competition, and distance. The triune God has called a people to live in the world to reflect the values of justice, equality, and sharing. Faithfully acknowledging their debt to the Creator, the church is supposed to stand on the side of those who are oppressed and marginalized. Not only to the feed the hungry and offer a cup of water to the thirsty but also to stand up against injustice as the Old Testament prophets did, and at times Jesus of Nazareth.

Thirdly, creation theology's stewardship principle sustains a lifestyle which acknowledges the deep link between our own well-being and the flourishing of nature. We would not be here unless nature had been here before for us. Due to space restrictions, I do not have the opportunity to develop this theme in any detail; I am just leaving for our consideration the need to think of the theological implications of sharing global resources in a manner that facilitates the flourishing and renewal of nature.

In Lieu of Conclusions: A Word of Caution

Having argued in this essay that a distinctively Christian vision of money, mobility, and global economics has to be guided by trinitarian-theological resources, I have also made myself vulnerable to an obvious criticism. It is as if I heard the reader say, "Right, what you argue sounds good but isn't that but a cheap and naïve use of the doctrine of the Trinity in the service of a better life on this earth?" My response is: Indeed, I am well aware of that danger—and make every effort to avoid it. In fact, we must resist the tendency in contemporary theology to make the Trinity serve all kinds of human programs and ideas (even if they are worthy in themselves). The Trinity is not meant to be a "social program." It is a foundational statement about the eternal God, based on revelation. Furthermore, even at its best, there is only a partial correspondence

14 Meeks, "Economy of Grace," 210.

between the divine and human communities: whereas the divine is perfect, ours are not, and so forth. That said, there is every reason to take a cautious look at the nature of divine community and wonder if something could be learned from it for the sake of advancing the life of men and women, all of whom have been created in Trinity's image!

Having tackled economic issues from a distinctively theological rather than, say, political or financial point of view, may also subject me to the criticism of remaining at a hopelessly generic level. Should we not be more specific? Perhaps we should. That said, I also know that the task of theological reflection is never to micro-manage issues in the world, not even in the church! Theology speaks of vision, values, orientations. Much work is therefore left for practitioners in an ever-changing globalized world and unique contexts in terms of "practical applications" of theological principles.

Bibliography

Botman, Russell H., "Covenantal Anthropology: Integrating Three Contemporary Discourses of Human Dignity," pp. 72–86. In *God and Human Dignity.* Edited by Soulen R.K. and Woodhead L., Grand Rapids: Eerdmans, 2006.

Browning, Bishop George. "Sabbath Reflections 5: Capitalism and Inequity versus a Gospel Mandate." Anglican Communion Environmental Network, 2012: http://acen.anglicancommunion.org/resources/docs/Sabbath%20Study%205.pdf (8/14/2013).

Brueggemann, Walter. *The Land: Place as Gift, Promise, and Challenge in Biblical Faith.* Overtures to Biblical Theology 1. Philadelphia: Fortress, 1977.

———. "The Liturgy of Abundance, The Myth of Scarcity." At http://www.religion-online.org/showarticle.asp?title=533 (3/12/2013).

Freetheslaves.net, FAQ's, http://www.freetheslaves.net/Document.Doc?id=37 (10/16/2013).

Giddens, Anthony. *The Consequences of Modernity.* Oxford: Blackwell/Polity Press, 1990) available at http://pol.atilim.edu.tr/files/kuresellesme/kitaplar/The_Consequences_of_Modernity.pdf (8/14/2013).

Hutton, Will, and Anthony Giddens, eds. *On the Edge: Living with Global Capitalism.* London: Jonathan Cape, 2000.

Kärkkäinen, Veli-Matti. *Trinity and Revelation. A Constructive Christian Theology for the Pluralistic World,* vol. 2. Grand Rapids: Eerdmans, 2014.

———, *Creation and Humanity. A Constructive Christian Theology for the Pluralistic World,* vol. 3. Grand Rapids: Eerdmans, 2015.

Lee, Sang Hyun. *From a Liminal Place: An Asian American Theology.* Minneapolis: Fortress, 2010.

Meeks, M. Douglas. "The Economy of Grace: Human Dignity in Market System," pp. 72–86. In *God and Human Dignity.* Edited by R.K. Soulen and L. Woodhead. Grand Rapids: Eerdmans, 2006.

———. *God the Economist: The Doctrine of God and Political Economy.* Minneapolis: Fortress, 1989.

Ritzer, George. *The McDonaldization of Society.* Revised New Century Edition. Thousand Oaks, Calif.: Pine Forge Press, 2004.

Siglitz, Joseph E. *Globalization and Its Discontents.* New York: W.W. Norton, 2002.

Waters, Malcolm. *Globalization.* London: Routledge, 1996.

PART 2

CHAPTER 2

Ethics and Global Economics

Vesa Kanniainen

The world is not equally fair to all its inhabitants: the different stages of development experienced by different countries means that income and wealth are unevenly distributed both across and within various regions; access to education and health are often restricted; and life expectancy and the mortality rate of children fluctuate considerably. In some areas people earn more than they can consume; those born on oil fields, for example, have access to huge unproduced wealth while others have to live in misery and squalor, especially in the developing countries. Even in industrialized capitalist nations, inequalities in income are on the increase. Though the distribution of happiness and that of income and wealth do not exactly correlate, it is clear that people cannot be happy when living in absolute poverty. Conversely, people in possession of high incomes accompanied by considerable stress are not necessarily happier than those at subsistence levels in developing countries with a less hectic lifestyle.

What I plan to do in this article is to focus on measurable phenomena like poverty and the mechanisms behind its changes during the second phase of globalization;[1] on the conflict between equity and economic efficiency; and on what research tells us about ourselves as human beings, and the development of our morality. Occasionally I highlight the relationship between scientific studies and views from the Bible in the belief that we are moral creatures and that we have consciences. We know this by virtue of the anger we feel in the face of unfair behavior towards ourselves or our co-citizens, whereby we express our moral feelings of empathy and altruism. A powerful source of this kind of anger lies in the abuse perpetrated by global companies which subject their employees to sub-standard working conditions, and we respond to this, not by merely regretting global poverty and the uneven access of people in distant countries to reasonable living conditions, but also by arranging consumer

1 In this article the 'second phase' of the globalization process refers to the relocation of productive capital across countries, and the growth of world trade, phenomena that have lasted about 40 years. The first wave of globalization took place towards the end of the 19th century, interrupted by the start of the First World War in 1914. I abstract other features of the globalization process like the convergence of values—both good and bad—and cultures.

© KONINKLIJKE BRILL NV, LEIDEN, 2016 | DOI 10.1163/9789004318496_004 boycotts against such firms and using modern social media to disseminate information about such behavior globally.

One can problematize whether the development of our world is guided by a battle between "good" and "evil", something which leads to our querying whether we obtain a better world when the former triumphs over the latter. Or is this a fallacious perspective? As an economist, my guide when examining this issue over the past thirteen years has been provided by my lecture series, *Ethics and Economics*. During this time I have developed a strong commitment to studying what research efforts in various fields can teach us about ourselves as human beings, and the economic mechanisms which arise from our behavior.

Global Inequality: World Poverty

No doubt the most burning ethical issue of today is that, currently, 1.3 billion people across the globe live in conditions of absolute poverty, defined as access to a daily income of US$2 or less. Although alternative levels have been suggested and used as measures, the important point is that all of them reference a state of *absolute* poverty, something quite different to the poverty of those in industrialized countries who have access to a menu of social security options. In my country (Finland), for example, the poverty rate has doubled in the past two decades, rising from 6% in 1993 to 13% in 2009, while the figures are even higher for the EU as a whole—16% in 2009. We should bear in mind, however, that here we are talking about relative instead of absolute poverty.[2]

Nonetheless, while the huge figure of 1.3 billion destitute inevitably places a corresponding burden on the consciences of many who are more fortunate, it hides an important development that has taken place during the second globalization phase. The world has changed considerably during this period and, remarkably, the finding is that the newly industrialized economies have been subject to greater and more rapid economic growth than the old industrialized countries. Indeed, Dollar and Kraay (2007) have reported that the economic growth of those developing countries that have participated in the processes of globalization accelerated from 2.9% during the 1970s, to 3.5% during the 1980s, to 5.0% during the 1990s. The growth rates of rich countries and such developing countries which did not participate in globalization declined over the same period. This observation is explained by the benefits accruing from the

2 Relative poverty is measured by the proportion of the population whose disposable income falls below 60% of the median income of the population.

processes connected with globalization which, though they have been highly criticized, have unarguably led to a substantial improvement in the standard of living for millions of people who used to exist in absolute poverty.

Thirteen Years with Ethics and Economics

I was once asked by a reporter whether I considered it immoral for a company to lay off workers. I replied with a typical economic answer related to business cycles though, *ex post*, I was not happy with my response. I wanted to understand more deeply what actually happens in the economy and, importantly, the place in it for issues of morality. Over the course of many years, I have tried to examine, explain, and analyze the problems of human beings and their behavior, finally reaching a major conclusion: one cannot address and understand economic phenomena without understanding what kind of creatures we human beings are. Furthermore, one cannot understand the human soul without understanding where we come from in terms of the past conditions in which our ancestors lived.[3] In undertaking the exploration of these issues, I have tried to develop a synthesis of a large number of studies in archeology, evolutionary studies, moral philosophy, psychology, biology, and economics. Ultimately, it appears to be possible to summarize key findings from these combined fields with just one sentence: human beings are selfish, greedy, and given to opportunism, but they are also equipped with feelings of altruism and empathy.[4] Janus-faced indeed!

Greed is classified as the fifth of the seven deadly sins in Dante's Divina Commedia. The Bible's New Testament talks about giving up wealth (Luke 5:1–11, 12:33, 14:33; Mark 2:13–17) and criticizes both the property which controls us (Mark 4:19, 10:25; Luke 8:14) and those who focus on its ownership (Matt 6:24; Luke 16:13). In the words of Jesus, it is easier for a camel to pass through the eye of a needle than for a rich person to enter the Kingdom of God. Yet we feel it in our heart when we observe injustice. This suggests that we indeed have a conscience. The Scot, Adam Smith, among the greatest of moral philosophers and the founder of economics as a new human science, called the conscience an *impartial spectator* in his influential work, *The Theory of Moral Sentiments*, in 1759. We want to do good for others, to make things right, but humans have

---

3 Though I have had the opportunity to "taste the tree of the knowledge", I am still left hungry.

4 In ethical economics, altruism refers to an action where a person pays a personal cost and yet still provides help, even to a genetically unrelated stranger. The case of the Bible's Good Samaritan is the classic example of such behavior.

an opportunistic gene: it is a matter of the threshold of temptation when Dr Jekyll becomes Mr. Hyde.[5] According to the Bible, a human being is a sinner, yet both the greed inside us and the ability to share are part of our makeup,[6] along with acknowledgment of the rules of fair play, one of which is something all global religions have endorsed: the Golden Rule: "Do unto others what you would have them to do unto you" (Mt. 7:12). In the language of research, this appeal represents the principle of reciprocity.

Meanwhile, Jesus offered advice to those who wish to change their lives: give up your wealth, give it to those in need, and follow him. Such a call appears radical. It should perhaps be interpreted in terms of the demand for temperance and a reordering of the values in one's life.[7]

The Economics of Stone-Age and Capitalist Systems

One cannot understand modern human economics without understanding how we used to live, though, naturally, one can only indirectly assess the lifestyles of our ancestors and the evolution of economic mechanisms. The key point, however, is that development from the past to the present serves a purpose. To put it briefly, more efficient institutions tend to replace those which are less efficient, a perspective that makes sense of studying the past. Residual markers of previous practice tell us how humans lived in earlier times, and we can, with thought, imagine additional mechanisms. Studying the markers, we come to realize that many of the economic and social mechanisms which we observe today must have been around for quite some time. In terms of such an inquiry, stone-age economics are a fascinating aid in explaining the capitalism of today.

Let us start, however, from the current world. The capitalist economic system is widely criticized for its uneven income distribution and its inability to provide well-being for all. The same criticism is directed at contemporary globalization processes. Those critical allegations are correct up to a point;

5 Adam Smith was the founder of what I would call an empirical moral philosophy in the sense that he accurately described the human being as he is in the real world. The idea of Dr Jekyll and Mr. Hyde appears in the novel by R.L. Stevenson (1886), another Scot, in which he examines the proposition that there may be two personalities within a single person, one apparently good and the other evil.

6 Numerous studies in psychology and economics have confirmed this view.

7 For many, if not for most, such an appeal is a challenging one. The economics of happiness has concluded that happiness tends to be relative. One's ownership, relative to that of one's neighbor, matters.

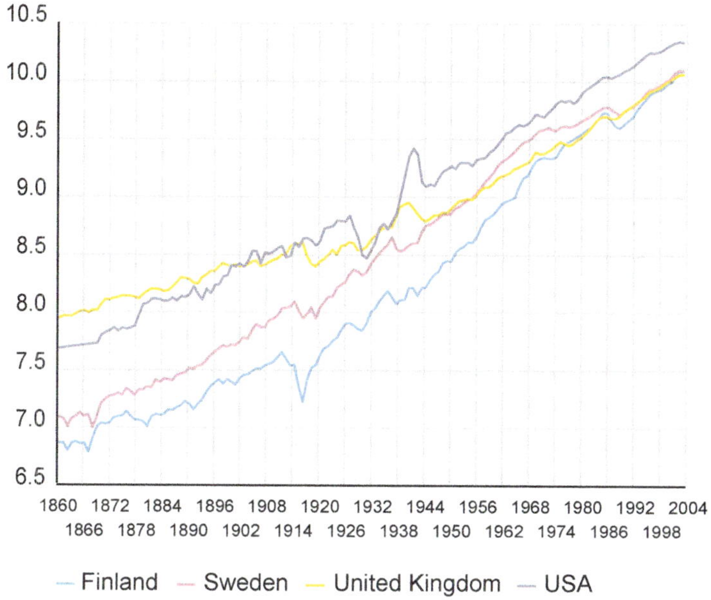

FIGURE 1 *The real gross national product per capita in Great Britain,* USA, *Sweden and Finland in 1960–2004.*
SOURCE: THE FIGURE IS BASED ON MADISON (2001), THE DATA HAS BEEN OBTAINED FROM BOLT AND ZANDEN (2013).

however, there is a caveat. By 2000, for example, the real standard of living in the developed countries had reached a level ten times higher than it was 100 years earlier (see Figure 1 above on the GDP per capita 1900–2000 in Europe). But is one hundred years a long period? Not really. From the perspective of human history, it is a tiny moment.

The second point to which I want to devote attention is the question of what we actually mean by the term "capitalism". In the interests of scientific exactitude, I have come to define capitalism as a system resting on three basic institutions: first, well-defined property rights; second, access to free contracting; and third, the principle of limited liability.[8]

8 The principle of limited liability in financial contracts underpins the growth of large-scale companies. By facilitating the diversification of risks, large financial resources have been collected to create the products and the material property to which we have access today: there is not a single, let us say communist, firm in the world able to produce modern products. When a Marxian academician travels, she flies in a capitalist airplane, she has an iPad or PC manufactured on capitalist principles, and her cosmetics are produced by a capitalist cosmetic company. Collective public goods are produced by central and local governments but only in a few cases do governments produce private goods, with public education and public health care the most noticeable exceptions.

While it has been a long journey from the economies of the ancients, the hunter-gatherers, to modern capitalism in terms of markets and sophisticated financial systems, there is, however, something apparently common to both: the principle of property rights. Once humans learned how to make fire, their social and economic life changed forever.[9] They presumably started to develop property rights over the food which they prepared for those who shared their hearths. At the same time the hunting of big game helped establish the principle of co-operation across a broader group because of its high risk. The catch being stochastic also led to the important principle of food sharing: the first insurance and risk management institution among humans,[10] strengthened by the need to protect small societies from outside threat. From a moral perspective, the important capital which developed was trust and reciprocity within a given society, facilitating exchange and fostering the important idea of the gratitude connected with indebtedness.

While this all sounds somewhat speculative, the idea of property rights unarguably had a breakthrough when people began to settle in one place in order to cultivate agricultural products, something which would not have been possible with free access to the fruits of someone else's work. While the hunters only had access to a minor type of capital—their spear or bow—the rise of agricultural production some 10,000 years ago in the area located in what was later Turkey, Mesopotamia and the Nile necessitated the ownership of the productive capital: land or "real property" in the modern sense. Everyone today understands the role played by private ownership in creating the incentives to make the effort required to take care of oneself and one's family.

The rest of the historical overview can be abbreviated by reference to innovations, the development of trade and markets (recall the Silk Road and mercantile maritime exploration), and the emergence of sophisticated financial instruments. What is important for us to see is that the developments I have described have served people in their natural desires to survive and guarantee the lives of their offspring. It is not that "bad capitalism" has been created by bad people but rather that the development of capitalism over time has been a process which has occasionally led to dreadful experiments accompanied by substantial pain and economic loss; some have even

9 Wrangham (2009) has a fascinating description of this process based on a large body of studies.

10 The Bible provides the first description of business cycles in terms of seven good years followed by seven years of crop failures, and the first description of building inventories as an insurance system.

threatened the break-up of the whole capitalist system.[11] Both the division of labor and exchange (trade) have always been fundamental economic processes, something understood since Adam Smith (1789). A perceptive observation on the subject is introduced by Vernon Smith (2005), a Nobel Prize winner in economics, when he wrote about two worlds of human exchange, a formulation that I am convinced provides an accurate perspective:

> First, we live in a world of personal, social exchange based on reciprocity and shared norms in small groups, families, and communities.
>
> Second, we live in a world of impersonal market exchange where communication and cooperation gradually developed through long-distance trade between strangers. In acts of personal exchange, we usually intend to do good for others. In the marketplace this perception is often lost as each of us tends to focus on our own personal gain.[12]

Morality—When the Scientific Approach Meets the Religious One

The purpose of an economic system is to produce well-being in both an efficient and equitable way. Its functioning, however, is conditional on the maintenance of trust. What the above analysis seems to indicate is that though our behavior in relation to other people is governed by norms of mutual cooperation, this may be threatened by opportunism. However, when you think about it, it is astonishing how much trust each one of us meets every day in the market economy, not to mention in the personal exchange of services, sharing of joint activities, family life, and interaction among friends. What are the mechanisms which facilitate all this trust and the creation of social capital? There are many. In personal exchange, should you cheat your friend or your spouse, you are likely to lose him/her. The penalty is severe. In the market place, deception is more difficult to penalize but the importance of the good reputation of a company or business enterprise works in favor of limiting or avoiding short-sighted opportunism and the temptation to cheat. In both cases, humans have been able to develop social norms which represent the social capital within society and maintain its social structures.[13] While they are not written

11 I am referring, for example, to the bankruptcy of the Lehman Brothers investment bank in the USA on September 15, 2008.

12 Smith 2005.

13 It has been recognized that some social norms can be counter-productive. Moreover, the strictest norms can probably be found within organizations such as the mafia and gangs.

contracts, everyone knows of the existence of norms: they coordinate our behavior, strengthen the social capital in a given community, and their presence is witnessed by the morality and the ethical principles which we follow. In scientific language, morality emerges endogenously from within a society. Where do the religious principles enter the picture?

While studying these mechanisms, I came across a publication by Richard Holloway (1999), an English bishop who also explains morality in terms of the internal logic of societies—without resorting to religious doctrine! Yet the message of the sciences and that of the church are not contradictory; rather they are complementary in that both acknowledge the logic of morality as an internal process, but merely have a different focus. While the sciences limit their task to the positivist aspects of life, and research on those issues, religions go one step further by crossing the line to concern themselves with the normative aspects.[14]

With these findings in mind, we have a platform on which to commence the interpretation of some burning issues of today, beginning at the global level.

Some Good News: The Effect of Globalization on World Poverty

It is an astonishing fact that absolute poverty, measured by the percentage of the global population living on an income of below $1–$2 daily, has been declining over the past 40 years and is down by 50% (see Figure 2). Similarly, global inequality measured by the Gini-coefficient has also been declining over the past 30 years (see Figure 3).[15] Moreover, the UN human development index has risen in all parts of the word.[16]

See also Figure 4 on the decline of world poverty. It is, therefore, not the case that standards of living, for example, always develop in an adverse direction.

Moreover, there is surprisingly positive news from some African countries. According to Euromonitor International 2013, seven out of the ten fastest-growing economies in the world are African, including Ethiopia, Mozambique, Tanzania, Congo, Ghana, Zambia and Nigeria. In addition, Africa is now the

14 Mr. Holloway did likewise in the latter part of his book. The line of demarcation here is known as the Hume's guillotine, named after another great Scottish philosopher, David Hume, also writing in the 18th century.

15 The Gini coefficient has been developed by economists to measure the inequality of income distribution.

16 The rise from the 1980s to 2010 has been 45% in the least developed countries, 23% in Sub-Saharan Africa, and 49% in South Asia.

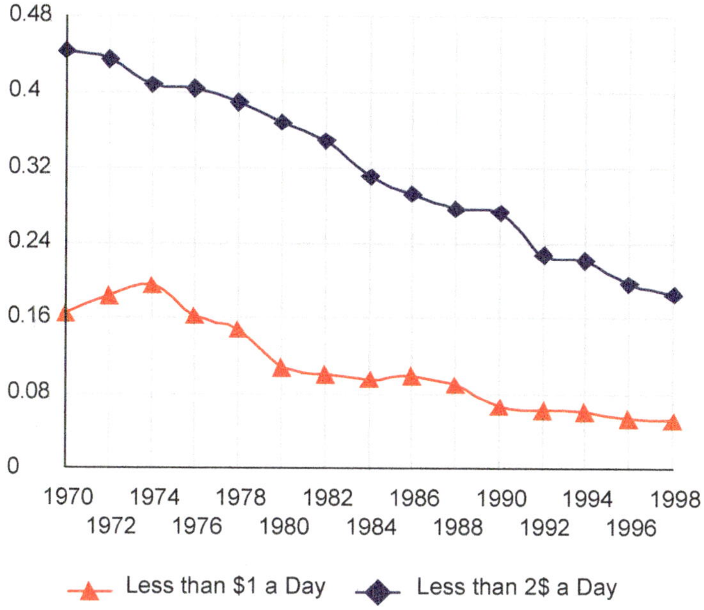

FIGURE 2 *World Poverty Rates.*
SOURCE: SALA-I-MARTIN, 2002, 2006.

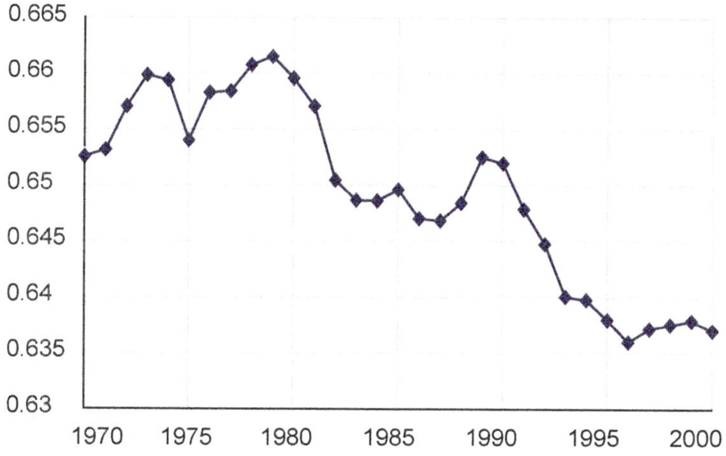

FIGURE 3 *Global Income Inequality: Gini.*
SOURCE: SALA-I-MARTIN, 2002, 2006.

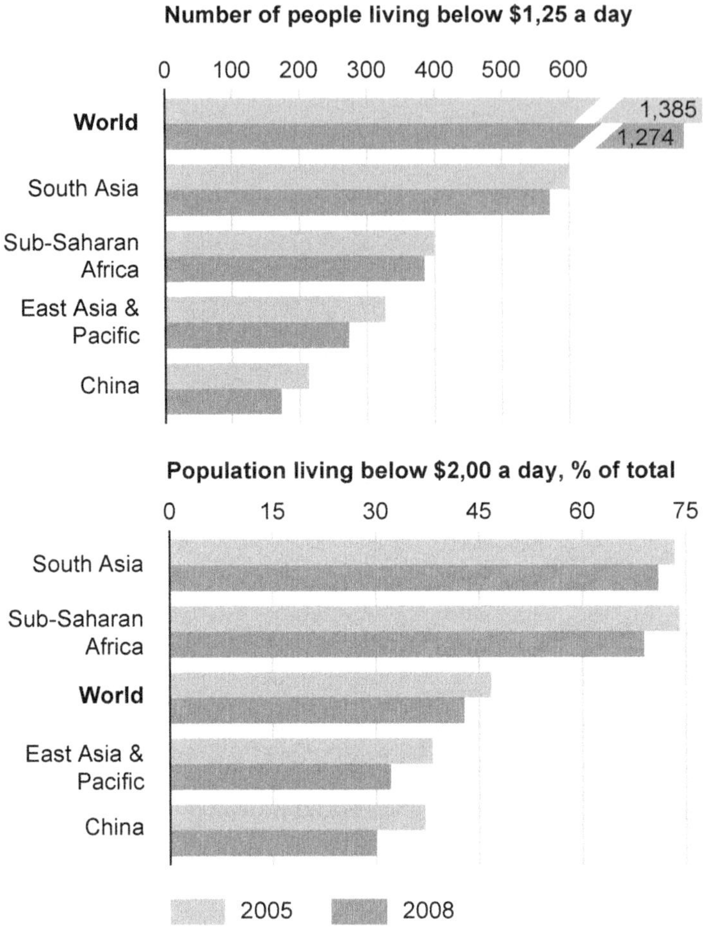

FIGURE 4 *World Poverty Continues to Decline.*
SOURCE: THE ECONOMIST, MARCH 3, 2012.

second fastest growing region, in economic terms, in the world, with GDP growth across its 54 countries estimated at 6% in 2012, according to the International Monetary Fund.

Why globalization? How do the principles of absolute and comparative advance dictate world development? One great insight provided by the prominent Enlightenment thinker, Adam Smith, lay in his description of the division of labor.[17] He claimed that people are different by virtue of their skills and, by

17 Some people appear skeptical about Adam Smith's metaphor of an "invisible hand" in the market place. The criticism is unfair on two grounds. Adam Smith wrote during a time when no modern economic research existed. Subsequently, and over the following two

exchanging their output, a win-win case becomes available. Economic exchange has for a long time been the key to development, and always will be, and the importance of this insight cannot be exaggerated. Practically all the products which we consume today are the results of exchange rather than self-production, and exchange benefits all parties. I myself do not produce any food, clothing, or technological devices—someone else has provided them all. On the other hand, I do produce teaching services for a university which pays me for doing so.[18]

At the global level, the idea of the division of labor is illustrated by international trade. It is important to understand that global exchange does not represent a zero-sum game but rather a matter of a win-win situation (for the skeptical reader, I refer to the Figures above). What is the logic, however? To explain the structure of international trade by the absolute cost advantage in production is very easy. Firms produce, or relocate to produce, in countries where the cost of production is lowest. If it is cheapest to produce product 1 in country A and product 2 in country B, it is easy to understand that their welfare is increased by moving the production of product 1 to country A, the production of product 2 to country B and arranging an exchange through trade. Adam Smith was again the first to notice this principle of absolute advantage. What is, however, more difficult to understand is that the exchange is a win-win case also where one country has the absolute cost advantage in the production of both commodities, a counter-intuitive conclusion successfully demonstrated by classical economists of the 19th century. Called comparative advantage instead of absolute cost advantage,[19] its benefits lie in the fact that everyone has a comparative advantage in something! No one is useless. There is, however, additional news that is both good and bad. Commencing with the latter: when firms relocate their production in search of an absolute or comparative advantage, the workers in the original country of production

centuries, the economic profession has identified reasons why markets fail in some cases; these include externalities, public goods, and information restrictions. Moreover, Adam Smith was after all right when he discussed what we might call the paradox of capitalism, i.e. that the outcomes of the selfish actions of individuals frequently benefit society as a whole. For the skeptical reader, I refer to Figure 1 above. On this matter, an excellent reference is also Mandeville (1714) who wrote earlier than Adam Smith.

18 For a convincing text on this subject, the reader is directed to Hartford (2008).

19 To illustrate this difficult mechanism let us take the case of a father and son wanting to build a playhouse together. The father is faster both at carrying the material and nailing the timber. Yet it pays to let the son carry the material and allocate the father's time to nailing instead the father doing both jobs. Though the father has the absolute advantage in both activities, he has the comparative advantage only in nailing while the son has the comparative advantage in carrying. Using the father's time to carry would waste his valuable nailing time. This is what we mean by an opportunity cost.

lose their jobs. Yet there is also good news; the factor prices (wages, the return on capital) tend to be equalized across countries.[20] The processes are slow but the mechanisms are there.[21]

Part of the globalization issue is connected to the problem of tax havens. International tax competition—the competition between national governments for firms and jobs—has been driving down the tax rates on profits, a problem exacerbated by the movement of ownership of companies and personal wealth to tax havens such as Luxemburg, Switzerland, and Jersey—even athletes are having their income taxed in Monaco. Where is the morality here? The relocation of taxable income to tax havens reduces national tax revenues and restricts the possibility of welfare provision for citizens. A reasonable prediction is, however, that the taxation of corporations will probably be eliminated in the long run—though taxation of capital income at the level of the owners will remain—provided they do not move; meanwhile, consumption and non-movable assets will be more heavily taxed. So, there is a problem. However, the case is even more complicated. Empirical studies indicate that a reduced tax burden on capital enhances global investment by companies, resulting in greater demand for labor, more jobs, and enhanced possibilities to pay wages to workers. Before we take a moral position, we should therefore analyze what the economists call the incidence of taxation: taxes aimed to fall on profits or capital income are thus being partly shifted to the workers in a highly complicated re-shuffle.

A final global issue that must be mentioned here relates to development: why is it so slow in the real world? My suggestion is that reasons for this are related to inefficient local institutions, lack of beneficial social capital, and the slow development of useful norms for development.

Some Bad News from the West

Income distribution in Western countries had been developing towards greater equality over a long period of time up until the past 30 years when it once again began to move towards increasing inequality (See Figure 5 on the 1% of top incomes in developed economies 1880–2009.)

---

20 These conclusions were analyzed by Stolper and Samuelson (1941).

21 In the real world, the politics of self-interest disturbs the process. For example, the protection of agricultural production in the EU or in the USA runs counter to the legitimate rights of developing countries to participate in international exchange.

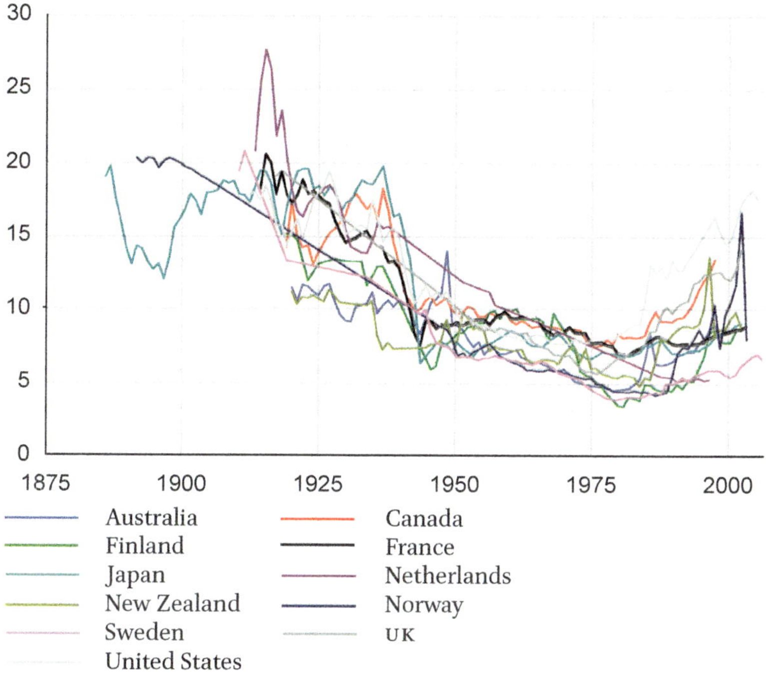

FIGURE 5 *Share of Top Incomes.*
SOURCE: THE FIGURE IS BASED ON ATKINSON, PIKETTY AND SAEZ (2011) AND IT IS REPRODUCED IN MALINEN (2012), "INCOME INEQUALITY IN THE PROCESS OF ECONOMIC DEVELOPMENT : AN EMPIRICAL APPROACH". THE DATA HAS BEEN OBTAINED FROM THE WORLD TOP INCOMES DATABASE, HTTP://TOPINCOMES.G-MOND.PARISSCHOOLOFECONOMICS.EU/

A French economist, Thomas Piketty (2013), has recently produced a voluminous and best-selling book on the rising inequality in the West entitled *Capital in the Twenty-First Century* in which he examines the source of this phenomenon. Why is the capitalist economy producing more inequality in the contemporary era compared to the equality it seemed to be encouraging earlier? I have three explanations to suggest in answer. Firstly, while globalization processes have reduced absolute poverty in the developing countries, this has taken place via an increase in the profit rate (return on capital) of global firms, thereby further enriching the owners of capital. Secondly, and at about the same time, the third industrial (digital) revolution has created a large number of new millionaires based on their special skills. Thirdly, the extraordinary financial boom in Western economies prior and up to 2007 made bankers and people working in financial spheres richer than ever.

Conflict Between Equity and Efficiency: The Key Issue within a Welfare State

Nowhere are the humans born with equal abilities and access to equal resources. Therefore, it is appropriate to try to equalize the starting line for everyone, certainly in terms of health care, education, and social security. This principle has been outlined by John Rawls, an American moral philosopher, in his famous "maximin" principle which states that societies should be judged on the basis of how they treat those in the weakest position. Despite efforts made in this direction, however, the starting line *ex ante* will always remains unequal—therefore, it is fitting that access to resources *ex post* should be more or less equalized But to what degree? There are limits to full equalization. Increasing equity through redistribution has its cost and, for reasons of efficiency, full equalization does not make sense. Those who work harder and those who contribute more should be rewarded, a course of action that also benefits society as a whole because it makes sense to preserve incentives to invest in education, to provide working effort, to take risks and to start entrepreneurial activity.

In Finland, 86% of those who are eligible for income support are of a working age and capable of working and yet it is not the case that paid employment is regarded as an option by everyone: some demand a "citizen salary", or find "bullshit jobs" unacceptable, or value leisure more highly than providing their fair share of labor. Easy access to social support creates passivity and the evidence indicates that this form of social selfishness has been increasing. Thus, while social justice is considered highly important in Nordic countries, and defense of the Nordic Welfare State is widespread, there is a problem: these prevailing values and the institutions implementing them may provide adverse incentives, making the taking of personal responsibility for one's welfare appear unattractive. Moreover, the political system is faced with strong lobbying efforts in favor of private benefits.

It is unarguable that people respond to incentives. Let me give just three illustrative examples. When government officials in Vietnam wanted to cut back the country's rat population by starting to subsidize anyone who killed rats, people responded by establishing rat breeding farms to increase the rat population in order to benefit from the subsidies. In another example: you may recall that the athlete Sergei Bubka from Ukraine improved his world record in the pole vault 35 times yet it was typically by only 1 cm at a time, not more. Why? A new record entitled him to a reward regardless of its magnitude and an additional centimeter was more valuable in the next sports event than in the current one. Finally, why has Grameen Bank of Bangladesh been so successful in generating small-scale loans? One explanation is that debt repayment is collectively monitored by a group of co-workers and that group monitoring creates the right incentives to take care of debt retirement.

To conclude, the economic system and its institutions should provide people with the right incentives to facilitate the exploitation of each person's strengths and develop their inherent skills. Only then can one expect success.

Fair Wage, Fair Salary: Why so Difficult?

Most people live on their wage or salary so why, therefore, is it so difficult to determine a fair return for workers, not to mention corporate managers? The issue is highly complicated despite the fact that the target is clear: having the right people in the right jobs. In brief, research suggests that somehow payment ought to be related to labor input while simultaneously making it clear that it is extremely difficult to properly measure the human effort involved in performing a specific task.[22] Incentivizing people can be defended but is it is not a straightforward option as incentives may produce undesired side effects (as in the "rats" example above), while managerial options are also often attended by unplanned corollaries.

Self-interest and Social Responsibility

In the globalized world, global companies are equipped with substantial economic power and sometimes also with political authority. One of the things at stake in this phenomenon is business ethics. In recent decades severe criticism has been directed at medical, chemical, or oil companies operating in the developing world that create adverse local effects. One justifiable claim has been that corporate social responsibility cannot be limited to economic responsibility towards the shareholders but must be extended to environmental responsibility and social responsibility more broadly.[23] Problems associated with working conditions or misuse of child labor have been brought to the attention of the media, leading to consumer boycotts, demonstrating that international transmission of information in today's globalized world is indeed a strong disciplinary device in the advancement of corporate social

22 For a convincing argument, see Harford 2008.

23 See also Porter and Kramer (2011).

responsibility.[24] Thus, even given that the main goal of firms is to make a profit, avoiding opportunism and being a good corporate citizen may, in today's world, be profitable and useful instruments in the game of market competition. Because information transmission in both commercial and social media has become highly efficient, companies can no longer neglect its repercussions. At the very least, consumers tend to have the power to punish.

"Give Me a One-Handed Economist"

Discussion of the conflict between economic mechanisms and the moral feelings inside us is sometimes disturbing. The world is a complicated one. Indeed, it is typical for economists repeatedly to state: "On the one hand ... but on the other ..." Frustrated by this fact, US President Harry S. Truman once cried out: "Give me a one-handed economist!" He never got one because such a creature is a paradox. Indeed, given the fundamentally perplexing nature of the world with which God has provided us, I can give you some free advice: never trust a one-handed economist.

Bibliography

Atkinson, A.B., Piketty, T. and Saez, E. "Top Incomes in the Long Run of History", *Journal of Economic Literature*, 49:1 (2011): 3–71.

Bolt , J., and Van Zanden, J.L., "The First Update of the Maddison Project; Re-Estimating Growth Before 1820", Maddison Project Working Paper 4, 2013.

Dollar, K., and Kraay, A. "Trade, Growth, and Poverty", *The Economic Journal* 114 (2004): 22–49.

Glazer, A., Kanniainen, V., Poutvaara, P. "Firms' ethics, consumer boycotts, and signalling", *European Journal of Political Economy* 26 (2010): 340–350.

Hartford, T. *The Logic of Life. The Rational Economics of an Irrational World*, New York: Random House, 2009.

Holloway, R. *Godless Morality. Keeping Religion Out of Ethics*, Edinburgh: Canongate Books, 1999.

Maddison, A. *The World Economy. A Millenial Perspective*. OECD 2001.

24 I can refer to Glazer, Kanniainen and Poutvaara (2010) for an analysis of the effects of consumer boycotts on business ethics in markets where consumers have moral preferences and where firms have to pay attention to those preferences to survive.

Malinen, T., *Income Inequality in the process of economic development: An empirical approach*, University of Helsinki, 2012.

Mandeville, B. *Fable of the Bees*, 1714. http://oll.libertyfund.org/index.php?option=com_staticxt&staticfile=show.php%3Ftitle=846&layout=html#chapter_66840.

Piketty, T. *Capital in the Twenty-First Century*, Cambridge, Massachusetts: The Belknap Press of Harvard University Press, 2013.

Porter, Michael E., and Kramer, Mark R. "Creating Shared Value", *Harvard Business Review 89*, nos. 1–2 (January–February 2011).

Rawls, J. *Theory of Justice*, Cambridge, Massachusets: Harvard University Press, 1971.

Ridley, M. "When Ideas Have Sex", a talk at TED (= video, accessible through the internet).

Sala-i-Martin, X. "The Disturbing 'Rise' of Global Income Inequality", *NBER Working Paper* 8904, 2002.

———. "The World Distribution of Income: Falling Poverty and... Convergence, Period", *Quarterly Journal of Economics*, CXXI (2006): 351–397.

Smith, A. *The Theory of Moral Sentiments*. Printed for A. Millar, in the Strand; and A. Kincaid and J. Bell. Edinburgh, 1759.

———. *An Inquiry into the Nature and Causes of the Wealth of Nations*, Modern Library ed. by Edwin Cannan. Fifth edition of 1789. London: Methuen and Co., Ltd., 1904.

Smith, V. "Human Betterment through Globalization." Foundation for Economic Education, 2005.

Stoper, W.F. and Samuelson, P.A., "Protection and Real Wages", *Review of Economic Studies*, 9 (1941): 58–73.

Wrangham, R. *Catching Fire. How Cooking made us human*, New York: Basic Books, 2009.

CHAPTER 3

Asian Perspectives on Global Economic Inequality

Felix Wilfred

The love of money is the root of all evil (1.Tim 6:10).

There are enough resources in the world for the need of all, but not for the greed of all.

M.K. GANDHI

You cannot consume beyond your appetite. The other half of the loaf belongs to the other person, and there should remain a little bread for the chance guest.

KHALIL GIBRAN

The Human Development Report of 2013 by the United Nations carries the title *The Rise of the South*.[1] It states that about 40 countries of the South whose development index was low in 1990 have shown remarkable improvement in human development in 2012; highlighted in particular are the cases of India, China and Brazil. However, this story of the "Rise of the South" could be misleading if we do not attend to ground realities which exhibit a range of inequalities that raise many questions about those countries which have achieved a level of development that has defied predictions. Inequality is the most crucial issue to be confronted as it jeopardizes any development they may have achieved. The undeniable fact is that about one billion people in the South live in extreme poverty, struggling to meet the bare necessities of life: food, clean water, shelter, basic health care and basic education. This state of affairs is due to persisting inequalities of which income inequality is only one of many, all of which are intertwined.

In this contribution, I shall try to analyze the connection between neoliberal economy and the phenomenal growth of inequalities in our global world, with reference to the South, and especially to Asia. In the second part we shall study some of the ways and strategies that need to be put in place,

1 UNDP, *Human Development Report 2013, The Rise of the South: Human Progress in a Diverse World* (New Delhi: Academic Foundation, 2013).

 | DOI 10.1163/9789004318496_005

so that inequalities are contained and we are able to move towards a global situation of greater equality, justice and harmony. In the final part, which is relatively short, we shall discuss on how religions could provide resources today for the project of a more equitable world.

Part 1: A World of Inequalities

The Case of Asia

Inequalities are of different kinds and each one has its own specific contours in each society, depending on its culture, tradition, history, etc. But what appears to be universal today is that in every society, money, market and competition are reinforcing these traditional inequalities in terms of gender, caste, ethnicity, education etc. Economic inequality has led to new forms of social inequality and asymmetry in political power.

Since the fast economic development of Asia has become the talk of the global world, let us begin by examining the case of this continent which is going through liberal economic transformation with its consequences in social, political and cultural fields.

In Asia, there is economic growth, but no poverty reduction. There does not seem to be any correlation between these two realities, resulting in a situation full of contradictions. China's colossal economy stands on political feet of clay. Taken up by the glamour of liberal economy and the goodies in the market, democracy seems to be the last thing Chinese youth are attracted to. Moreover, the pursuit of a crass liberal economy has led to serious violations of human rights, land-alienation, suppression of minorities, and gross disparity among the various Chinese regions and populations.

India, on the other hand, has not used the opportunities offered by its democratic political system (the largest democracy in the world) to overcome inequality and pursue the wellbeing of all its citizens. The democratic system is corrupted by liberal and capitalist forces. India, which has pursued a liberal economy since the 1990s, has economic growth, but the poor are deprived of their basic needs and their rights. Against many parameters of development, India trails far behind Bangladesh where there is greater equity in growth and development.

This discrepancy between growth and poverty in Asia, and in the global world at large, could be illustrated by drawing on the concept of the Human Poverty Index (HPI) introduced by UNDP in 1997.[2] There is not only the human

---

2 UNDP *Human Development Report of 1997*. New York: Oxford University Press, 1997.

development index (HDI) of a country but also a Human Poverty Index (HPI). "What is the difference between the HDI and HPI? The HDI measures progress in a community or country as a whole. The HPI measures the extent of deprivation, the proportion of people in the community who are left out of progress... HPI draws attention to deprivations in three essential elements of human life...—longevity, knowledge and a decent living standard".[3] Often there is no correspondence between the two. A country which shows a high percentage in HDI may have a low Human Poverty Index due to persistent structures of inequality. Only a comparison between the two indices will show how well or inequitably the benefits of development are distributed.

Inequalities are also divided along an urban-rural axis. Asian societies have been rural-based, so much so Gandhi said that the heart of India beats in its villages. Today, in Asian countries as well as in many developing societies, the rural gets marginalized whereas the lion's share of the benefit of economic growth goes to the relatively well-off sections in urban areas. What the rural population gets from the present-day form of development are but some crumbs. We need to pay attention to the rampant social inequalities in Asian societies on the basis of ethnicity, region, caste, religion, etc. The marginalized groups suffer many disabilities, because they have not been provided the capabilities in terms of health, knowledge, life-span, etc.[4]

The Price of Greed and the Struggle for Basic Needs

"The Price of Greed" is how *Time* magazine characterized the financial crisis the world has been experiencing since 2008.[5] Greed begets more greed and finally the price has to be paid. Unfortunately, it is the poor of the world who are today paying a hefty price for the avarice of the rich money-spinners, speculators and business interests. This is shown by the bail-out measures of the various states. It is a strange irony that the tax money of the poor is spent to save the greedy rich. It is again greed that lays off workers in times of crisis to save costs and maintain profits unaffected. What we fail to realize in normal times is that it is the same greed that is at work in the mainstream economic system.

There are 2170 billionaires around the world whose combined wealth has doubled in the past five years—up from 1.85 trillion pounds to 3.88 trillion

---

3 UNDP, *Human Development Report 1998* (New York – Oxford: Oxford University Press, 1998): 25.

4 Cf. Amartya Sen, *The Idea of Justice* (New York: Allen Lane, Penguin Books, 2009).

5 'The Price of Greed' *Time* (29 September, 2008); see also Joseph E. Stiglitz, *The Roaring Nineties: Why We're Paying the Price for the Greediest Decade in History* (New York: W.W. Norton & Company, Inc. Penguin Books, 2003).

pounds.[6] The number of billionaires in India has doubled in the past fifteen years indicating the phenomenal concentration of wealth in a country with 400 million people living below poverty line. This fact has led Christine Lagarde, director of the IMF to state that the net worth of the Indian billionaires is large enough to eliminate the country's absolute poverty twice over.[7] Something similar was stated by UNDP way back in 1997 in its annual report.

> The world has more than enough resources to accelerate progress in human development for all and to eradicate the worst forms of poverty from the planet. Advancing human development is not an exorbitant undertaking. For example, it has been estimated that the total additional yearly investment required to achieve universal access to basic social services would be roughly $ 40 billion, 0.1% of world income, barely more than a rounding error. That covers the bill for basic education, health, nutrition, reproductive health, family planning and safe water and sanitation for all.[8]

Greed not only turns priorities upside down, but also expresses itself in gorgeous consumption patterns. Consumerism is increasingly reaching out to the rural hinterlands too. The greed ingrained in the system of capitalist economy followed by Asian states has risked such crucial areas of the wellbeing of the poor such as nutrition, health-care, basic education, development of women, and the security of marginal communities.

We could think of overcoming inequalities only when there is restraint on human greed and greater focus on the common good. Restraint on greed is indispensable today to enable the freedom of all—especially the weaker ones—and provide them opportunity for the flowering of their freedom and capabilities which is true development.[9] There is a further reason for a curb on the endless pursuit of economic growth. Experience and study have increasingly led to the realization that economic growth and prosperity, if pursued beyond a certain limit, can become a threat to all stakeholders and their

---

6 *The Times of India* (1 April, 2014): 10.

7 Christine Lagarde, http://businesstoday.intoday.in/story/indian-billionaires-wealth-can-end-countrys-poverty-twice-imf/ accessed on 1 December, 2014.

8 UNDP, *Human Development Report of 1998* (New York: Oxford University Press, 1998): 37; see also the incisive analysis of the shocking and scandalous situation resulting from the current economic policies, Naomi Klein, *The Shock Doctrine* (New York: Penguin Books, 2007).

9 Cf. Amartya Sen, *Development as Freedom* (New York: Anchor Books, 2000).

happiness.[10] Further, from a psychological point of view, the more unequal a society is, the higher its level of distress.[11]

Social Consequences of Inequality

Greed is accompanied by violence because, in order to wrest control of possessions, one needs to employ violent means. The imbalance and asymmetry of power to which greed leads is a situation of injustice. It exploits the poor and marginalizes them. The greed that is deeply embedded in the capitalist system of economy continues to generate violence at all levels and in every part of the world. This is something obvious. A Buddhist text brings out very lucidly where the path of violence, greed and exclusive possession lead to:

> Thus from the not giving of property to the needy, poverty became widespread, from the growth of poverty, the taking of what was not given increase, from the increase of theft, the use of weapons increased, from the increased use of weapons, the taking of life increased.[12]

Greed brings forth unequal societies, and inequality is a permanent source of violence. The other becomes an enemy to be destroyed or a competitor to overcome. Increasing numbers of analyses show that countries and societies with greater inequality are also the ones prone to crime and violence. In societies in which there is less inequality, the quality of life turns out to be higher.

Another social consequence of inequality is the destruction of *social coherence and quality of life*. This is something observed not only in Asia and other developing countries, but also in the Western countries, something so well brought out in the work of Richard Wilkinson and Kate Pickett.[13] Inequality kills opportunity even though people abound in talents. Talents can flourish only in a society of equal opportunities. Inequality harms the community in as much as it prevents the talents of the marginalized individuals, groups and

---

10 Cf. Tim Jackson, *Prosperity without Growth: Economics for a Finite Planet* (London – New York: Earthscan, 2009).

11 Cf. John de Graaf – David Wann – Thomas H. Naylor, *Affluenza: How our Consumption is Killing us and How We Can Fight Back*, 3rd edition (San Francisco: Berrett-Kochler Publishers, 2014).

12 Quoted in Paul F. Knitter and Chandra Muzaffar, (Eds.) *Subverting Greed:Religious Perspectives on the Global Economy* (New York: Orbis Books, 2002): 63.

13 Cf. Richard Wilkinson and Kate Pickett, *The Spirit Level: Why Greater Equality Makes Societies Stronger* (New York: Bloomsbury Press, 2010); Joseph E. Stiglitz, *The Price of Inequality* (New York: W.W. Norton & Company, Inc. Penguin Books, 2012).

communities from playing an active part in the life of the community and contributing to its growth.

Further, the social condition of the working class has suffered enormously under the present-day global economic dispensation and its tendency to create inequalities. The gains of workers movement over a century and half through many struggles are thrown to the winds today. We are back again to the initial years of the industrial revolution in terms of exploitation of the working class. Maximization of profit that took a great toll is once again at work with the globalization of liberal economy. The workers' welfare and quality of life have gone down drastically, and their condition is characterized by a sense of deep insecurity.

The Case of Privatization

Inequality increases when, without attending to the basic needs, a country goes on with privatization. In a country which has problems with malnutrition, basic health-care and low literacy, privatization has disastrous consequences. With privatization, inequality grows beyond limits. Let me illustrate the point with an example from the field of health care.

The practice of privatization is not something abstract, but something to be viewed in context and against the social history of a people. China, for example, spends 2.7% of its GDP on public health care, whereas India just 1.2%. The market economy has put pressure on the health care of the people in India, encouraging private health care which most poor people cannot afford. Unlike most developed countries—Britain, Japan, Korea, and developing countries like Brazil and China, India has not built up any solid base for public health-care. Jumping into private health-care, as India seems to be doing now, has enormous consequences for the life and wellbeing of the poor.[14]

In British colonial times, there were recurrent famines in India in which millions perished. After political independence, India has within a few decades gained not only self-sufficiency but also has become an exporter of food. With better nutrition, there has come about a drastic reduction of child-mortality, and the average life-expectancy in India has risen from just 31 years when the British left, to 67 years now. The gains India has made in these respects, thanks to a strong public sector, are, however, being compromised by increasing privatization. India needs to build up a strong public health care system before launching into privatization of health which is bound to leave millions of poor

14 See Jean Drèze and Amartya Sen, *An Uncertain Glory: India and Its Contradictions* (Princeton: Princeton University Press, 2013): 37.

in the lurch, since the private health-care based on the capitalistic principles of competition and profit is unaffordable to them.

Crony Capitalism and the Political Fallout of Democracy

Inequality results when there is disproportionate sharing of political power and the concentration of it in a small group of elites. What follows is the absence of effective public policies aimed at the reduction of poverty.

In India, natural resources are heavily exploited by the business lobby with the blessings of corrupt politicians. The illegal mining and shipping of iron ore to China by Uday Vir Singh, who made a profit of 2 billion within a short period, is only the tip of an iceberg. The point is that this sell-out of national resources was possible only because of his proximity to the state apparatus and to politicians whose palms were substantially greased.[15] Democracy per se does not guarantee the overcoming of inequalities; rather, it creates conditions conducive to their overcoming. However, where democracy remains simply a political ideal without impact on the economic agenda, it can become a convenient cover-up for corrupt practices, something being amply demonstrated by the sham "democracies" in several countries of the globe.

We have not only the philosophy and anthropology of competition to challenge, but also crony capitalism. Here riches and money are made not so much through competition, as by connections involving the state, its power and bureaucracy. In short, corruption and bribery have become new sources for riches and the creation of billionaires in poor countries. Whereas in developed countries the wealth made by crony capitalism is much less, in developing countries it has gone up very high and very fast—something which explains the phenomenal growth of billionaires, in India, China, Hong Kong, Singapore, Malaysia, Indonesia and so on.[16]

Part II: Towards Overcoming Inequalities

From Competition to Cooperation and Solidarity

It is well-known that the neo-liberal ideology animating the mainstream economic system is based on competition as a general law or principle. What happens in the economic realm, it is argued, is nothing but concretization of a general law of nature. Competition is associated with growth, greater effectiveness and productivity.

15 See *The Economist* (March 15, 2014): 21.

16 Ibid., *The Economist.*

It is important to examine more closely the arguments fielded in favour of competition to be able to unmask the myths behind it. It is said that competition is something that is inherent in human nature, and therefore it is inevitable. Human nature is prone to be lazy, greedy and aggressive. In this connection, competition is seen, with reference to Darwinian socio-biology, as something that underlies the survival of the fittest. For, it injects a force of dynamism to overcome what is at the level of nature. Numerous studies have shown, however, that the so-called natural tendency to compete, win and set oneself apart is nothing but a socially learned behaviour pattern.

If we are to assume (and not concede) that the competitive spirit is natural, we should, on the basis of no less strong evidence, conclude that the spirit of cooperation too is natural. Apart from scientific studies to this effect, even ordinary observation makes it evident that cooperation is ubiquitous and something without which the human species cannot survive. In fact, so many peoples and cultures of the world manifest in their ways of life and traditions such a spirit of cooperation that we are forced to question whether the tendency of competing is not peculiar to a few cultures, and whether this limited experience is extrapolated as a general principle. Christian vision, for example, sees human beings not as competitors but as members of a family, sharing the same origin and journeying together towards a common destiny.

A second important argument that seems to lend plausibility for competition is the situation of scarcity. At first sight it may appear that precisely because there is want and the means are scarce, competition could be justified. On the other hand, an actual lack of material resources could be viewed as an environment in which human agency directed at solidarity and participation could flourish.[17] Contrary to the Malthusian prognostics of doom for humanity because of the geometrical growth of population and arithmetic production of food, we realize in the light of Christian faith that scarcity triggers the spirit of generosity and sharing, especially among the poorest of the poor. Moreover, it provokes human economic agency as an extension of God's work of ongoing creation. For, the situation of scarcity can lead to maximizing the use of available resources through a process of participation and sharing so as to sustain life for all. Christian Scriptures highlight the centrality of justice and love to get the better of poverty and destitution. Christian faith anchored in the tradition of covenant, election and in the vision of the Kingdom of God calls for personal self-sacrifice in economic relations. There would be no poor (Dt. 15:4) if only humans took their obligations to reach out to the other

17 Albino Barrera, *God and the Evil of Scarcity: Moral Foundations of Economic Agency* (Notre Dame, Indiana: University of Notre Dame Press, 2005).

seriously. Chronic Malthusian scarcity is prima facie evidence of moral failure whether by sins of omission or commission.

These considerations on competition lead us to conclude that the present economic system is not something that is inevitable. The serious consequences we experience in the form of the suffering of the innocent should set in motion another system of economy that is based on the spirit of cooperation, solidarity and sharing. Precisely because there are limited resources, human beings, forming one family, should share what is available equitably; competition is not at all called for. On the contrary, it is counter-productive. The vision of society that the symbol of the Kingdom of God evokes is one of communion, mutuality, and reciprocal support. Nowhere does the Bible tell us to follow the law of competition, which is diametrically opposed to the Kingdom of God. What transpires through the scriptures and Christian tradition is a call to cooperation in love and in the spirit of interdependence.

Capitalism is premised on an anthropology that views the other as competitor. Solidarity, instead, is based on an anthropology of human interdependence and cooperation for the common good, and on an internal ethics oriented towards the other. In fact, the Chinese sage Mencius gives a telling example of a child at the brink of falling into an open well. We reach out our hands to save it, not for any external motive of gaining favour with the parents of the child and neighbours, nor for fear of being blamed for not helping. An inner voice simply tells us that this child should not perish; it needs to be saved.[18]

Welfare Measures and Resistance

Even when the state tends to act independently, as in the case of providing welfare measures to the benefit of the poor (food subsidies, healthcare, old age pensions, etc.), this is being stoutly resisted by the corporates on the plea that it is bad economics. Good economics, according to them, is one which can produce best results, and this is possible only through free competition. In short, the argument is that the best way to create a developed and prosperous society is to teach the poor to compete! Such an argument is blind to the initial unequal condition of competition. Speaking of the argument of competition and meritocracy, the Mandal Commission in India critiqued it with a picturesque image of a race where the able-bodied and the physically challenged participate in the same race, and the winners are rewarded.[19] This is

18 Mencius, *The Works of Mencius*, Book 2, Part 1, Chapter 6.3. Translated by James Legge, 1815–1897, with Critical and Exegetical notes (New York: Dover Publication, Inc., 1970).

19 *Reservations for Backward Classes: Mandal Commission Report of the Backward Classes Commission, 1980* (Delhi: Aklank Publications, 1991).

obviously senseless, since it ignores the initial unequal conditions of competition. Market economy and laissez faire capitalism do the same.

It is argued that allowing the market to follow its own laws automatically brings equilibrium, and any intervention in the logic of market is bad economics. This philosophy of free market, represented by the Chicago school of economics and by Milton Friedmann and the like, fails to understand, among other things, the vastly differing initial conditions. Believing that the functioning of market will bring with it equality is simply utopian and is contradicted by the conditions of the masses of poor in Asia and in other continents. An unrestrained market is not an instrument of equality as claimed by pundits of laissez-faire economy, but its cause.

Participative Economic Life

In the mainstream global economy and market, some people, some groups, and even some continents (Africa, for example) do not count. The reason is the presumption that they have nothing to contribute to accumulation of wealth, the linchpin of modern economy. They are the excluded. A healthy economy, on the contrary, is one in which there is a dynamic flow of wellbeing throughout the social body. This can take place when all parts of the body are involved in this movement.

Social inequality and other evils derive from the fact that people are excluded from participating as active agents in the economic life of the country. Either the economy is viewed as something that is to be directed by the experts in the field or by a group of elites whose economic activities overlap with the fulfillment of their own self-interest without benefiting the people. Yet, a primary form of participation takes place when people become active contributors to the economy through employment. Therefore, the situation of unemployment is one that restricts the opportunity for people to be participant in the economic life of their society or the country, which is as important for their dignity and self-esteem as for the realization of their needs. Hence, any policy that deprives people of employment in the name of increasing profit or accumulation of capital is a process of exclusion, and needs to be challenged. Displacement of millions of people from their traditional means of livelihood in the developing societies of the South, and the lack of opportunities for growing numbers of young people are symptoms of the deep malaise afflicting the current political economy. It calls for immediate attention.

Economy and Democracy

Democratically inspired economic life contributes to the overcoming of inequalities. India is a world experiment in the complex relationship between democracy and poverty reduction. The experiences here show that a formal democratic system can coexist with capital accumulation and exploitation, and with mass poverty and destitution all around. This is an anomaly. Participative economy, on the other hand, is of vital importance for sustaining a substantive democracy.[20] An important study on democracy in South Asia brings out this point lucidly.[21]

> Continued co-existence of mass democracy and mass poverty is both a challenge and paradox of democracy in South Asia. While the working of democracy has not led to freedom from want, it may have given more space for struggles for securing better economic conditions. A manifold mismatch informs the relationship between democracy and freedom from want: between the objective economic condition of the citizen and their sense of satisfaction, between objective and subjective placement in the economic hierarchy…, and between popular preferences on economic policies and the policies pursued by the state. While this mismatch between the 'objective' and 'subjective' economic conditions of the people creates a space of democratic contestation, it also allows for state inaction on poverty and destitution.[22]

As for India, in the immediate post-independence period, a state or a political party was judged in terms of its ability to alleviate the poverty and misery of the people. On the contrary, in the last few decades, under the spell of neo-liberalism, this ideal was simply ignored and not acted upon. Fortunately, there is a dawning realization that democracy should mean abolition of want and destitution. It is important to sustain this democratic spirit. The masses of people who are becoming more and more concerned, due to their increasing pauperization, about the adverse economic policies, are putting continuous pressure on the elected representatives and the state to pursue policies that will respond to their situation and needs. Holding the state accountable for its economic decision-making will be an important exercise in democracy.[23]

---

20 Cf. Pranab Bardhan, *Scarcity, Conflicts and Cooperation: Essays in the Political and Institutional Economics of Development* (Delhi: Oxford University Press, 2005). This book goes into the external environment of politics and governance required for economics, and appears to be of neo-liberal inspiration.

21 *State of Democracy in South Asia: A Report* (Delhi: Oxford University Press, 2008).

22 Ibid., *State of Democracy in South Asia.*

23 Inequality and discrimination remain the greatest challenges for development and growth of peoples and nations. Cf. UNDP, *Human Development Report 2014, Sustaining*

As it is, the present economic system does not incorporate and value the economic contribution of certain segments of people. Most glaring is the exclusion of the household work of women in the maintenance of the family and society. Women's economic contribution to the family in terms of household work like cooking, cleaning and caring remain hidden and invisible. Were one to take into account the economically measurable income that would be generated if women were to do the same work outside the domestic walls, the very understanding of economy is bound to change.

In sum, we may not leave the economy as a matter to be decided by experts. Which economy works and is beneficial is to be indicated by people, especially the victims. Hence the representation of all, especially the weaker sections and groups, is important to the framing of economic policies in democratic spirit. Listening to the voices from below is an indispensable means of overcoming the economic inequality of our days. If there is an absence of participation by the people in shaping economic life, it is often due to social exclusion. Social inclusion and economic participation mutually reinforce each other.

Strengthening the Commons

Way back in 1968 Garrett Hardin wrote a celebrated article in the journal *Science*, entitled "The Tragedy of the Commons".[24] He said that common resources like pasture land, forests, air, water, fisheries etc. which had served the community for millennia have entered into a situation of crisis because, due to greed, some members have started overexploiting them. This results in destruction, which is ultimately to nobody's advantage. For him, what caused this tragedy was the absence of well-defined property rights. Decades later, Elinor Ostrom, who was awarded Nobel Prize for economics in 2009, came back to the question. She showed that the real tragedy is in the destruction of the *community-based systems* of *conserving the commons*.[25] These systems had the advantage of turning the people into active participants using common resources responsibly. It allowed the violators to be easily identified and dealt with—something that created greater accountability for, and control over, the commons.

Human Progress: Reducing Vulnerabilities and Building Resilience (New York: Oxford University Press, 2014). The report's findings point to why governments must enact and enforce laws.

24 Garrett Hardin, "The Tragedy of the Commons", in *Science* 162 (1968): 1243–1248.

25 Cf. Elinor Ostrom, *Governing the Commons: The Evolution of Institutions for Collective Action* (Cambridge: CambridgeUniversity Press, 1990).

Situating the community as the important player and most effective manager of the common resources challenges the primacy given to individual actors in the neo-liberal economy. Community management itself of what is common is an expression of culture and it helps overcome the violence that competition and conflicts between individuals could cause. In former times, before neo-liberal economics, the state and the market were viewed as protecting natural resources from overuse and destruction. The community management of commons comes as an alternative to these two traditional actors, whose credibility has come into question, especially in these times when nature's regenerative capacity is stunted by exploitative human interventions.[26]

From Profligacy to a Sustainable Way of Life

When the Club of Rome warned in the 1960s of severe limits to growth, it came as a shocking realization. Unfortunately, it has not led to any significant change in the economic realm; much less to any radical rethinking of the reigning neo-liberal paradigm. For the mainstream economy, it is business as usual. If India, China, Brazil, etc. were to follow the logic of mainstream economy and chart for themselves a course of progress as in the developed nations, it is plain that the resources available are far from adequate, and probably two or more earths in addition to the present one would be required to sustain such a model of development. If every Chinese and every Indian were to own a car, our earth will literally turn into a gas chamber choking people to death. What we need is not sustainable development, but the practicing of *a sustainable way of life*.

Let me illustrate the point with reference to India whose neo-liberal economy has created an environment for the flourishing of consumerism and opulence in a sea of misery, to the advantage of the well-to-do classes and castes. It is changing the face of India and its traditional ethos. Pavan Verma tells us how the Indian middle-class of the immediate post-independence period lived with the ideals of Gandhi and Nehru, and how restraint and moderation characterized their lives. This has undergone such a change today that the middle-class has become a class of competitors, with Bill Gates, Ambanis and Mittals as their new icons of success. Instead of restraint and moderation, they are given to instant gratification and more and more to vulgar exhibitionism and ostentation.

> Indians love the spiritual halo ascribed to them by foreigners, but are in truth among the world's most ingenious and resilient entrepreneurs,

26 See Tim Jackson, *Prosperity without Growth: Economics for a Finite Planet* (London & Washington: Earthscan, 2009).

> with their feet on the ground and their eyes on the balance sheet. Indeed, in the world view of Hinduism, Artha, the acquisition of wealth, is among the four highest purusharthas or goals of life. There is no biblical injunction in Hinduism to the effect that it is more difficult for a rich man to reach heaven than it is for a camel to go through the eye of a needle. On the contrary, Lakshmi, the goddess of wealth and prosperity, is ubiquitous in homes across the country.[27]

What is most disturbing in today's world is its amnesia of the poor, the callous indifference and the absence of any sense of community and solidarity. Zygmunt Bauman tells us about the shift from the "other" to self-fulfillment, of which consumerism is an expression.

> The concept of responsibility and responsible choice, which resided before in the semantic field of ethical duty and moral concern for the Other, have shifted or have been moved to the realm of self-fulfillment and calculation of risks. In the process, the "Other", as the trigger, the target and the yardstick of responsibility recognized, assumed and fulfilled has all but disappeared from view, elbowed out or overshadowed by the actor's own self. 'Responsibility' now means, first and last, responsibility to oneself... while responsible choices are first and last, those moves serving the interests and satisfying the desires of the self.[28]

If such is the case, the poor have nothing to gain from this economy of consumerism. The kind of economy the poor envision is one in which the fulfillment of basic needs will be the priority, and not the gratification of consumerist instincts.

Forward to Labour and Employment

The greed capitalism embodies has brought the world to a situation in which accumulation of wealth has taken absolute priority over labour and employment. With liberalization, the South has also fallen into the trap of sacrificing the livelihood and employment of millions for the profit of a small percentage

27 Pavan K. Varma, *The Great Indian Middle Class* (Delhi: Penguin Book, 2007): xxi.

28 Zygmunt Bauman, *Consuming Life* (Cambridge: Polity Press, 2007): 92. See also *Id., Does Ethics Have a Chance in a World of Consumers?* (Cambridge Massachusetts: Harvard University Press, 2008).

of its rich. In the process, the South has thrown to the winds the wellbeing of the workers, as exemplified in the case of Special Economic Zones.[29]

There has been also a drastic increase of unemployment worldwide in these years. Moreover, during the past years productivity growth has exceeded wage growth, affecting the lives of the labourers, and this is particularly so in the case of women. This trend is glaring in India and Brazil. The world trend, as per the report of the International Labour Organization, shows that the proportionate share of women's wages has sharply declined: "Income gap between the top and the bottom ten percent of wage earners increased in 70 percent of the countries for which data are available."[30] Furthermore, the health of employees is not a priority with the government, nor with employers. As a result, employees with low wages are sometimes forced to spend as much as 80% of their wages on health care, leaving little for food and other basic necessities.[31]

Charting a new economic course means bringing the question of labour and employment to centre-stage. The private sector cannot throw overboard the labour movement's legacy of over one hundred and fifty years, which has ensured just wages, security, and health-care for workers and employees. In a situation of crisis, private corporations and enterprises tend to cut wages and other benefits frantically, increase working hours, and also layoff workers. This trend needs to be arrested and economic participation on the part of the people will help to check such anti-labour practices in the future. Besides, state intervention is important. It should hold the private sector responsible for the violation of the basic norms of social justice. The widely discussed notion of corporate responsibility is often a matter of make-believe in many countries of the South. It does not really address the question of social justice in the field of labour nor respond to the exigencies of the common good.

An Economy of Care and Mutuality

The present economic system is totalitarian in character. It transforms everything and everybody into commodities, and pulls the whole world into its net.[32]

---

29 Preeti Sampat, "Special Economic Zones in India" in *Economic and Political Weekly*, vol. 43, 28 (July 12, 2008): 25–30.

30 Quoted in T.K. Rajalakshmi, "Wake-up Call", in *Frontline* (March 13, 2009): 86–87. "For instance in the United States in 2007 the chief executive officers (CEOs) of the fifteen largest companies earned over 500 times more than the average worker" ibid., 87.

31 Cf. T.K. Rajalakshmi, "The Other Half" in *Frontline* (April 24, 2009): 90–92.

32 Ray Kiely, *Empire in the Age of Globalization: US Hegemony and Neo-liberal Disorder* (Hyderabad: Orient Longman Pvt. Ltd., 2007).

A future course of an economy sensitive to the needs of the poor calls for rethinking priorities and consequent reallocation of resources. In a country like India where large masses of people are still illiterate and where poverty prevents children from attending school, it should be a norm that education be accorded high priority with allocation of adequate funds. Similarly, taxation and fiscal policies should be continuously re-evaluated so as to benefit the poor rather than increasing the advantage of the already rich and well-to-do.

The worst thing the present neo-liberal economy does is to reduce the relationship between producers and consumers in terms of market. This is an impoverization of human relationality and a very dangerous reductionism. Feminist critique challenges the reductionism that commercializes the human dimensions of life. The present crisis is basically a consequence of a mechanistic economy that needs to be redeemed by foregrounding mutuality and genuine care, which are often devalued as the 'feminine'. A feminist redemption of this situation in terms of the wellbeing of humanity and the earth would mean bringing the soul back into the economy by prioritizing mutuality and solidarity. This ethics of care, woven into our way of life, will be the new software by which a new economy will operate. Part of this software must be the evolution of a new relationship with the earth and all that this implies, because the economy of care also extends to the whole of nature.

Challenge to the Discipline of Political Economy

Our foregoing reflections lead us to interrogate the state of mainstream economics of present times and of social sciences in general. Christian theology could make a contribution by provoking the present economy to abandon its claimed neutrality. There is a scandalous superficiality in the present state of these sciences. They fail to address the human condition suffered by the weak and the marginalized. Today's economics has become a matter of theories, numbers, equations and models.

Fortunately, the self-assurance of the present economy is shaken. There seems to be a sudden black-out, and the financial game has come to a halt. With all the sophistication vaunted by economics, and its claims of prescience and predictive capabilities, it is today dumbfounded and is not able to explain the current financial disaster that now affects the economies of the entire world including, alas, those of the poor and developing nations. Even more, it is clueless today as how to get out of the deep mire into which it has sunk the world. The present discipline of economics dominated by neo-liberal ideology is far from capable of pulling the world out of this quagmire. There is a need for a radical transformation of the science of economics along with other social sciences. The reason is spelt out clearly by the Gulbenkian Commission on the Restructuring of the Social Sciences:

> For, unlike the natural world as defined by the natural sciences, the domain of the social sciences not only is one in which the object of study encompasses the researchers themselves but also one in which the persons they study can enter into dialogue or contests of various kinds with these researchers. Matters of debate in the natural sciences are normally solved without recourse to the opinions of the object of study. In contrast the peoples … studied by social scientists have entered increasingly into the discussion, whether or not their opinion was sought by scholars, who, indeed, frequently considered this intrusion unwelcome.[33]

Economics requires constant dialogue with the entirety of society and its various strata. We need voices from the ground and alternative perspectives that will wake up these sciences from their slumber in the abstruse world of self-isolation.

Part III: Religion and Overcoming of Global Inequalities

Religions have, unfortunately, often contributed to legitimizing accumulation of wealth, and have supported practices of greed. Wealth is said to be sign of God's blessing, and poverty and deprivation a result of sin. A classic example is the ambiguous position of Christianity vis-à-vis colonialism in its greed, plundering and genocide during the process of the appropriation of the "wealth of nations". The "prosperity Gospel" of today is perhaps an echo of traditional legitimization of riches. If in the past, fate and sin were seen as causes of poverty and inequality, today, under the aegis of liberal economy, they are interpreted by blaming the victims: because the poor are lazy, incompetent and inefficient, lacking in entrepreneurship, they remain poor. Some trends in Christian theology reflect this kind of explanation.

I do not mean to imply that this occurs only in Christianity. Other religions are not exempt; in both ideology and practice all have succumbed to the lure of wealth. Hinduism, for example, teaches that the condition of poverty or wealth is the result of *karma* (past action), a view which can deter human involvement and active agency in fighting inequality. If I singled out Chritianity, it is simply

33 Immanuel Wallerstein et al., *Open the Social Sciences: Report of the Gulbenkian Commission on the Restructuring of the Social Sciences* (Delhi: Vistaar Publications, 1997).

because of its overwhelming influence in history through its association with colonialism. Its theology and explanations regarding poverty and wealth have had a profound *Wirkungsgeschichte* (historical effect) on the presentday global situation and thought.

On the other hand, we also find that all religions concur in the deep wisdom that attachment to riches is harmful to human beings and society. Greed (*lobha*) and acquisitiveness (*aparigraha*) have been viewed in some streams of Indian religious tradition as contradicting the call to a life of *dharma*. They are to be countered by the generosity of sharing (*dana*) and wisdom (*prajna*) that redeem us from delusion. Buddhism speaks of the insatiable thirst (*trsna*) for riches which leads us astray and causes us to suffering (*dhukka*) instead of happiness. *Dana* is to be understood not simply as almsgiving; it has a depth of signification, which combines as it does the Christian understanding of social justice with compassion.

Jesus Christ tells his disciples, "Watch out! Be on your guard against all kinds of greed; a man's life does not consist in the abundance of his possessions" (Luke 12:15). Capitalism is nothing but organized greed with all the evil it produces. We are reminded of the words in the Letter to Timothy which help us to understand what is deeply at work in capitalism: "Love of money is the root of all kinds of evil" (1Tim 6:10). No wonder then that Jesus said that it is easier for the camel to go through the eye of a needle than the rich to enter into the Kingdom of God (Matt 19:24; Mark 10:25; Luke 18:25). The ugly nature of avarice gets exposed in times of crisis such as we are currently living through. How could the well-being of humanity be based on an economic system whose structuring principle is greed?

Freedom from greed and attachment is the cornerstone of Jesus' social teachings. He does not command this only to his close disciples; it is meant for all those who want to follow him. There is even more to his teaching. By enjoining renunciation and detachment, Jesus responds to a basic human and societal issue which rests on a deeper vision of human beings and society. Jesus commands his disciples to free themselves from greed and attachment, because that will make them authentic human beings. The servitude which greed and attachment represent diminishes and corrodes human and societal life here on earth.[34] Therefore, the exhortation against avarice and attachment are not to be interpreted as something esoteric or fostering otherworldliness.

---

34 Roelf Haan, *The Economics of Honor: Biblical reflections on Money and Property* (Michigan: William B. Eerdmans Publishing Company, Grand Rapids, 2009); Craig L. Blomberg, *Neither Poverty Nor Riches: A Biblical Theory of Possessions* (Leicester, England: Inter Varsity Press, 1999).

Further, his teachings on the dangers of riches and the need for detachment and renunciation are not meant simply as spiritual principles for individuals. They are principles for the life of the community as well. Absorbing the teachings of Jesus, the early Christians tried to create an ideal community free from greed and accumulation.

It appears to me that today religions in general and Christianity in particular could bring in four kinds of resources to stem the tide of global inequalities:

1) Prophetic challenge to the dominant economic order with all its consequences;
2) Drawing from its scriptures and traditions a sense of hope for a world which is heavy-laden with inequalities. It can bring the message of hope that change is possible and necessary.
3) Collaboration with new social movements and civil society initiatives—something very important especially where Christianity is in a minority situation. It is also important in the traditionally Christian regions of the West in order that they regain their lost credibility. Programs of advocacy appear to be important as an integral part of Christian mission to bring about greater global equality.
4) Bringing spiritual resources to restrain the economy from the path of accumulation and opulence, and through spiritual forces and inculcation of values, orient it towards a transformative social order and deeper inter-human relationships.

Theology too has an important role to play in transforming a world marked by gross inequalities. An engaged theological critique of the dominant political economy as well as the theoretical conceptions it has attempted to develop can be assisted by feminist perspectives. One important thing theology needs to be aware of is that economy is not gender neutral. In its critical study and analysis of both macro and micro-economy (which would include the process of production, distribution, consumption, trade, etc.), theology needs to be aware of gender inequality as operative in the very economic structures. The unequal power relationships patriarchy creates is operative in all economic processes. The dominant economic system simply reproduces and reinforces existing unequal gender-relationships of power.

Theology and economics need to come together today and reinforce each other. We are reminded of what Gandhi had to say about the relationship between religion and economics: "Whereas religion to be worth anything, must be capable of being reduced to terms of economics, economics to be worth anything must also be capable of being reduced to terms of religion and spirituality".[35]

Faith and theology that help the flourishing of life, cannot subscribe to a death-dealing totalitarian economy. Just as political totalitarianism needs to be opposed in the name of faith (think of the National Socialism of Hitler's Germany), so too in the name of the same faith, an economic system that spells suffering and death to the innocent should be resisted. Along with resistance which can take different forms, there also needs to be efforts made to devise alternatives.[36] A sign of hope is that in different parts of the world, significant movements and micro-initiatives are emerging that challenge the claim of the inevitability of the present economic order. For me, "Money and Mission" would make sense from this perspective. Money is a symbol of the economy and Christian mission is called today to make its contribution to transform it in the direction of life and the flourishing of the humans and nature. This is really a global mission, and mission in every part of the world—as much in the South as in the North.

Conclusion

The Berlin wall was pulled down. It brought an era to an end. But Europe is encircling itself today with new walls of defense against immigration from the South. As long as the North was not touched, there was little concern about the issue of global inequality. Today, the issue of immigration from the South is putting pressure on the North, unsettling its people in their self-enclosed islands of affluence. With the mobility that characterize the modern world, the wave of migrations will grow and storm the fortresses of the North—something that is causing serious preoccupation for Europeans and those in the Northern hemisphere.[37] The predicament of migrants and refugees is ultimately the

35 *Young India*, 15 September, 1927. As quoted in Chritopher Key Chapple – Mary Evelyn Tucker, *Hinduism and Ecology* (Cambridge Massachusetts: Harvard University Press, 2000): 227.

36 Joerg Rieger, *No Rising Tide: Theology, Economics, and the Future* (Minneapolis: Fortress Press, 2009); see also Sasika Sassen, *Globalization and its Discontents* (New York: The New Press, 1998). The author questions the axiom "Rising tide raises all boats" (attributed to J.F.K. Kennedy) and shows its fallacy in the prevailing economic system.

37 The Syrian refugee crisis has led to some rethinking on migration and attempts to loosen somewhat the tight EU grip on asylum regulations. Efforts by the German Chancellor, Angela Merkel, to call for an exception to be made in the case of Syrian refugees has

portrayal of a world of abysmal inequalities. Lampedusa remains a constant reminder of tragedies inequality can bring about. The North is feeling the heat, so to say, of what could become a conflagration unless the issue of inequality is addressed at its roots, and in its structures.

More than in the past it is becoming evident that greater equality is good and even essential as much as for the South as for the North. So, the battle against inequality is a global one which requires numerous forces of solidarity, support and intervention. With all its ambiguities in the past, religions do possess many resources that could be channeled to shape a world with a sharper sense of equality and justice, following a sustainable way of life attentive to the groans of nature and the needs of the poor of the earth.

Bibliography

Bardhan, Pranab. *Scarcity, Conflicts and Cooperation: Essays in the Political and Institutional Economics of Development.* Delhi: Oxford University Press, 2005.

Barrera, Albino. *God and the Evil of Scarcity: Moral Foundations of Economic Agency.* Notre Dame, Indiana: University of Notre Dame Press, 2005.

Bauman, Zygmunt. *Consuming Life.* Cambridge: Polity Press, 2007.

———. *Does Ethics Have a Chance in a World of Consumers?* Cambridge Massachusetts: Harvard University Press, 2008.

Blomberg, Craig L. *Neither Poverty Nor Riches: A Biblical Theory of Possessions.* Leicester, England: Inter Varsity Press, 1999.

Chapple, Chritopher Key – Mary Evelyn Tucker, *Hinduism and Ecology.* Cambridge Massachusetts: Harvard University Press, 2000.

Drèze, Jean, and Amartya Sen. *An Uncertain Glory: India and Its Contradictions.* Princeton: Princeton University Press, 2013.

Graaf, John de – David Wann – Thomas H. Naylor, *Affluenza: How Our Consumption is Killing Us and How We Can Fight Back.* 3rd ed. San Francisco: Berrett-Kochler Publishers, 2014.

earned general goodwill for Germany whose people practice "Willkommenkultur" (Welcome culture) in spite of some Neo-Nazi attacks on asylum camps; this is accompanied by an extreme reluctance to admit refugees by most other EU members (except perhaps the Nordic countries). Germany alone has taken 40% of all refugees in EU territory. That said, the number of refugees a defensive EU has acceped is much smaller than in other parts of the world. For example, Turkey alone has about 2 million Syrian refugees; Lebanon 1.5 million and Jordan 629, 0000. Such facts are generally not known.

Haan, Roelf. *The Economics of Honor: Biblical Reflections on Money and Property.* Michigan: William B. Eerdmans Publishing Company, Grand Rapids, 2009.

Hardin, Garrett. "The Tragedy of the Commons", in *Science* 162 (1968): 1243–1248.

Jackson, Tim. *Prosperity without Growth: Economics for a Finite Planet.* London & Washington: Earthscan, 2009.

Kiely, Ray. *Empire in the Age of Globalization: US Hegemony and Neo-liberal Disorder.* Hyderabad: Orient Longman Pvt. Ltd., 2007.

Klein, Naomi. *The Shock Doctrine.* New York: Penguin Books, 2007.

Knitter, Paul F., and Chandra Muzaffar, eds. *Subverting Greed: Religious Perspectives on the Global Economy.* New York: Orbis Books, 2002.

Lagarde, Christine. http://businesstoday.intoday.in/story/indian-billionaires-wealth-can-end-countrys-poverty-twice-imf/ accessed on 1 December, 2014.

Mencius, *The Works of Mencius*, Book.2, Part I. Translated by James Legge, 1815–1897, with Critical and Exegetical notes. New York: Dover Publication, Inc., 1970.

Ostrom, Elinor. *Governing the Commons: The Evolution of Institutions for Collective Action.* Cambridge: Cambridge University Press, 1990.

Rajalakshmi, T.K. "The Other Half" in *Frontline* (April 24, 2009): 90–92.

———. "Wake-up Call", in *Frontline* (March 13, 2009): 86–87.

Reservations for Backward Classes: Mandal Commission Report of the Backward Classes Commission, 1980. Delhi: Aklank Publications, 1991.

Rieger, Joerg. *No Rising Tide: Theology, Economics, and the Future.* Minneapolis: Fortress Press, 2009.

Sampat, Preeti. "Special Economic Zones in India" in *Economic and Political Weekly*, vol. 43, 28, July 12, (2008): 25–30.

Sassen, Sasika. *Globalization and its Discontents: Essays on the New Mobility of People and Money.* New York: The New Press, 1998.

Sen, Amartya. *Development As Freedom.* New York: Anchor Books, 2000.

———. *The Idea of Justice.* New York: Allen Lane, Penguin Books, 2009.

State of Democracy in South Asia: A Report. Delhi: Oxford University Press, 2008.

Stiglitz, Joseph E. *The Roaring Nineties: Why We're Paying the Price for the Greediest Decade in History.* New York: W.W. Norton & Company, Inc. Penguin Books, 2003.

———. *The Price of Inequality.* New York: W.W. Norton & Company, Inc. Penguin Books, 2012.

The Economist. March 15, 2014.

The Times of India. 1 April, 2014.

UNDP. *Human Development Report 2014, Sustaining Human Progress: Reducing Vulnerabilities and Building Resilience.* New York: Oxford University Press, 2014.

———. *Human Development Report 2013, The Rise of the South: Human Progress in a Diverse World.* New Delhi: Academic Foundation, 2013.

———. *Human Development Report 1998.* New York- Oxford: Oxford University Press, 1998.

———. *Human Development Report of 1997*. New York: Oxford University Press, 1997.

Varma, Pavan K. *The Great Indian Middle Class.* Delhi: Penguin Books, 2007.

Wallerstein, Immanuel, et al. *Open the Social Sciences: Report of the Gulbenkian Commission on the Restructuring of the Social Sciences.* Delhi: Vistaar Publications, 1997.

Wilkinson, Richard, and Kate Pickett. *The Spirit Level: Why Greater Equality Makes Societies Stronger.* New York: Bloomsbury Press, 2010.

Youngs, Gillian. *Global Political Economy in the Information Age: Power and Inequality.* New York: Routledge, 2006.

CHAPTER 4

Christian Mission in a World Under the Grip of an Unholy Trinity: Inequality, Poverty and Unemployment

Tinyiko Sam Maluleke

A Missionary Pathology

Inside Valdezia—a 30km radius village in the northern part of South Africa near the border with Zimbabwe—is a mission station established in 1873 by Swiss missionaries.[1] Key among the regime of values and behaviours studiously cultivated and implemented by the Swiss missionaries among their adherents was a strict aversion to wealth, a frowning upon commercial activity and a turning away from anything that could remotely resemble "the love of money" (1 Tim 6:10). Members of the church were not encouraged to go into business and business enterprises were not allowed.[2] Such was the determination of the missionaries on this matter that until the early 1990s, only an Indian family from the neighbouring town was permitted to operate the only general dealer store in the area.

In part, the missionary theology of diffidence towards wealth lay in the 18th and 19th-century movement's search for, and attempt to reinvent, pristine cultures and peoples untouched by corrosive modernity and the unseemly aspects of its civilization. It was part of a desperate attempt to "protect" their African converts from the corrosive effects of modernity[3]—especially modernity's "worship" of money. Desperately, the missionaries tried to push back and postpone the tide of modernity while at the same time dispensing a gospel which lured their converts away from the worship of Mammon (Mt. 6:24). Converts were supposed to "stay clean" of the possible "contamination" that comes with frequent contact with money. In the process it was hoped that whatever

1 See Gandjean *La Mission romande: Ses racines dans le sol suisse romand. Son épanouissement dans la race thonga.* Lausanne: G. Bridel, 1917.

2 See Maluleke *A Morula Tree Between Two Fields: The Commentary of African Writers on Missionary Christianity.* Pretoria: University of South Africa, 1995.

3 Cf. Harries *Butterflies & Barbarians. Swiss Missionaries & Systems of Knowledge in South-East Africa.* Oxford: James Currey, 2007.

 | DOI 10.1163/9789004318496_006

remnants of the pristine African community that were left would be salvaged and sustained. Accordingly, the liturgy, hymnology and theology of churches that resulted from Swiss missionary work were deeply imbued with a diffidence towards wealth and worldly things as well as an orientation towards things heavenly.

As an example, I produce below excerpts from two of the most popular hymns in the church born out of the work of Swiss missionaries, then and still.

[4]Hymn 168 *A hi Tsakeni Vamakwerhu*[5]—Let Us Rejoice

A hi tsakeni vamakwerhu—Let us rejoice brothers and sisters
Hina vana va Xikwembu—We the children of God
A hi languteni le henhla—Let us look up above
Laha hi kongomelaka—Where we are heading

(Chorus) *Le henhla, Le henhla*—Up above, up above
Yesu a ta hi nghenisa—Where Jesus will welcome us
Le kaya, Le Kaya—Oh home beautiful home
Hi ta va ni ku kwetsima—Where we shall be made holy

Hymn 202 *Tshika Wena Moya Wa Nga*—Be Strong Oh My Spirit

Tshika wena moya wanga—My dear spirit do not despair
Tshika ku kanana— And have no doubts
Languta mahlweni ntsena—Focus only ahead of you
Laha u yaka kona—Where you are headed

Chorus
Kule ni misava leyi—Far far away from this world
Kule ni tiko leri—Far far away from this country
Hi ta byi kuma vutshamo—We will have a place
Endlwini ya Tatana—Inside our father's house

More than a hundred years later, these types of hymns have lent themselves to easy appropriation in the growing "Pentecostalisation" of Christianity in Africa.[6] This overly other-worldly theology was in keeping with the liturgical

4 Tinsimu Ta Vakriste. 1989 Braamfontein: Sasavona.

5 This language is called Xitsonga, one of the 11 official languages in South Africa.

6 See Asamoah-Gyadu, *Contemporary Pentecostal Christianity: Interpretations from an African Context.* New York: WIPF and Stock, 2013.

theologies of similar missionary enterprises in other parts of Africa and elsewhere at that time. It was, in part, a dimension of the European pietistic and revivalist movements out of which many 19th-century missionary societies sprang. These movements tended to be theologically and doctrinally conservative.

Incoherence and Contradictions

But the missionary drive for the shunning of wealth and the elimination of the love of money was fraught and riddled with contradictions. To begin with the missionaries were, like all European missionaries of their era, several removes richer than their (potential) African converts—regardless of how the missionaries may have regarded their own wealth status. In the eyes and in the experience of their converts, the missionaries were not seen as impartial and neutral towards wealth and money. Indeed one of the very first acts of "mission" by missionaries upon arrival in the mission fields was an act of wealth-acquisition, namely, the purchasing of a piece of land from and around which missionary activities would be launched. This is exactly what the Swiss Missionaries did upon arrival in the northern part of South Africa. This, at a time when the local people were losing the last pieces of land they owned. This "first act of mission" stood in sharp contract to the missionary theology of diffidence towards wealth. If we add to this their education, typewriters, ox wagons (and later cars), piped water, electricity and huge mansions, the missionaries struck a very wealthy pose.

An old call-and-response folksong testifies to the extent to which the locals realised how embedded the missionaries were in the consumerist culture they were seeking to "protect" the locals from.

> *Khangelani, movha movha*—Behold the car, behold the car
> *Khangelani, movha ku duma ka wona*—Behold the wonder of its unique roar
>
> (Twice) *Emovheni lowu ku na valungu*—Inside the car, are white people
> *Lava tisaka rito ra Xikwembu*—Bringing the word of God

The song makes a potent connection between the missionaries, missionary work and the car. This telling picture is completed by the famous saying of Africans: "When the missionary came to our land, we had the land and they had the bible. They said, let us pray and after the prayer we had the bible and they had the land." African converts were not blind to the complicity between mission, wealth acquisition, so-called civilisation, Western commercialism and land dispossession.

Nor were potential African converts that well insulated from the effects of modernity by the mid-19th century, by which time many African communities were already confronted with particular faces of modernity such as conscription, colonialism as stated in the foregoing, and land dispossession. In Southern Africa, many able-bodied men of the community were conscripted into the burgeoning mining industry as a result of which they were away from home for most of the year in the mines of Kimberly and Johannesburg. Others were conscripted into the army during both the first and second world war. As well as suffering the horrors of war and the indignity of mine work, these men became unwitting purveyors and "evangelists" of modernity in the rural community. Modernity, in some of its most unseemly guises, was already in place.

There are other ways in which the fundamental contradictions in the anti-wealth gospel of the missionaries were manifested because the evangelising activities of the missionaries included the inculcation of certain artisan, agricultural and horticultural skills among the converts and their children—activities which not only generated income for the mission but also enabled many beneficiaries to make a living out of their skills. It could be argued that the very fact of starting schools and hospitals was antithetical to the quasi-monastic anti-wealth theology of many missionary societies. Generally, education improved the job and earning prospects of the converts, thus undermining the logic of the anti-wealth project.

Part of the result of the well-meaning but self-contradictory anti-wealth project was the creation of a pathologically neurotic, guilt-ridden passive-aggressive attitude towards money, wealth and towards the church itself. Perhaps traces of this pathology persist to this day, manifesting through a lingering dependency syndrome, a fundraising paralysis, an inability for purposeful wealth creation as well as a failure to integrate faith and broader community development. The result is a church which is unable to factor the place of resources in support of mission, in service to the less fortunate in society, in a constructive and theological way: one that is hapless about general community development and clueless about economics and politics.

Another result of this pathology is a church which, once the missionary perks and privileges are gone, is both unwilling and unable to mobilise the resources it needs for its existence let alone for mission work. It is as if, although the church stands smack in the middle of community, literally and metaphorically, it remains a foreign entity—foreign because of its origins and foreign because of its heavenly rather than earthly outlook. In part this is what

John Gatu of Kenya foresaw and attempted to prevent with his call for a missionary Moratorium in Africa as early as the 1970s.

Doing Theology and Church in the 21st Century

The background we have sketched above produced a church leadership and intelligentsia without the theological and ecclesiastical aptitude and wherewithal to mount a comprehensive critique of power, culture, politics, economics and development, let alone the ability to posit and generate alternatives. What we have in many places in the South is a desperate and disparate church without the capacity to mount an authoritative and alternative vision of the world based on a comprehensive critique of global power arrangements.

And yet it is true that the churches of the South are growing explosively, especially the indigenous and charismatic Pentecostal churches (Bediako 1995). There is also truth in the oft-quoted suggestion by renowned mission historian Andrew Walls that the Christian centre of gravity has shifted from the North to the South. On account of numbers and dynamism alone, Southern Christianity has long overtaken Christianity in the North. In this regard, the designation "World Christianity" ought to be redefined and expanded. Currently, appellations like "World Christianity" and "World Music" are predominantly meant to signify the marginal and the non-mainstream (Maluleke 2010). "World" is the section in the music store where you find the exotic, the unclassifiable, the non-European and the non-American.

Similarly, the focus of many a "World Christianity" chair is the exotic, little known, unclassifiable little "Christianities" in "remote" (from North America and Europe) corners of the world. It would be more accurate to describe the whole of Christianity as World Christianity, meaning that Christianity is now truly a world religion to the extent that it is found on every continent, in both urban and rural centers. But for this reality to dawn fully, all of Christianity must take ownership of it—i.e. the churches and the academy, the North and the South. Sadly this has not yet happened. Largely, the South still behaves as if it were home to marginal and exotic Christianity and the North still behaves as if it were the center of Christianity in the world. To the extent that the money and wealth are still in the North, the shift in the Christian centre of gravity from North to South has not been able to displace the dominance of the North in Christian missiological discourse.

Though in terms of numbers and dynamism the Christian center of gravity has indeed shifted, poverty and inequality are most acute and severe in the South. This is true when the North is compared to the South, true within the North and certainly true within the South itself. Generally, Christianity has thus become a faith whose wealthiest adherents and institutions reside in the North at a time when its poorest adherents and institutions are to be found in the South. It has become a religion with a wealthy minority and a poor majority. Indeed, within the South the same wealth divisions reproduce themselves—with a wealthy and wealth-controlling Christian minority amidst a sea of a poverty-stricken majority. This warped situation is, we wish to suggest, both the cause and consequence of an incoherent and a weak theology of money and wealth.

A church establishment so acutely divided along wealth lines and a community which mirrors global wealth divisions will necessarily find it difficult to engage missiologically with issues of poverty and inequality. This reality lies at the heart of Christian theological incoherence on matters pertaining to poverty. The same reality also lies at the heart of the much lamented loss of nerve (Bosch 1980) when it comes to mission action and theology. The end of the cold war, following the apparent triumph of the neo-liberal capitalist system in the late eighties, seemed to endorse the global economic status quo. While the rich have become richer around the globe, the poor and their poverty have been multiplied.

Christian Mission in an Unequal World

Few have mapped the contours of mission theology and discourse over the past century with more erudition than the late South African missiologist, David Bosch (Bosch 1980 & Bosch 1991). In his earlier work David Bosch seemed to have settled, albeit uncomfortably, for the evangelical versus ecumenical divide as the best illustration of the situation of Christian mission in the 20th century. However, it was in his *magnum opus*, written in the glare of the approaching 3rd millennium, that Bosch (1991) fully recognized the thousand flowers of mission theory and praxis already in bloom. In this work Bosch ditched the binary evangelical vs. ecumenical language. In its place came a more nuanced approach and a deeper analysis that took account of variety and context—his so-called "emerging ecumenical missionary paradigm". In this work Bosch appreciates 21st-century Christianity as "World Christianity" (without using this term) as well as the role and place of theologies other than the mainstream theological traditions. The role of the "younger churches" both as shapers and practitioners of mission (theology) also receive greater recognition in this piece.

Up to the late 20th century Christian mission discourse tended to be framed mainly in terms of the religious conditions and affiliations of the world and its inhabitants. It is from this frame of thinking that we have inherited the language of several binary and familiar descriptions of the world as consisting of the saved and the lost, the reached and the unreached, the heathen and the Christianized, the born again and those doomed to an eternity in hell. These types of contrasting distinctions were often used whenever Africans (and other peoples practicing the so-called "tribal religions") were under consideration (Friesen 1996). Questions of inequality and poverty—even for the mercurial David Bosch (1991)—were not fully factored into theological and missiological discourse. Admittedly, Bosch gave considerable space to "younger churches" and the radical theologies of liberation such as the Black Theology of Liberation in the USA and South Africa as well as Latin American Liberation theologies in Africa, Latin and North America.

He also hints strongly at the shift of the Christian center of gravity but does not sufficiently square this up, in our opinion, with the challenges of inequality between North and South, within the North and within the South. This reality, more than anything, has shaped the ebb (and whatever flow remains) of ecumenical theology in the 21st century. The emerging ecumenical paradigm, which Bosch foresaw, has been struggling to be born since the turn of the new century because the world is unequal and unipolar. It has not quite emerged because while the Christian numbers are in the South the money is still in the North. Wealth and power matters today in Christian mission as it has always done in past. We cannot mount a mission discourse that is oblivious to the inequality of the world in which Christian mission is to be carried out.

This has been the central thrust of the message of liberation theologies. Unfortunately since these theologies are born in the South and amongst the poor and marginalised in the North, they have tended to be 'ghettoized' so that they are referred to mainly as illustrations of the exotic possibilities in emerging Christian theologies. Yet these are theologies emanating from the vibrant centers of Christianity in the 21st century. How is it possible that theological voices from the vibrant centers of Christianity are rendered merely exotic while the jaded theologies of Europe continue to rule the roost globally? In fact in the mainstream theological academy theologies of liberation tend to be regarded as a fad that has come and gone. The restless theological train of the South has been curiously moved on to "newer" but equally exotic theologies such as "public theology", "contextual theology", "reconciliation theology" etc.

The answer has to do with money, wealth and poverty. Why are the Christians of the South unable and not allowed to do mission in the North, despite their numbers and their evident enthusiasm? The answer has to do with money, wealth and poverty. Why is western-led ecumenism seemingly fading away at this crucial moment? The answer has to do with the changing financial priorities of the rich Christians in the North. It all has to do with Mission and money—the money of mission and the mission of money, the money in mission and the mission in money.

World Inequality, Poverty and Degradation at a Glance

Even with the possibility of error margins, global statistics of the wealth gap issued by authoritative bodies are shocking.[7] A recent Oxfam article[8] based on the authoritative Credit Suisse's 2013 Global Wealth Report[9] paints a rather bleak picture. Some of the startling facts emanating from the Oxfam analysis are worth highlighting:

- The richest 85 people in the world are worth more than the poorest 3.5 billion;
- Nearly half of global wealth is owned by 1% of the world population;
- The wealth of the 1% richest people in the world is 65 times the total wealth of the bottom half of the world's population;
- Seven out of ten people live in countries where economic inequality has increased in the last 30 years;
- Between 1980 and 2012, the richest 1% increased their share of income in 24 out of 26 countries for which Oxfam has data;
- 95% of the post-financial crisis growth experienced in the USA since 2009 has been captured by the richest 1% while the bottom 90% became poorer.

These are massive observations on the condition of the world we live in. Granted that wealth is only one form of power, these observations still give important clues as to how other forms of power are structured in our world. The massive gap between those who have power and those who do not is replicated in many other spheres of life. It is sometimes argued (by some advocates of capitalism) that "some economic inequality is essential to drive growth and

---

7 Accessed on 17th of January 2015 http://www.washingtonpost.com/blogs/wonkblog/wp/2014/01/22/10-startling-facts-about-global-wealth-inequality/.

8 Accessed on 17th January 2015 http://www.oxfam.org/sites/www.oxfam.org/files/bp-working-for-few-political-capture-economic-inequality-200114-summ-en.pdf.

9 Accessed on 17th January 2017 https://publications.credit-suisse.com/tasks/render/file/?fileID=BCDB1364-A105-0560-1332EC9100FF5C83.

progress, rewarding those with talent, hard earned skills, and the ambition to innovate and take entrepreneurial risks."[10]

It is, however, clear that in current global configurations the situation has become extreme and distorted. Surely God is not so mean as to allocate talent and innovativeness only to 100 out of 7 billion people! In a world where wealth and opportunity is concentrated in the hands of so few, you can bet that economic and social policy will also be structured in such a way as to favour the rich. Australian filmmaker John Pilger (2006) and others have pointed out that the current global economic system amounts to "socialism for the rich and capitalism for the rest."[11] This, they argue, was aptly illustrated when European and North American governments used taxpayers' money to rescue banks and big business in the aftermath of the 2008 financial meltdown—a meltdown caused not by the poor but by the selfsame rich. Yet while the post 2008 bail-outs are a dramatic illustration of the socialism-for-the-rich and capitalism-for-the-rest syndrome, this syndrome is more common than meets the eye. Consider the tax cuts and subsidies given to big business in many countries as well as the huge salaries, perks and healthy bonuses given to CEOs and executives as opposed to the lot faced by the workers and the unemployed. All these are illustrations of a form of socialism reserved for the rich while the rest are condemned to capitalism.

This is a system designed to concentrate wealth in the hands of a few, resulting in massive poverty and lack among the majority. It is a system built for the rich and powerful without much regard to the poor except perhaps for their labour and buying power. More importantly it is a system which resembles a narrowing pipe. Because it is designed to reward a tiny minority while punishing the vast majority, it is really a global system designed to create exclusion and poverty for the majority. There is a sense in which the rhetoric of democracy and rule of law either does not give sufficient recognition to the deliberate systemic constraints or serves to obfuscate the inherent problems in the system.

Oxfam has observed that this system has the potential to render democracy and the rule of law meaningless to the vast majority of the world's citizens. In a survey of six countries, (Spain Brazil, India, South Africa, UK and the USA) Oxfam noted that many citizens experienced the laws and regulations of their countries as institutions designed to benefit the wealthy. Such laws and

---

10 See Oxfam Report.

11 See Jones, Owen, 29 August 2014, 'It's Socialism for the rich and capitalism for the rest of us in Britain' *The Guardian. UK Edition*, http://www.theguardian.com/books/2014/aug/29/socialism-for-the-rich. Accessed on 18th January 2015.

regulations pertain to issues such as financial deregulation, the tax system, rules that enable the rich to evade tax, so-called austerity measures designed to hurt the poor, policies that put women at a disadvantage as well as policies that enable the "capture" of a country's oil and mineral wealth.

And yet, even the likes of Oxfam and Credit Suisse seem to run out of ideas when it comes to recommendations on how to deal with the global problem of inequality. The nub of their recommendations appears to be a moral appeal to the rich and the powerful to be a little kinder and a little more responsible. For example, Oxfam appeals to "those gathered at Davos" to:

- Not dodge taxes in their own countries;
- Not use their economic wealth to seek political favours;
- Make their investments public;
- Agree to pay more tax based on their income;
- Lobby their government to use taxes constructively by providing such benefits as universal healthcare, education and social protection;
- Demand a living wage for workers in their companies.

Clearly the foregoing are nice and noble appeals. However, to appeal to the consciences of the rich and the powerful, urging them to make these commitments and concessions, comprises a fundamental misunderstanding of the logic of the global system that produces inequality. It is not in the interest of the rich not to dodge taxes—especially if it is not illegal to do so. Asking the rich not to use their wealth to seek political favours is to misunderstand the partnership between wealth and politics in many democracies. The very elections—the fundamental basis of a democratic government—often rest on secretive or undeclared funding of the parties and the candidates. In some instances the wealthy have moved into politics and campaigned for themselves or their representative to take up political power.

Unless there is appropriate national and international legislation, why should the rich reveal the full extent of their wealth? Asking the rich and powerful to call for a living wage is like asking cats to go and teach mice how to avoid being caught by cats. Clearly therefore, while organisations like Oxfam and the research arm of Credit Suisse are clearly familiar with the extent of the inequality problem, they are not much wiser when it comes to proposals designed to change the system.

Global inequality has several devastating ramifications—ramifications that take on different guises in different countries and regions. While the vast majority of the citizens of the world are victims, there is a hierarchy of victims all over the world. From a labour point of view, we could argue that it is the working classes of the world who are the victims of inequality. In this regard, global worker and labour movements such as the International Labour Organization (ILO)[12] seeking to unite workers globally around common problems are pursuing a just and valid cause and course. And yet the labour movement must also be vigilant that it does more than pursue palliative solutions without addressing the root causes of the problems facing the working class.

South Africa as an Example

An Overview

In a book purported to be give us the "long view" on South Africa, Landman bravely proposes eight basics that South Africa or any country requires in order to become a "modern successful society". These are:

- A sound economy;
- Economic growth that exceeds population growth;
- Adequate employment;
- An open society;
- Uninhibited creative individuals;
- Unlearning old values and learning anew;
- Strong social capital;
- Addressing inequality.[13]

Although inequality is included, it is, according to Landman, but one of eight important non-negotiable elements.Landman's operating assumption is that the economy of democratic South Africa is doing far better than the economy under Apartheid. Whereas between 1975 and 1993 South Africa progressively became 11% poorer (:30), its per capita income has "grown by a third since democracy despite the 1998 global crisis and the 2009 recession." More fundamentally, Landman bases his observations on a number of economic postulations and beliefs already implied in the preceding list which are core to what has been termed the neo-liberal economic theory.

These include the following four creeds of neo-liberal economic policy:

- The wealthier a country is, the better the chances for democracy (therefore democracy has a good chance of survival in South Africa);

---

12 http://www.ilo.org/global/lang--en/index.htm accessed on 19th January 2014.

13 Landman 2013, 19.

- Growing national wealth makes social development possible;
- The (creative) individual (not the tribe) is king;
- New values spurned by economic development must be embraced not resisted.[14]

Landman insists that the challenge in South Africa is that, owing to robust demographic growth, both unemployment and employment have grown. And yet, in spite of what Landman says, economic growth in South Africa has not created sufficient jobs, hence an unemployment rate that remains above 25%—i.e. nearly 5 million people are unemployed.

With the worst Gini coefficient of all the BRICS (Brazil, India, China, South Africa) countries, at 0.70, South Africa is one of the most unequal countries in the world. Up to 50% of South Africa's income goes to 10% of the population. Yet here too Landman would like to suggest South Africa is not doing as badly as often suggested.

> The rich are certainly getting richer, but the poor are getting less poor. Over the last few years, the inequality between me and Bill Gates has certainly increased. But I am not poorer than I was twenty years ago.[15]

Consistent with his general views, Landman presents all sorts of mitigating arguments and numbers to suggest that, through government redistribution in social grants and the provision of free services, South African inequality can be rolled back.

Distinguishing between financial capital (in the bank), human capital (in the head) and social capital (between people), Landman devotes some time and space to the latter. For him, South African social capital is visible in the popularity of the culture of establishing rotating credit associations. These become nodes of communal, spiritual and financial support groups that act as glue for communities struggling with the effects of poverty. I suppose this is where Landman would also locate the churches, as key builders of social capital. The basic point he makes is that for a modern society to be successful, social capital is as important as financial and human capital. For Landman, South Africa has more social capital than it is given credit for, even by South Africans themselves. But is this analysis correct? We do not agree.

---

14 Landman 2013:37–39.

15 Landman 2013, 135.

Example of the Weakening South African Labour Movement

The South Africa example of the challenges facing the labour movement is perhaps instructive. The biggest trade union confederation in the country, the Congress of South African Trade Unions (COSATU) has a formal alliance with the African National Congress (ANC) the ruling party in South Africa. Whatever the lobbying benefits such an alliance brings to COSATU, twenty years after the instigation of democracy, the disadvantages of the alliance have become crystal clear. Several recent developments may serve to illustrate the problem. Firstly, in an attempt to stem youth unemployment, the South African government has sought to provide subsidies for big business who/to employ young people. This move has been bitterly opposed by COSATU on at least two grounds, namely that once again tax payers are 'rewarding' big businesses for 'refusing' to do what they should have done naturally; and using thefunding from this 'cheap labour' subsidy, big business is going to undermine organised labour. Nonetheless, the ruling party has proceeded to implement the subsidy system regardless of the protestations of COSATU, their alliance partner, to the detriment of the working class.

Secondly, two years ago, the post-Apartheid government of South Africa permitted (or instructed) the police force to use live ammunition on protesting mining workers, killing 34 miners in Marikana—a mine owned by Lonmin, outside Rustenburg—in the Marikana massacre. Here was a classical contest between workers and mine owners. Refusing to go to work, the miners took off and held a vigil on a hill outside the mining buildings. While there was violence in which ten people were killed in the week before the massacre, the killing of 34 miners in one evening was chilling.[16] Ironically some of the police involved in the massacre are members of a police union belonging to COSATU. Therefore, on the Marikana hill, not only did we have COSATU fighting against COSATU (assuming that at least some of the workers [previously] belonged to COSATU-affiliated unions) alliance partners were also at war with each other. Nothing demonstrated the limits of labour alliances with ruling parties better than this bloody incident. Having formed a new union, at that time still to be recognized, the striking workers were in fact also turning their backs on COSATU, its affiliates and the government which they had voted into power. On the face of it, the Marikana strike was about wages, but it was also a protest about several systemic problems facing miners in South Africa

16 The South African government appointed a judicial commission of inquiry to investigate the Marikana shootings. That commission has submitted its report to the President and that report has since been made public. See, http://www.sahrc.org.za/home/21/files/marikana-report-1.pdf, accessed 25 February 2016.

today. These include the conditions under which the miners live and work, the huge salary gap between the lowest paid miners (such as rock drillers) and the mining executives, the rapprochement between union leaders and Lomnin management, as well as the cozy relations between government and mining companies. The involvement of someone like Cyril Ramaphosa, a former mine trade unionist and now the Deputy President of South Africa, as a mine owner in the Marikana saga was also instructive.

Two further examples of the precariousness of a labour movement that is too closely enamoured with the ruling party will suffice. About two years ago, the South African government finalised its plans to institute vehicle E-tolling around Johannesburg—a tender for which has been awarded to an Australian company. Sham consultations with communities were held. It was clear that the government had made its mind up ahead of the consultations. One of the most vociferous opponents to the E-tolling scheme was COSATU. COSATU argued that the E-tolling methodology—because it "will add to the burden of the poor", "exclude the poor from using the best public infrastructure", will force the poor back into a "totally inadequate public transport system"—is "privatisation through the backdoor" and "the most expensive way of recovering road costs".[17]

A citizen's organisation formed to oppose E-tolls called the Opposition to Urban Tolling Alliance (OUTA) also argued that the system was irrational, noting that the tolled free-ways are not new routes, the system is poorly planned, there are no viable alternative routes for those who cannot afford the tolled highways, and that there were better and cheaper methods of funding road construction and maintenance.[18] Once again, although COSATU and the ruling party are in alliance and although the ruling party prides itself in its connectedness to the general populace, all the pleas and arguments of COSATU and OUTA were ignored as gantries were installed in several places on the Johannesburg highways, establishing the E-Tolls system.

Finally, after several years of tensions between some members of COSATU and the government, tensions that have put considerable strain on their alliance, the biggest COSATU union, the national Union of Metal Workers in South Africa (NUMSA) was expelled from COSATU in 2014. Its expulsion is not only likely to weaken COSATU further but may in fact spurn a new political movement to the left of the ruling party. It is possible much labour instability may lie ahead as part of the restructuring of the labour scene in South Africa. Two of the 'official' reasons for the expulsion of NUMSA are that, in violation of an agreed COSATU principle, it was recruiting in sectors designated to other

17 http://drum.co.za/news/reasons-for-opposing-e-tolls-vavi/.

18 http://www.outa.co.za/site/about-outa/why-we-oppose-e-tolling/.

COSATU unions, and that it had publicly urged its members not to back the ruling party in the 2013 general elections. That is how bad things have become between some trade unions and the ruling party. NUMSA has been critical of government policies, especially as these pertain to worker rights. By extension it has also been critical of the nature of the alliance between COSATU, the ruling party and the South African Communist Party (SACP). The absorption of leaders of the SACP into the government has been a particular sore point.

The Example of a Weakening Ecumenical Movement

Additional to the weakening of the labour movement outlined above has been a weakening of the ecumenical movement and the prophetic impact of the churches. To be fair, the decline of ecumenical cooperation is a global phenomenon that seems to be one of the outcomes of the end of the cold war in the late 1980s. Since then all the major ecumenical bodies in the world seem to have taken a knock. The most obvious symptom is loss of financial sponsorship. The churches and (government) agencies which used to fund these bodies appear to have lost their own sources of income, lost their funding agendas or changed their priorities. As a result, ecumenical bodies such as the World Council of Churches (WCC) and their continental and national equivalents have sharply declined in income, output and influence over the past quarter of a century.

The South African ecumenical movement has been no exception—it too has been affected by the domino effect of the global processes we have just outlined. More uniquely, the South African ecumenical context of the past 25 years has been dominated by the ending of Apartheid and the entrance of South Africa into the global trade and financial community. Suddenly the South African ecumenical movement and the churches were without much of the funding they had hitherto enjoyed. Furthermore the ecumenical movement 'lost' some of its influential leaders to the South African democracy project. To illustrate this superficially, some of the ecumenical leaders who were absorbed into the new government and its many arms include the following:

Desmond Tutu—headed the Truth and Reconciliation Commission
Frank Chikane—became a director in the office of the President
Brigalia Bam—became the chairperson of the Independent Electoral Commission
Smangaliso Mkhatswa—became a Mayor
Tom Manthata—joined the Human Rights Commission
Itumeleng Mosala—became a Vice Chancellor and later a director in government

These are but a few examples. Whether these people were 'lost' to the churches by virtue of their serving in these capacities is a matter we have debated and still need to debate. The truth of the matter is that the ecumenical movement suddenly had to replenish its leadership core. But more than the loss of money and a handful of critical leaders, the ecumenical organisation was also at a crossroads theologically. If prophetic witness and liberation theology was what was needed during the years of Apartheid, what kind of stance should churches and theologies take in light of the changed situation? Was liberation theology still relevant after the end of the cold war?

If the new situation vexed the churches it was only because the churches realised that the advent of democracy did not translate into the elimination of poverty, inequality and the disease burden for the poor. A new tricky relationship started to develop between the churches and the new democratic government. Previously the new government had assumed that purely because it was a popular government (unlike the Apartheid regime) the churches would be in solidarity with it. Uncomfortable with some of the policy options and priorities of the new government, however, some in the churches started talking not about "solidarity" but "critical solidarity".

For its part the new government and the ruling party launched several initiatives aimed at managing religions in general and the churches in particular. The new secularist constitution came in handy for the new government in its efforts to equalise and relativise religions. The fact that a form of Christianity and a particular kind of Christian theology were supportive of Apartheid did not always help the churches. And yet the prophetic witness of the churches during Apartheid is incontestable—personified in the contributions of the likes of Desmond Tutu, Beyers Naude, Wolfram Kistner, Khoza Mgojo, Allan Boesak and Itumeleng Mosala. Three notable government initiatives over the 20-year period of democracy were: the formation of the National Religious Leaders Forum (NRLF), the Moral Regeneration Movement (MRM) and the formation of the National Interreligious Council (NILC). The first two were created during the presidency of Nelson Mandela as invitations for faith organisations to help the government in the construction of a moral and ethical society. Both of these first two initiatives have now collapsed. Though intended to be an inter-religious body, the NILC was deliberately put up as an alternative to the South African Council of Churches (SACC).[19] In fact the SACC was not invited to participate in it. Instead the more non-confrontational churches from the ranks of the Charismatic and the Pentecostal denominations were

19 'Mataboge, Mmanaledi 2009, Mail and Guardian' Why the ANC dumped the Council of Churches' http://mg.co.za/article/2009-09-18-why-anc-dumped-council-of-churches.

invited. Part of the reason the new government can afford to treat the SACC with some disrespect is that it has become very weak. Without financial sponsorship (in fact some of its former overseas sponsors would rather support the new government directly), very thin at the leadership level and almost theologically bankrupt, the SACC is but a shadow of its former self.

Theological Grounding of Christian Mission in an Unequal World

> We are living in a world in which faith in mammon threatens the credibility of the gospel. Market ideology is spreading the propaganda that the global market will save the world through unlimited growth. This myth is a threat not only to economic life but also to the whole creation.[20]

In the important WCC document from which we quote above, several key affirmations on the nature of Christian mission and its basis in the Holy Spirit are shared. For our present purposes, three concluding affirmations (paragraphs 106, 107 and 108) emanating from this document are noteworthy. The first of these recognises "mission movements emerging from the global South and East"; the second recognises "marginalised people as (prophetic) agents of mission"; and the third affirms "that the economy of God is based on values of love and justice" which is opposed to the "idolatry in the free-market economy." In another equally important document of the WCC,[21] the role of the church in mission is explored. The document outlines the role of the church as being primarily that of proclaiming the Good news in word and in deed.

In his *Apostolic Exhortation*,[22] proclaimed in 2013, Pope Francis makes similar points, calling for the "structural causes of poverty" to be addressed and the "special place of the poor in God's people" to be respected. Economic policy, says the Pope, ought be shaped, not by the "unseen forces and the invisible hand of the market" but by concern for "the dignity of each human person" and the pursuit of the common good. Economy "should be the art of achieving a fitting management of our common home, which is the world as a whole."

20 *Together towards Life: Mission and Evangelism in Changing Landscapes.* Geneva: World Council of Churches, paragraph 7, 6.

21 Faith and Order Paper No. 214, *The Church: Towards a Common Vision.*

22 *Evangelii Gaudium: Apostolic Exhortation on the Proclamation of the Gospel in Today's World.* 2013 Rome: Vatican.

Implications and Conclusions

Firstly, we need to recognize the need to respond to the inequalities in our world, not only in action but theologically and missiologically. This will mean unlearning destructive theologies and missiologies, whether they be "pie-in-the-sky" or those that teach us to fake diffidence towards wealth and money. It also means recognising the violence and dispossession that occurred in the process of evangelisation.

Secondly, we need to recognise that while the Christian centre of gravity has shifted to the South, the wealth centre of gravity remains in the North. This means that while the global Christian majority live in poverty, the Christian minority of the North lives in wealth. This is a recipe for many theological and sociological challenges.

Thirdly, although the number of Christians is growing exponentially in the South, the churches of the South are some of the most under-resourced in the world. This creates many theological, spiritual and practical challenges for the church. It certainly is one of the reasons why churches and church organisations in the South are unable to respond effectively to the prevailing socio-political situation.

Fourth, the impact and inequality is yet to be adequately accounted for and grappled with in missiology. This is probably a sign of the extent to which the North still sets the missiological and theological agenda.

Fifth, World Christianity, not as reference to the exotic and the marginal but rather as an expression of global Christian reality, needs to become hegemonic in theological education and research. This is arguably an important step if we are to be able to respond theologically and practically to global inequality.

Sixth, economic matters—matters of what Pope Francis calls "the art of achieving a fitting management of our common home"—are central, and not incidental, to theological reflection.

Seventh, in our engagement with economic matters we must always stand ready to evaluate economic policies encouraging the propensity to create inequality and antagonistic tothe goal of protecting human dignity.

Eighth, while no country in the world can address its economic and social challenges in isolation, it is important to have a firm grasp of the national and local economic scene. Global inequality always shows up next door and in our local village. This is the reason why we have spent some time on the South African situation.

Ninth, the church's ability to participate meaningfully in God's mission, especially its prophetic calling, depends on its structural and theological strength. In this regard, the church's engagement with cognate civil society organisations becomes important. We need to keep track of the strengths and weaknesses of these organisations.

Tenth, like all other organisations, churches must be weary of being trapped ideologically and blinded either by the worship of Mammon or by alliances forged with governments and other organisations in society.

Finally, it is important that our participation in mission is always guided by and based on Biblical reflection. Equally important is the necessity to subject the pursuit of wealth—for both Church and state—to environmental sustainability.

Bibliography

Adebajo, Adekeye. *Africa's Peacemakers. Noble Peace Laureates of African Descent.* 1st ed. London: Zed Books, 2014.

Asamoah-Gyadu, Kwabena. *Contemporary Pentecostal Christianity: Interpretations from an African Context.* New York: WIPF and Stock, 2013.

Bediako, Kwame. *Christianity in Africa.* London: Regnum, 1995.

Bhorat, Haroon & Kanbur, Ravi (eds.). *Poverty and Policy in Post-Apartheid South Africa.* 1st ed. Cape Town: HSRC, 2006.

Biko, Hlumelo. *The Great African Society: A Plan for a Nation Gone Astray.* Jeppestown, Johannesburg: Jonathan Ball, 2013.

Bonk, Jonathan. *Missions and Money. Revised and Expanded.* 2nd/Revised ed. Maryknoll, New York: Orbis Books, 1991.

Bosch, David J. *Witness to the World. The Christian Mission in Theological Perspective.* London: Marshall, Morgan & Scott, 1980.

———. *Transforming Mission.* Maryknoll, New York: Orbis Books, 1991.

Buhlungu, Sakhela. *A Paradox of Victory: COSATU and the Democratic Transformation in South Africa.* Pietermaritzburg: UKZN, 2010.

Buhlungu, Sakhela & Tshoaledi, Malehoko (eds.). *COSATU's Contested Legacy. South African Trade Unions in the Second Decade of Democracy.* Cape Town: HSRC Press, 2012.

Carpenter, Joel (ed.). *Walking Together. Christian Thinking and Public Life in South Africa.* Abilene: Christian University, 2012.

Chitando, Ezra (ed.). *Mainstreaming HIV and AIDS in Theological Education. Experiences and Explorations.* Geneva: World Council of Churches, 2008.

Dibeela, Prince & Lenka-Bula, Puleng & Vellem, Vuyani (eds.). *Prophet from the South. Essays in Honour of Allan Aubrey Boesak.* 1st ed. Stellenbosch: Sun Press, 2014.

Dickson, Kwesi A. *Uncompleted Mission. Christianity and Exclusivism.* Nairobi: Acton, 2000.

Dube, Musa W. (ed.). *Other Ways of Reading. African Women and the Bible*. 1st ed. Geneva: World Council of Churches, 2001.

Dube, Musa W. *The HIV & AIDS Bible. Selected Essays*. 1st ed. Scranton: University of Scranton, 2008.

Evangelii Gaudium: Apostolic Exhortation on the Proclamation of the Gospel in Today's World. Rome: Vatican, 2013.

Faith and Order. Paper No 214, *The Church: Towards a Common Vision.*

Fanon, Frantz. *Black Skin, White Masks*. London: Pluto Press, 1967.

Friesen, Stanley. *Missionary Responses to Tribal Religions at Edinburgh 1910*. New York: Peter Lang, 1996.

Gibson, Nigel C. *Fanonian Practices in South Africa. From Steve Biko to Abahlali base Mjondolo.* Scottsville: University of Natal, 2011.

Gandjean, A. *La Mission romande: Ses racines dans le sol suisse romand. Son épanouissement dans la race thonga.* Lausanne: G. Bridel, 1917.

Gore, Al. *The Future*. New York: Random House, 2013.

Gumede, William & Dikeni, Lesley (eds.). *The Poverty of Ideas. The South African Democracy and the Retreat of Intellectuals*. Auckland Park, Johannesburg: Jacana, 2009.

Haddad, Beverley (ed.). *Religion and HIV and AIDS. Charting the Terrain.* Scottsville: UKZN Press, 2011.

Harries, Patrick. *Butterflies & Barbarians. Swiss Missionaries & Systems of Knowledge in South-East Africa*. Oxford: James Currey, 2007.

Harsh, Ernest. *Thomas Sankara. An African Revolutionary*. 1st ed. Ohio: Ohio University, 2014.

Keum, Jooseop. *Together towards Life. Mission and Evangelism in Changing Landscapes.* Geneva: World Council of Churches, 2013.

Khoza, Ruel J. *Let Africa Lead. African Transformational Leadership for 21st Century Business.* 2nd ed. Sunninghill, Johannesburg: Vezubuntu, 2005.

Kürschner-Pelkmann, Frank. *Reinhard Bonnke's Theology. A Pentecostal Preacher and His Mission. A Critical Analysis.* 1st ed. Nairobi: All Africa Conference of Churches, 2014.

Landman, JP. *The Long View. Getting beyond the drama of South Africa's Headlines.* Auckland Park, Johannesburg: Jacana, 2013.

Mahajan, Vijay. *Africa Rising*. Fifth printing ed. New Jersey: Prentice Hall, 2009.

Maluleke, Tinyiko Sam. *A Morula Tree Between Two Fields: The Commentary of African Writers on Missionary Christianity.* Pretoria: University of South Africa (unpublished thesis), 1995.

———. "The Africanization of Christianity and the fate of Mission. Ten Theses on African Christianity." In, Küster, Volker (ed.), *Mission Revisited: Between Mission History and Intercultural Theology.* Münster: LIT Verlag, 2010, 105–116.

Mandela, Nelson. *Long Walk to Freedom*. London: Little Brown Company, 1994.

Mashau, TD. and Kritzinger, Klippies (eds.). *Pavement Encounters for Justice. Doing Transformative Missiology with Homeless People in the City of Tshwane.* 1st ed. Parrow. Cape Town: AcadSA, 2014.

Mataboge, Mmanaledi. Mail and Guardian' Why the ANC dumped the Council of Churches', 2009. http://mg.co.za/article/2009–09–18-why-anc-dumped-council-of-churches

Mbeki, Thabo. *Africa. The Time has Come.* Cape Town: Tafelberg, 1998.

———. *Africa Define Yourself.* Cape Town: Tafelberg, 2002.

Mngxitama, Andile & Alexander, Amanda & Gibson, Nigel C. (eds.). *Biko Lives! Contesting the Legacies of Steve Biko.* New York: Palgrave Macmillan, 2008.

Mosala, Itumeleng. *The Bible in Black Theology.* Grand Rapids: Eerdmans, 1987.

Mphahlele, Es'kia. *Africa My Music. An Autobiography 1957–1983.* 3rd ed. Braamfontein, Johannesburg: Ravan, 1984.

Mugambi, JNK. *From Liberation to Reconstruction. African Christian Theology After the Cold War.* 1st ed. Nairobi: East African Educational Publishers, 1995.

Ngcaweni, Busani (ed). *The Future We Chose. Emerging Perspectives on the Centenary of the ANC.* Pretoria: Africa Institute of South Africa, 2013.

Oduro, Thomas & Pretorius, Hennie & Nussbaum, Stan & Born, Bryan. *Mission in an African Way. A Practical Introduction to African Instituted Churches and the Sense of Mission.* Toronto: Christian Literature Fund, 2008.

Pilger, John. *Freedom Next Time.* London: Black Swan, 2006.

Pöntinen Mari-Anna. *African Theology as Liberating Wisdom. Celebrating Life and Harmony in the Evangelical Lutheran Church in Botswana.* Leiden: Brill, 2013.

Ranger, Terence O. (ed.). *Evangelical Christianity and Democracy in Africa.* Oxford: University Press, 2008.

Saayman,Willem and Kritzinger, Klippies (eds.) *Mission in Bold Humility. David Bosch's Work Considered.* 1st ed. Maryknoll, New York: Orbis Books, 1996.

Sachs, Jeffrey. *The End of Poverty. How we can make it Happen in Our Lifetime.* 1st ed. London: Penguin, 2005.

Sanneh, Lamin & Carpenter, Joel A. (eds). *The Changing Face of Christianity. Africa, the West and the World.* Oxford: University Press, 2005.

Schaaf, Ype. *On Their Way Rejoicing. The History and Role of the Bible in Africa.* 1st ed. Carlisle: Paternoster, 1994.

Schreiter, Robert J. *The New Catholicity. Theology between the Global and the Local.* 3rd ed. Maryknoll, New York: Orbis Books, 1997.

Soyinka, Wole. *The Burden of Memory, the Muse of Forgiveness.* Oxford: University Press, 1999.

———. *Of Africa.* Yale: University Press, 2012.

Tinsimu ta Vakriste. (*Church Hymnary*). *Swiss Mission in South Africa.* Braamfontein: Sasavona, 1989.

Tutu, Desmond. *God is not a Christian. Speaking Truth in Times of Crisis.* 3rd ed. London: Rider, 2011.

Volf, Mirosloav. *Exclusion & Embrace: A Theological Exploration of Identity, Otherness and Reconciliation.* 1st ed. Nashville: Abingdon, 1996.

Vähäkangas, Mika & Kyomo, Andrew A. (eds.) *Charismatic Renewal in Africa. A Challenge for African Christianity.* Nairobi: Acton, 2003.

Wa Azania, Malaika. *Memoirs of a Born Free. Reflections on the Rainbow Nation.* 1st ed. Auckland Park, Johannesburg: Jacana, 2014.

Wickeri, Philip L. (ed.) *The People of God Among All God's People: Frontiers in Christian Mission.* London: Council for World Mission, 2000.

Wickeri, Philip L., Wickeri, Janice K., and Niles, Damayanthi M.A. *Plurality, Power and Mission. Intercontextual Theological Explorations on the Role of Religion in the New Millennium.* 1st ed. London: Council for World Mission, 2000.

Wilmore, Gayraud S. & Cone, James W. *Black Theology. A Documentary History, 1966–1979.* Maryknoll, New York: Orbis Books, 1979.

Yoder, John Howard. *The Politics of Jesus.* 2nd ed. Grand Rapids: Eerdmans, 1972.

Yousafzai, Malala. *I am Malala. The Girl who Stood Up for Education and was Shot by the Taliban.* London: Weidenfeld & Nicolson, 2013.

CHAPTER 5

Poverty and Power: African Challenges to Christian Mission

Gerrie ter Haar

In December 2012 I was in Helsinki to deliver a keynote speech at this same venue on a related subject, for a different audience but with some of you present. The title of my presentation then was "Poverty and Prosperity in Africa."[1] In that paper I looked at the relation between religion and the economy from an African perspective, in which economic prosperity is seen as related to spiritual growth and believed not to be achievable without creating the right spiritual conditions. I argued that for many African believers spiritual growth is an intrinsic part of human progress, in which spiritual wealth goes together with material prosperity.

In the present paper I continue the argument. This time my focus will be less on the money aspect and more on the mission aspect of churches in Africa, and especially on the way African-initiated churches (i.e. home-grown churches) consider their mission in the world today. For present purposes I take 'mission' to be understood in the broad sense as proposed to me in the original invitation as "Christian churches' and groups' responsibility towards the outside world".

Western Power and African Dependency

In recent decades, the historical mainline churches have come to understand their mission largely in terms of 'development', that is, as an effort to enhance the quality of life and further the material welfare of the global poor. However, churches in Africa as well as African theologians have been especially sensitive to the degree of dependency implied in development relations. As early as 1986 the All Africa Conference of Churches (AACC) published a report with its own analysis of the causes of poverty in Africa, in which it criticized the

1 Gerrie ter Haar, "Poverty and prosperity in Africa", in Tomas Sundnes Drønen (ed.), *Religion and Development: Nordic Perspectives on Involvement in Africa*, New York: Peter Lang, 2014, 11–25.

 | DOI 10.1163/9789004318496_007

churches' continuing dependence on outside assistance and the lack of strategies for developing long-term programmes rooted in a vision of social transformation.[2] Even longer ago, in the 1970s, Emmanuel Milingo, then Archbishop of Lusaka,[3] had asserted that Africa had been turned into a continent of beggars and to an alarming degree been made dependent on Western development aid. As a long-standing critic of development policies in Africa he criticized both Western and African development agents and blamed the African political elite for keeping their own people poor.[4] In that sense he did not see any difference between Africa's new political leaders and the old colonial masters: "They have sat in the chairs of the former rulers, and have assumed both the power and the riches of the colonialists, meanwhile they have left their people in the same misery in which they lived for many years."[5] During a thanksgiving service at the 17th anniversary of Zambian independence in 1981 he lashed out at the country's elite, accusing them of perpetuating a system of self-enrichment through nepotism.[6] It is worth noting that even today, more than half a century since most of Africa gained independence, many African states are dependent on international aid for half their budgets.

It is only recently, and for a variety of reasons, that Western development agents have begun to realize that they may have to change their policies in such a way as to adapt them to the specific context of Africa, incorporating an African worldview, which is often religious. Moreover, this remains a controversial matter. Meanwhile, African views of development have hardly been able to make a significant impact on international development programmes and policies. Since the 1970s, the World Bank and the International Monetary Fund (known as the Bretton Woods institutions) have been largely responsible for the ideological direction of development debates worldwide. Their influence has often resulted in policies that have been widely seen as externally imposed. In Africa, the Structural Adjustment Programmes (SAPs) of the 1980s

2 *Report on the Root Causes of Hunger and Food Insufficiency in Africa*, Nairobi: All Africa Conference of Churches, 1986.

3 Milingo had been appointed Archbishop of Lusaka in 1969. He was removed from his seat by the Vatican due to a controversy about his healing ministry. The various aspects of the conflict have been analysed in Gerrie ter Haar, *Spirit of Africa: The Healing Ministry of Archbishop Milingo of Zambia*, London: Hurst & Co./Trenton, N.J.: Africa World Press, 1992.

4 An early and most outspoken example are the series of lectures presented in 1976 in Canada (London, Ontario) to students of the Divine Word Centre that were originally published in mimeograph, and republished in 1994 in Australia: Emmanuel Milingo, *Development: An African View*, Broadford, Victoria: Scripture Keys Ministries.

5 Emmanuel Milingo, *Liberation through Christ: African Point of View*, Lectures given at the Divine Word Centre, London, Ontario, Canada, 12–16 April, 1977, 35. Mimeographed.

6 Ter Haar, *Spirit of Africa*, 207.

in particular have been widely criticized, including by church organisations, for their negative effect on African populations, notably the poorest among them. These programmes have sometimes been referred to as Satan Amongst the People, in a typical African play on words that provides existing jargon with an alternative and more realistic meaning.[7] Equally typical, the criticism is voiced in a religious mode, using a symbolic language familiar to most people in Africa.

The historical mainline churches in Africa—that is, the former mission churches—have tended to follow the lead of the Bretton Woods institutions in some of their fundamental assumptions concerning the nature of development. They share a rationalist approach to development, in addition to a strong belief in history as an evolutionary process. For many years this did not allow for any consideration by secular organisations of the role of religion in development. But religion, as African theologians and philosophers have continuously shown, is central to traditions of African thought and therefore crucial in addressing development issues in Africa.[8] From such a perspective development and progress must have a spiritual foundation to be really effective. In an African context poverty is not considered simply as a lack of material resources, nor is poverty exclusively seen as the result of dispossession and deprivation. It includes *spiritual* poverty, an aspect that is often ignored,[9] even by leading development experts who have otherwise described poverty as a multifaceted phenomenon. Robert Chambers speaks in this regard of a 'poverty trap' that contains five dimensions: material poverty, physical weakness, isolation, vulnerability, and powerlessness.[10] Other development experts, such as John Friedmann and Amartya Sen, have added or emphasized other aspects, notably lack of social power and lack of freedom.[11] None of them takes into account the importance of the spirit world that many Africans believe to

7 John Mihevc, *The Market Tells Them So: The World Bank and Economic Fundamentalism in Africa*, London and New Jersey: Zed Books, 1995, 236.

8 Patrick Wachira, "Development without foundation: Relationship between philosophy, culture and development", in David W. Lutz, Paul M. Shimiyu & George Ndemo Osengo (eds.), *Rethinking Integral Development in Africa*, Nairobi: Consolata Institute of Philosophy Press, 2011, 359–72.

9 See Gerrie ter Haar, "Religion and development: Introducing a new debate", in Ibid. (ed.), *Religion and Development: Ways of Transforming the World*, London: Hurst &Co./New York: Columbia University Press, 2011, 3–25.

10 Robert Chambers, *Rural Development: Putting the Last First*, Harlow: Longman, 1983; see also Ibid., "Poverty Unperceived: Traps, Biases and Agenda", IDS Working Paper 270, July 2006.

11 John Friedman, *Empowerment: The Politics of Alternative Development*, Cambridge, Mass.: Blackwell, 1992; Amartya Sen, *Development as Freedom*, New York: OUP, 1999.

exist, and its possible relation to their experience of poverty. Spiritual poverty is a concept that also resonates with African Christians' missionizing in Europe today, who experience Europe as a spiritual desert that will not be able to gain true prosperity unless its people return to God.[12] Most importantly, the concept of spiritual poverty reflects an African understanding of poverty as relational: for human beings to prosper—materially and spiritually—they must maintain a balanced relationship with their environment and all that is in it. This includes the spirit world, or the world of God.

It is often reluctantly that Western development organisations have begun to engage with the reality of religion in Africa, not least because it manifests itself in culturally unfamiliar ways. Even in Christian development circles, many feel uncomfortable in this respect, especially in regard to churches that have freed themselves entirely from Western tutelage and are mapping their own path to social transformation. This becomes most visible in the life of the latest generation of AICs or African independent churches, for which I have coined the term African *international* churches.[13] These have emerged in the era of globalization and amid the socio-economic conditions that have accompanied it. They do not conform to the traditional image of AICs of the first generation, which were shaped by the circumstances of their own time, a century ago. The field of action of the new-generation AICs is no longer the local environment but extends to the whole world, and their existence has given a new boost to the missionary movement, albeit in ways that are not always appreciated in the West. African international churches have often been criticized for the way they understand the mission of the church.[14] But the real reason for suspicion may well be in the changing power relations that are implied. African Christians today have the power to implement their task according to their own understanding of the gospel. The commandment to spread the gospel among all nations[15] is a necessity in their view and forms the basis of all other aspects of their work, including their development activities. For them, African dependency on Western power has become a thing of the past.

---

12 This is a reference to Ezekiel 37: 1–3. See Gerrie ter Haar, *Halfway to Paradise: African Christians in Europe*, Cardiff: Cardiff Academic Press, 1998, ch. 1: "A valley of dry bones".

13 Ter Haar, *Halfway to Paradise*, 21–26.

14 A well-known critic is Paul Gifford, esp. his book *Ghana's New Christianity: Pentecostalism in a Globalising African Economy* (London: Hurst & Co., 2004).

15 This is a reference to the Great Commission as recorded as in the Bible, esp. Matthew 28.

From Power to Participation

Over the years development organisations have become aware of the need to bring about a change in the relationship between donors and recipients and have tried to overcome some of the obstacles to such a realignment. In the 1970s a new approach to development was introduced that quickly gained in popularity, in which participation became a central concept. Characteristic of participatory development programmes is a bottom-up approach rather than the traditional top-down one, accompanied by efforts to involve the poor in decisions affecting their lives. Participation is thus seen as a way of empowering the poor. Churches and Christian organisations have embraced participation as a leading concept in their development programmes in an attempt to turn historical relations of dependency into a relationship built on equality. Various observers have suggested that the concept of participation derives its power from the fact that it is generally seen as morally good, in contrast to the top-down processes dominant in the first decades after the end of colonial rule.

But like all ideas and practices, participatory development has also come under critique; in particular its claims to the transfer of power have been questioned. One well-known critic is Ilan Kapoor, a professor of Critical Development Studies in Canada, who has highlighted the manipulative influences of development practitioners on the participatory process.[16] He argues that the aspiration to renounce power and privilege has the paradoxical effect of reinforcing rather than diminishing these very qualities. According to him it renders participatory development into a *dis*empowering method rather than an empowering one. Participatory development, Kapoor maintains, easily becomes a vehicle for the 'self-empowerment' of the development agents themselves, instead of a methodology for the empowerment of the 'other', as grassroots participants are left with an illusion that they are in control of the processes that take place around them. In reality, as other critics also allege, most partnerships exist on an uneven playing field, with the partner who controls the finances often determining the terms of the relationship. Issues of power relations within the relationship are seldom raised.[17] It is exactly this misrepresentation of power relations, according to Kapoor et al., that opens up

16 Ilan Kapoor, "Participatory development, complicity and desire", *Third World Quarterly*, vol. 26, nr. 8, 2005, pp. 1203–20. See also Ibid., "Concluding Remarks: The power of participation", *Current Issues in Comparative Education*, vol. 6, nr. 2, 2004, 125–29.

17 Cf. Fiona Bailey & Anne M. Dolan, "The meaning of partnership in development: Lessons for development education", *Policy & Practice*, nr. 13, 2011, 30–48.

the space for manipulation in participatory development. The development agents remain the masters of ceremony.[18]

While this debate is normally conducted in secular terms, a qualitative study in 2010 by Arne Zocher, then a master's student at Aalborg University, took the debate in an unusual direction by introducing into it the concept of mission.[19] Following the theoretical framework proposed by Ilan Kapoor, he found that religious development workers are very similar in their behaviour and attitudes to their secular counterparts. Participatory development, in this case, serves to meet the religious desires of development practitioners themselves. For many of them, it entails a process of personal transformation that brings them closer to God. Following Kapoor, he suggests that the self-empowering experience of religious transformation can result in the practitioners' increase of influence and power, thus making the concept of participation even more effective as a manipulative method.[20] The same, I would suggest, might apply to the concept of partnership, another buzz-word today among development practitioners, religious and non-religious, to describe the new relations between what used to be seen as the developed and the yet-to-be-developed world. Both concepts carry the suggestion of equality and mutuality, and both conceal their hidden powers.

Although Zocher's research was not carried out in Africa, but in Bangladesh, and though his qualitative study was based on a single case and is thus limited in scope, he opens up an interesting way of looking at the connection between development work and Christian mission by critically examining the concept of participatory development in religious organisations as a bottom-up alternative to the top-down power relations of the colonial period. In the final analysis, Zocher argues, religious development practitioners prefer participation because it provides a sophisticated vehicle for proselytization and conducting Christian mission among non-Christian populations. Participation and proselytization both entail the production of ideology as part of a process aimed at changing—i.e. manipulating—people's consciousness. Development work, and especially participatory development, provides Christian development organisations as well as individual missionaries with an instrument that conceals the process of proselytization. Its manipulative quality makes

18 Kapoor, "Participatory development", 1207.

19 Arne Zocher, "Participation is Dangerous: A Qualitative Study on Christian Development Practitioners and Participatory Development", M.A.Thesis, Aalborg University, 2010. Available at http://projekter.aau.dk/.

20 Ibid., 91ff.

participatory development the preferred model for religious development practitioners and a potential means to carry out mission activities.

Zocher's argument implies that in this respect there is no substantial difference between the more subtle development approach of the historical mainline churches, which tend to make a rigorous distinction between development and proselytization, and the rather less subtle development-*cum*-proselytizing efforts of modern charismatic churches, such as many of the international AICs. In effect, one may say, historical mainline churches and international AICs are both attempting to attract people through their social activities. African international churches, however, are frequently criticized for their overt proselytizing, which they themselves consider in terms of Christian witnessing and as central to their sense of mission. Social responsibility is an integral part of their Christian mission, as can be seen from their development activities, but in all cases squarely based on the Bible. The external criticisms show how the position of the new AICs has changed over the years, as they have moved from the periphery to the centre of society and become ideological competitors with the historical mainline churches. In contrast to the classical AICs, the leaders of the new-generation AICs are neither poor nor uneducated, nor are many of their members, but like their classical predecessors, they too are firmly rooted in an African worldview, in which the spiritual dimension is prominent.

The spiritual autonomy of the new AICs is a powerful driver of social change in Africa, and, in view of their own aspirations, this may have global effects in the long run.[21] Preaching the gospel and turning people to Christ are considered the foundational condition for bringing about change, both individually and socially. Inner personal change is seen as a precondition for the successful transformation of society. The one cannot go without the other, as the material and spiritual aspects of life are deemed to be inseparable. The same is true with regard to development, which for many Africans is not only a material but also a spiritual matter, a commitment that can be fulfilled only with help from the spirit world: hence the emphasis in AICs on the power of the Holy Spirit, a type of power in which they can fully share. Spiritual empowerment is an effective strategy from such a perspective, since it opens up avenues to achieve the 'good life', which is what development is all about. It is also a *participatory* strategy, one in which human beings work together with the Holy Spirit to improve their lives. In that sense too, there is no relation of dependency, but of mutual engagement between the human and the spirit world, or the world of God.

---

21 Not only are these churches spread around the world, but in the present day and age religion has generally become a global social and political force.

Mission and Prophecy: Two Sides of the Same Coin

African international churches leave no doubt about the fact that their primary task in the world is to preach the gospel. Their founders are often seen as prophets. Both the missionary and the prophet are believed to carry the word of God, if necessary to an unwilling audience. The prophetic function is an important one in African-initiated churches, whether in Africa or outside. Independent churches in Africa have often been founded as a result of a profound spiritual experience by their leader, who claims to have received a call from God to take His message to the people. A person who responds to such a divine call is considered a prophet. That is to say: these are not self-acclaimed prophets, but it is the hearers, the audience, who recognize in them the qualities ascribed to a prophet in the Bible. Prophets are not tellers of fortunes, although they are seers, people whose eyes have been opened to see what others cannot. In their own perception the true task of the prophet is simply to speak the word of God. "People call me a prophet", one of my interviewees told me, "because they see that I can predict things, they see certain qualities that they can only identify with biblical prophets, such as humility and the ability to suffer myself. They call me a prophet from their own personal observation. It is something which comes with the experience by which people see you."[22] According to the same source, a prophet, as a spokesperson of God, called to take His word to the hearers, must not only preach the word of God but also practise it. Armed with the Bible, a prophet "has to go out with the word of God to make others safe". Mission and prophecy are two sides of the same coin.

Preaching and practising the gospel, with a social awareness informed by the Bible, constitute what many African Christians believe to be the Church's prophetic task, to be distinguished from the Church's missionary task, which is deemed more specific. While the task of a missionary is limited in terms of prophetism (notably to the element of preaching the word of God), the task of a prophet is limitless, as he or she has to diagnose the ills of society and make these known to the people, while at the same time indicating means by which those ills can be addressed. The Ghanaian pastor Himmans-Arday—founder of

22 Interview with Ghanaian Rev. Daniel Himmans-Arday held on 26 July 2000. See Gerrie ter Haar, "Prophets in the modern world: An anthropological perspective on prophetism in African-initiated churches in Western Europe", in J. Brosseder (ed.), *Verborgener Gott Verborgene Kirche? Die kenotische Theologie und ihre ekklesiologischen Implikationen*, Stuttgart: Kohlhammer, 2001, 68–80, quotation 78.

the oldest African international church in the Netherlands[23]—compares the task of a prophet with that of a newspaper reporter. Like a newspaper reporter, a prophet observes the ills of society and broadcasts them to the world. The difference is that a newspaper reporter halts at that point, because, in his words: "they don't have a clue of how to stop it. But the man of God having read these things must pray to God for a clue."[24] The prophet has to find a way by which social ills can be cured. If he is not doing that, he is not benefitting society and thus not living up to his prophetic task. At the same time, questions of social justice, so prevalent in biblical prophetism, cannot be separated from matters of charity. As Himmans puts it: "Bring justice but add charity, bring charity but add justice to it".[25]

Combining justice and charity, based on their own reading of the Bible, seems a general principle of the African international churches that missionize around the world. A notable example is the Redeemed Christian Church of God (RCCG), originally from Nigeria but now considering the whole world as its mission field. Europe is an important part of the mission field: with reference to the metaphor used by the prophet Ezekiel, the spiritual condition of Europe is frequently described by the new AICs as a "valley of dry bones".[26] In their perception, Europeans are unable to see their own spiritual poverty and to appreciate the help they may need from Africa to enrich them, since they see Africans only as people who are trying to escape from the material poverty of their own continent.

In order to meet the challenge to fulfil its mission—in terms of its responsibility to the outside world—in Europe, the Redeemed Christian Church of God has established the Europe Mainland Mission as its missionary arm. In its own estimation the first phase of its mission activities—taking the nations of Europe for Christ—is almost completed. In other words, the church has established an institutional presence in many European countries. It is now entering the second phase: incursion into the major cities of northern Europe in particular. Hence the focus has been shifted from entering new countries to expanding missionary work in specific regions. For this purpose the church has launched a strategic plan introducing, among other things, training and

---

23 The True Teaching of Christ's Temple in Amsterdam, which started in the early 1980s as a house congregation.

24 Ter Haar, "Prophets in the modern world", 75–76.

25 Ibid., 76.

26 See footnote 12. A further elaboration can be found in Gerrie ter Haar, "Een dal vol beenderen: Een Afrikaanse visie op westers Christendom", *Nederlands Theologisch Tijdschrift*, vol. 51, 1997, nr. 3, 177–93.

performance assessments of mission leaders, and a web-based reporting system to enhance accountability. A number of training institutes have been founded: the European Leadership Academy, the School of Disciples, and most recently (October 2013) the School of Missions. Worldwide there is a strong focus on engaging young people, especially students. One innovative instrument is the virtual network called Campus Koinnect, which has its own social media site (a kind of alternative Linked-in) that welcomes visitors from all parts of the world, in more than 80 languages, to form a global Koinnect Community.[27]

Under the same concept of mission, RCCG carries out conventional development projects and programmes worldwide, such as helping people to develop entrepreneurial skills, setting up education centres, and providing in various ways for poor and disadvantaged groups such as orphans.[28] As such it is similar to secular or religious mainstream development organisations, but its methodology is fundamentally different, being based on the Bible as the true Word of God and on the belief in the power of the Holy Spirit as His divine instrument. Spiritual guidance is combined with systematic planning and organization, similar to a global business run on modern management principles. A global reach and an innovative use of modern media (RCCG is on YouTube, Twitter and Facebook) are some of the church's remarkable mission features. But the most striking of all is the total independence of the new African missionary movement from Western development agents, whether religious or secular. There are many areas, however, where secular and religious approaches to development overlap. In an article some years ago I made a comparison between the principles conventionally applied by secular development agents and the religious principles and practices of development as applied by an African actor. These include aspects such as transformation, self-realisation, agency, relationality, social trust, and human dignity and freedom. I showed that the differences are not so much in the final objectives but in the *ways* followed to achieve them, that is, in the method.[29]

---

27 A summary of this vision is stated in the 2014 RCCG diary "Europe Mainland Mission", published by the RCCG House of Wonders in Amsterdam. See also www.rccgmainlandeurope.org and www.campuskoinnect.org.

28 Cf. Dele Olowu, "Faith-based organisations and development: An African indigenous organisation in perspective", in Ter Haar, *Religion and Development*, 55–80, esp. 70–73.

29 Gerrie ter Haar, "The *mbuliuli* principle: What is in a name?", in Barbara Bompani and Maria Frahm (eds.), *Development and Politics from Below: Exploring Religious Spaces in the African State*, Basingstoke: Palgrave Macmillan, 2010, 40–55.

Poverty and Power

The methodology of modern African missionaries derives from a biblically informed analysis of social ills. Their spiritual autonomy makes it possible for them to analyse the world in terms that are meaningful to themselves, if not always to others. Their perception that a spiritual deficiency is at the heart of every crisis extends to their analysis of poverty. In contrast, leading development academics generally do not consider the spiritual causes of poverty, ignoring the power that the spirit world holds for many people in Africa and many other parts of the world.[30] References to the 'spirit of poverty' are frequent in AICs, implying a form of evil from which Africans can liberate themselves through communication with the spirit world, in this case through active engagement with the Holy Spirit. It is a strategy often involving some form of exorcism as a spiritual liberation to make space for the in-dwelling of the Holy Spirit. In their view, it is a Bible-based strategy. So, for that matter, are offering and tithing, which are seen by these churches as part of the biblical teachings on economic justice,[31] though often criticized by outsiders in the same way that deliverance is. These are only some of the many Bible-based strategies for the alleviation of poverty and the redress of social ills that are common in AICs, where the human and the divine combine forces for success in life.

Through their holistic approach African missionaries provide a recipe for self-empowerment for the many people around the world in need of spiritual and material support. From their perspective Christian witnessing is at the centre of their work, including their social projects and programmes. As Bryant Myers has observed, "What we put at the center of our program is also our witness. [...] If money is the focus, then money is perceived to be the key to transformation [...], if it is development technology, then technology will be worshiped as the source of transformation."[32] African missionaries put the gospel message at the heart of everything they are doing, in the belief that this, and nothing else, is the key to transformation. In doing so they are developing new models not only for understanding the world but also for *changing* it. Their spiritual autonomy reflects a new and final phase in the decolonization

---

30 As Bryant L. Myers from World Vision already observed in 1999 in his book *Walking with the Poor: Principles and Practices of Transformational Development* (Maryknoll, New York: Orbis Books), 85.

31 See Kent A. van Til, *Less than Two Dollars a Day: A Christian View of World Poverty and the Free Market*, Grand Rapids, Michigan: Wm. B. Eerdmans, 2007, 83.

32 Myers, *Walking with the Poor*, 208.

of Africa, which, I suggested many years ago, may be described as the decolonization of the mind.[33]

From an African point of view, we may say, poverty is not simply a concept referring to a lack of material resources. It also includes more than the immaterial dimensions that have been added by leading development academics over time to the core of the development concept, such as vulnerability and isolation, or lack of access to social power and lack of freedom. For many Africans poverty also encompasses a lack of access to the power of the spirit world. It is for this reason that the Christian development expert Bryant Myers has added spiritual poverty as a sixth dimension to Robert Chambers's well-known five dimensions scheme of poverty.[34] This is an important addition because, as Myers states, "No system[ic] account of poverty is complete without a holistic view of the spiritual and the material at the level of people and the social systems within which they live".[35] While development experts do nowadays generally include in their understanding of poverty the concept of empowerment, spiritual empowerment remains outside their frame of reference. Yet it is precisely this dimension that African missionaries fully understand and address, reflecting the holistic approach to human development that the earlier quoted African bishop Milingo advocated decades ago.

Conclusion

Evangelical Christianity has had a long and prominent history in Africa since the days of the early missionary movement.[36] Evangelical Christians are essentially 'gospel people'.[37] In his classic study on the subject, historian David Bebbington identified four main characteristics of Evangelical Christianity: biblicism (i.e. a special regard for the Bible), conversionism (i.e. the belief that lives need to be changed), activism (i.e. the belief that the gospel needs to be expressed in effort), and crucicentrism (i.e. a stress on the sacrifice of Christ

---

33 In a review of Gifford's book *Ghana's New Christianity: Pentecostalism in a Globalising African Economy*, published in *African Affairs*, vol. 105, nr. 420, 2006, 486–87.

34 Chambers, *Rural Development*; Friedman, *Empowerment*; Sen, *Development as Freedom*. See above p. 87.

35 Myers, *Walking with the Poor*, 69.

36 Andrew F. Walls, *The Missionary Movement in Christian History: Studies in the Transmission of Faith*, Maryknoll, New York: Orbis Books, 1996.

37 Derek J. Tidball, *Who Are the Evangelicals? Tracing the Roots of Today's Movement*, London: HarperCollins, 1994, 11.

on the cross).[38] Originating in eighteenth-century Britain and imported into Africa in the days of colonialism, this tradition is being redynamized by the African international churches and taken out of the African continent back to Europe again. The evangelical tradition has met with worldwide interest, especially engaging younger generations, who show a remarkable similarity with AIC members in their understanding of the gospel message and who embrace its activist stance. Their faith-inspired activism is the pendant of the secular-based NGOs, once more highlighting the point made above that the difference lies in the *path* taken to achieve goals, including development goals,[39] rather than in the goals themselves. They have turned the traditional statement 'I believe in God' into its logical pendant 'God believes in me', and therefore we will manage together. Modern evangelical churches portray Jesus as the coach for success, rather than as saviour of the poor, through the power of the Holy Spirit. It underlines the argument I have often made about turning spiritual power into spiritual capital.[40]

Peter Berger has defined spiritual capital as a sub-set of social capital, referring to the power and influence created by participation in a religious tradition.[41] Surely Berger did not have in mind the power and influence ascribed to the Holy Spirit, which drives so many modern African missionaries, thereby perpetuating the traditional spirit orientation that is so characteristic of African religiosity generally. But surely too, empowerment by the Holy Spirit can be seen as a form of invisible capital and thus be added to the existing canon. For that purpose I have defined spiritual capital as 'people's ability to

38 This has become known as the 'Bebbington Quadrilateral'. See David Bebbington, *Evangelicalism in Modern Britain: A History from the 1730s to 1980s*, London: Unwin Hyman, 1989.

39 Such as the eight United Nations Millennium Development Goals: eradicating extreme poverty and hunger, achieving universal primary education, promoting gender equality and empowering women, reducing child mortality, improving maternal health, combating HIV/AIDS, malaria and other diseases, ensuring environmental sustainability, developing a global partnership for development.

40 Including in Ter Haar, *Religion and Development: Ways of Transforming the World* (2011). To be sure, spiritual power, like any form of power, can be used for constructive as well as destructive purposes. The discussion is about the *potential* of religion, not about the great variety of real manifestations, which are both good and bad, like all human efforts.

41 Peter L. Berger and Robert W. Hefner, "Spiritual capital in comparative perspective", a paper written for the Spiritual Capital Research Program of the Metanexus Insitute. Available at www.metanexus.net. See also Peter L. Berger and Gordon Redding (eds.), *The Hidden Form of Capital: Spiritual Influences in Societal Progress*, London and New York: Anthem Press, 2010.

access resources believed to reside in an invisible world, which can be mobilized for the common good through forms of active engagement with them'.[42]

The older missionary movement, as Andrew Walls has pointed out, was the product of a particular phase of Western political, economic and religious development.[43] The new missionary movement, this time spearheaded by African and other non-Western Christians, is a product of its own time and place. African Christians today live in a globalized world, whether in or outside the African continent. Many of them belong to one of the large African international churches, the most recent type of AICs.[44] These are the product of their own time and circumstances, economically and politically, which also informs their understanding of the missionary task of the church in the 21st century. Conventional views of poverty and prosperity, of health and wealth, are challenged by African Christians who now have the power to follow and implement their own views in theology, including mission theology. As former archbishop Milingo formulated it many years ago: "We thank her [Europe] for what she has done for us, and we appreciate her worries and anxieties about us. But we believe that she, as a grandmother to us, should now worry much more about her problems of old age, than about us."[45]

Bibliography

Bailey, Fiona and Anne M. Dolan. "The meaning of partnership in development: Lessons for development education", *Policy & Practice*, nr. 13, (2011): 30–48.

Bebbington, David. *Evangelicalism in Modern Britain: A History from the 1730s to 1980s*, London: Unwin Hyman, 1989.

Berger, Peter L. and Gordon Redding (eds.). *The Hidden Form of Capital: Spiritual Influences in Societal Progress*, London and New York: Anthem Press, 2010.

Berger, Peter L. and Robert W. Hefner. "Spiritual capital in comparative perspective", Spiritual Capital Research Program, Metanexus Insitute. Available at www.metanexus.net. Accessed in August 2014.

Chambers, Robert. *Rural Development: Putting the Last First*, Harlow: Longman, 1983.

———. "Poverty Unperceived: Traps, Biases and Agenda", IDS Working Paper 270, July 2006.

---

42 Ter Haar, *Religion and Development*, 20.

43 Walls, *The Missionary Movement*, 259.

44 For an elaboration of this typology, see Ter Haar, *Halfway to Paradise*, esp. 21–26; also Ibid., "Poverty and prosperity in Africa", 14–15.

45 Milingo, *Liberation through Christ*, 8.

Friedman, John. *Empowerment: The Politics of Alternative Development*, Cambridge, Mass.: Blackwell, 1992.
Gifford, Paul. *Ghana's New Christianity: Pentecostalism in a Globalising African Economy*, London: Hurst & Co., 2004.
Kapoor, Ilan. "Concluding Remarks: The power of participation", *Current Issues in Comparative Education*, vol. 6, nr. 2, (2004): 125–129.
———. "Participatory development, complicity and desire", *Third World Quarterly*, vol. 26, nr. 8, (2005): 1203–1220.
Mihevc, John. *The Market Tells Them So: The World Bank and Economic Fundamentalism in Africa*, London and New Jersey: Zed Books, 1995.
Milingo, Emmanuel. *Liberation through Christ: African Point of View*, Lectures given at the Divine Word Centre, London, Ontario, Canada, 12–16 April, 1977. Mimeographed.
Milingo, Emmanuel. *Development: An African View*, Broadford, Victoria: Scripture Keys Ministries, 1994.
Myers, Bryant L. *Walking with the Poor: Principles and Practices of Transformational Development*, Maryknoll, New York: Orbis Books, 1999.
Olowu, Dele. "Faith-based organisations and development: An African indigenous organisation in perspective", in Gerrie ter Haar (ed.), *Religion and Development: Ways of Transforming the World*, London: Hurst & Co./New York: Columbia University Press, 2011, 55–80.
RCCG diary "Europe Mainland Mission", RCCG House of Wonders in Amsterdam, 2014.
Report on the Root Causes of Hunger and Food Insufficiency in Africa, Nairobi: All Africa Conference of Churches, 1986.
Sen, Amartya. *Development as Freedom*, New York: OUP, 1999.
Ter Haar, Gerrie. *Spirit of Africa: The Healing Ministry of Archbishop Milingo of Zambia*, London: Hurst & Co./Trenton, N.J.: Africa World Press, 1992.
———. "Een dal vol beenderen: Een Afrikaanse visie op westers Christendom", *Nederlands Theologisch Tijdschrift*, vol. 51, nr. 3, (1997): 177–193.
———. *Halfway to Paradise: African Christians in Europe*, Cardiff: Cardiff Academic Press, 1998.
———. "Prophets in the modern world: An anthropological perspective on prophetism in African-initiated churches in Western Europe", in J. Brosseder (ed.), *Verborgener Gott Verborgene Kirche? Die kenotische Theologie und ihre ekklesiologischen Implikationen*, Stuttgart: Kohlhammer, 2001, 68–80.
———. Review of Paul Gifford's book *Ghana's New Christianity: Pentecostalism in a Globalising African Economy*, *African Affairs*, vol. 105, nr. 420, (2006): 486–487.
———. "The *mbuliuli* principle: What is in a name?", in Barbara Bompani and Maria Frahm (eds.), *Development and Politics from Below: Exploring Religious Spaces in the African State*, Basingstoke: Palgrave Macmillan, 2010, 40–55.
——— (ed.). *Religion and Development: Ways of Transforming the World*, London: Hurst & Co./New York: Columbia University Press, 2011.

———. "Religion and development: Introducing a new debate", in Ter Haar, *Religion and Development*, 3–25.

———. "Poverty and prosperity in Africa", in Tomas Sundnes Drønen (ed.), *Religion and Development: Nordic Perspectives on Involvement in Africa*, New York: Peter Lang, 2014, 11–25.

Tidball, Derek J. *Who Are the Evangelicals? Tracing the Roots of Today's Movement*, London: HarperCollins, 1994.

Van Til, Kent A. *Less than Two Dollars a Day: A Christian View of World Poverty and the Free Market*, Grand Rapids, Michigan: Wm. B. Eerdmans, 2007.

Wachira, Patrick. "Development without foundation: Relationship between philosophy, culture and development", in David W. Lutz, Paul M. Shimiyu & George Ndemo Osengo (eds.), *Rethinking Integral Development in Africa*, Nairobi: Consolata Institute of Philosophy Press, 2011, 359–372.

Walls, Andrew F. *The Missionary Movement in Christian History: Studies in the Transmission of Faith*, Maryknoll, New York: Orbis Books, 1996.

Zocher, Arne. "Participation is Dangerous: A Qualitative Study on Christian Development Practitioners and Participatory Development", M.A. Thesis, Aalborg University, 2010. Available at http://projekter.aau.dk/. Accessed in August 2014.

CHAPTER 6

The Mission of the Church Amidst European Social and Economic Crisis: The Case of Greece

Evi Voulgaraki-Pissina

"Theology is the interpretation of the eternal in terms of the transient". This is a very succinct but comprehensive definition of the function of theology given by a Greek Orthodox Professor of Missiology.[1] The tension between eternity—the "place of light, [the] place of green pasture, [the] place of refreshment, whence pain and sorrow and mourning are fled away", as we describe and praise it in the Orthodox funeral service, the *Trisagion* for the Dead—and the turbulent world we live in, is self-evident. Furthermore, the tension is even greater, a real gap to be bridged, when the 'eternal' does not simply reflect the Kingdom of God, but God the Creator Him/Herself, and when 'transient' can refer to a very rapidly moving course of events, a very turbulent and high river.

And that is the case all over Europe, especially in the shadowy, unstable peripheral parts of the old Continent. With particular regard to my homeland, Greece, issues such as a steep deterioration in living conditions, an anxiety that bedevils reality and daily life—which casts a blight upon the far or near future—a frightening loss of things long taken for granted and a great need for adaptation to new social conditions, all cause a shift in our understanding of life, society, anthropology and theology.

In this article, I shall try to illuminate this interrelation and interaction of the eternal and the transient amidst the on-going social and economic crisis, bearing in mind the keynote question of the mission of the Church under the given circumstances. The article examines how mission can be best applied within a turbulent situation, and *vice versa*: how conditions of extreme impoverishment and injustice, such as now apply in Greece, influence and mark our missiological understanding.

Following the Chalcedonian Christological doctrine, a holistic understanding of mission reflects the inseparable unity of the two natures, divine and human, in the one person of Jesus Christ. It links *martyria* (witness) with social

1 Βουλγαράκης, « Ο Σημερινός Θεολογικός Λόγος για τη Σωτηρία » [Voulgarakis, "Contemporary Theological Soteriology"], 111.

 | DOI 10.1163/9789004318496_008

diaconia and the quest for justice. It reveals the spiritual and the material element that inseparably constitute the basis of Christian life. It becomes a genuine expression of Christian spirituality and loving ethos. It manifests itself as the 'Liturgy after the Liturgy', bringing the eschatological perspective into daily life.[2]

The first part of this presentation is an introduction to current Greek reality. The second part makes a critical closer examination of the various ways the needs of society are being addressed by the Church as the Body of Christ, focusing on the grassroots and institutional side of the Church with particular attention to its Hierarchy. The third and last part will focus on theoretical missiological problems, particularly on the bearing of the economic crisis and the experience obtained by dealing with people's urgent needs, on our theological understanding of mission.

The Current Greek Reality

Conceptualizing the Greek Crisis

Conceptualizing the Greek crisis is a major and general challenge. Since it erupted, it has been perceived through a multitude of interpretative lenses. Strongly conflicting accounts and a general blur at the level of sheer facts have made interpretation of the situation, let alone discovery of a way out or a remedy, a very ambiguous matter.

A narrative of quite unfavorable and derogatory character, from a Greek viewpoint, has been presented *par excellence* in the mainstream mass media. However, one should welcome a certain progress achieved in the area of information on the Greek crisis worldwide, which has recently become more pluralistic, deeper in understanding, more self-critical than judgmental, and now seems finally to perceive the consequences of certain austerity policies leading to a dead-end. Because of this fairer view, the whole discussion of Greece has lately been slightly more oriented to questions than to certainty.[3] Derogatory language and implications of guilt have been used as a means to impose dehumanizing measures. The famous phrase by German chancellor Angela Merkel, that Greeks should be punished for being naughty and that Greeks should

---

2 Keum, *Together towards Life*, 4. Vassiliadis, "An Orthodox Assessment," 174–178.

3 Today multiple perspectives are reflected even in the EU Parliament official site, e.g.: "Greece: Troika Success Story or a Warning." Furthermore, Lapavitsas, "Greece does not yet need Another 'Rescue' Package." Locks, "Austerity: A German Prescription for a Greek Tragedy." Charrel, "Errements européens et erreurs de la « troïka »."

do their homework,[4] along with deeply insulting material published in some European, especially German media,[5] were tools, perhaps weapons, of major psychological importance in the first phase of the Greek crisis. Regarded as a sign of hostility instead of solidarity, such a negative press also caused the Greek people to feel very estranged from a theological and philosophical point of view—regardless of whether their adherence to the Orthodox faith was sincere or merely cultural. Such remarks are racist in their exaggeration and generalizing character and increased the sense of mistrust and resentment.

Here, one should bear in mind some subtle differences in theology and mentality between East and West. I am not referring so much to modern theology, which is to a large degree homogeneous, but rather to a historical inheritance. The East has inherited its law and structure predominantly from Rome. Due to a lesser emphasis on legal, let alone legalistic, thinking, soteriological issues have traditionally been much less raised in the East. Besides, the idea than one is being blessed with material affluence by the Lord as a sign of His/Her gratification, (an idea originating in some cases in the Old Testament, e.g. Abraham, etc.,) was not further developed, generally speaking, in the Eastern tradition. This idea and the consequent striving to succeed are mostly interlinked with the idea of predestination and have in the past inspired certain types of Western Christian spirituality and ethos.[6] Furthermore, the notion that one is guilty when one is poor and unsuccessful in secular terms is completely alien to Eastern Christianity. Poverty, illness, or suffering are considered a testing and a challenge for God's beloved, in an ascetic spirit of *harmolipi*, the mingling of joy and sorrow, which conceives the descent into the tomb as the path to Resurrection. The idea of sin, as understood in the light of Orthodox theology (and modern ecumenical theology, to a large extent), differs significantly from the concept of guilt and is not related to it.[7] The authority of Law is also differently appreciated. "The final state of Law is anomy, the dissolution of

---

4 "Griechische Finanzmisere." Pop, "Merkel: 'loves' Europe, insists on 'Homework'." "Athen muß sein Hausaufgaben machen."

5 Disregarding populist yellow newspapers, I shall limit my documentation to the notorious cover of *Focus* magazine, an obscene Photoshop remake of the statue of Venus of Milos with the caption: "Betrüger in der Euro-Familie," *Focus: Das moderne Nachrichtenmagazin*, No. 8/10 (February 22, 2010).

6 Weber, *The Protestant Ethic and the Spirit of Capitalism*. Furthermore, Brink and Höpfl, *Calvinism and the Making of the European Mind*.

7 We consider "the Fall as an inheritance essentially of mortality, rather than of sinfulness, sinfulness being merely a consequence of mortality": Meyendorff, *Byzantine Theology*, 145. Cf. Weaver, "The Exegesis of Romans 5:12 Among the Greek Fathers." Shults, *Reforming Theological Anthropology*, 192.

every bastion of consciousness, total homelessness": this is how Vassili Psyllis, a prominent young Orthodox theologian, sums up the feeling about the law especially in the light of existing unlawfulness.[8] For us, Jesus Christ is mainly the liberator from the burden of the Law, "for the entire law is fulfilled in keeping this one command: 'Love your neighbor as yourself'" (Gal. 5:14).

Returning to our main train of thought: as to the small steps taken and the little progress achieved, one has to state that many European officials and IMF executives admit mistakes and miscalculations on various levels, although they are far from showing willingness to change direction.[9] The TINA [There Is No Alternative] Thatcherite principle was used to shrink the options down to the one chosen by the troika of IMF, European Central Bank and the European Commission.[10] This joint EU-IMF mechanism is questionable as to its very legitimacy.[11] Yet, while the TINA principle is increasingly discussed and challenged at an international level, in Greece the media cartel controls information to an unprecedented degree. This has been the case especially after the black-out of public TV, which also generated a huge wave of local and international reaction, the EBU (European Broadcasting Union) being part of it for quite a while.[12] Younger people use the Internet to obtain and disseminate

---

8 Psyllis, « Συναίρεση Θανάτου II » ["Contraction of Death II"].

9 "Schulz: Europe is not a Community of Austerity." Schulz's double talk is only of rhetorical importance. It applies to a period of time that has quite different value for the sufferers and for the managers of the crisis at different levels. The sufferers are urging a solution. The managers of the crisis are in no hurry. They seem to feed present needs with expectations, vague future plans and hopes of an almost metaphysical nature. Similarly, EU and IMF official evaluations of the Greek program include self-criticism, yet at the same time an unwillingness to modify. "Bowles: 'Troika's Overall Response to the Crisis has lacked Transparency.'" "Greek Officials welcome IMF Report."

10 A recent moderate example is the article by the managing director of the European Stability Mechanism Mr. Regling: "Alternatives to Austerity the managing director of the European Stability Mechanism Mr. Regling: "Alternatives to Austerity would be even More Painful."

11 "The Troika: How Europe's bailout Power Broker works". A 04'30" video, by the European Parliament/EuroparlTV on http://www.europarltv.europa.eu/en/player.aspx?pid=71f24322–51f0–47fb-933d-a2c300d507e4, posted January 31, 2014. Further critique in an official statement by the European Parliament: "Troika helped to avoid the Worst, but flawed Structure harmed Recovery."

12 "The European Broadcasting Union (EBU) believes that independent public service media (PSM) is indispensable for democracies, culture and societies. This is why on 11 June, when the Greek government abruptly shut down ERT, the EBU felt it had no option but to immediately take action to prevent Greek screens from remaining black, by carrying the satellite signal being produced by former ERT staff and streaming it on our

information, but parts of the less active population, especially the elderly, are true victims of the terrorizing newspeak on television in combination with fictional governmental "success stories."

People are facing a psychological war. Even when reality dawns clear and unmistakably, people are confused by doubts, as well as by depression and self-resignation. But the war is not confined only to the psychological level. The situation is being experienced literally as an atypical war situation, a subjective assessment nevertheless supported by the objective economic figures and financial statistics. Greek society is suffering an extreme deterioration of life conditions, including violent impoverishment—euphemistically called internal deflation—disrespect for private property through disproportionate and unfair taxation, destruction of public infrastructure, a governmental disregard for the law (in both legal and moral senses) and for the functioning of democracy, all in a way that is usually unknown in peacetime. The number of suicides has doubled and is currently the highest in Europe, in all amounting to a real humanitarian disaster.[13]

Evaluating the Numerical Data

Greece started out with an alarming average debt at just under 104% of its GDP (Gross Domestic Product) during 1994–2009; the European Commission estimates the debt to have reached 176.2% of GDP in 2013 and releases the 'optimistic' forecast that it may fall to 170.9% in 2015![14] This is enslavement to eternal debt, a situation that strangulates any economic planning. Unemployment reached 28% among the economically active population in November 2013, by far the highest in Europe.[15] The volume of GDP has been sinking constantly ever since 2008; in 2011 and 2012 it sank by more than 7% each year.[16] According to calculations of the yearly figures, the overall reduction is up to 25% since 2008. More important, the reduction of disposable income is estimated to

---

website": "Greece: EBU Looking Forward, not Back." The EBU seized broadcasting on August 21, 2013, but people continued to watch the ERT [Public Television] program online until November 7, when the main broadcasting headquarters were evacuated by the police. ERT radio is still broadcasting as a pirate radio station.

13 The dimensions of the darkest problem in Greece today are highlighted, despite the obscurity of official statistics, in the survey: Αλεβιζοπούλου, Ιωακειμίδου and Σπύρου, « "Να έχουμε και Νεκρούς" » [Alevizopoulou, Ioakimidou and Spyrou, "We may as well have Dead"], 66–75. Further, Economou, Madianos, Theleritis, Peppou and Stefanis, "Increased Suicidality Amid Economic Crisis in Greece," 1459.

14 "Greece: Troika Success Story or a Warning Against too Much Austerity?"

15 "Unemployment statistics."

16 "Real GDP Growth Rate—Volume: Percentage Change on Previous Year."

exceed 40% in the same period of time (37.2 % for the years 2010–2013).[17] This means that working people, let alone the unemployed, have lost more than one third of their income. The landscape as far as small and medium-sized enterprises are concerned is also devastating.[18] This is the result of the Troika rescue policies, which can by no means be compared to economic figures of peaceful times, but to those of a period of war. Simply said: The remedy has proven to be lethal. The rescue has been and still is killing us.[19]

The production structure and the infrastructure of the country are rapidly being destroyed. The catastrophe is unique anywhere in the world, even compared to previous IMF intervention paradigms. Political and economical analysts mention the structural problems of the EU, the fact that the surplus of one is the other's deficit, the clash between centre and periphery, north and south, the lack of democracy within European structures, the retreat of politics before the advance of the markets and capital.[20]

Charting the Political Landscape

The problem of the unworthiness and corruption of our own politicians is linked very closely to forms of dependence, whence power *de facto* derives. The political parties that have been administering the situation have in fact been

17 "Real Adjusted Gross Disposable Income of Households per Capita." One has to note in this case that the figures concerning Greece are characterized as provisional, yet an expert analysis can approximately calculate the overall reduction. Calculated per capita there is a reduction of 22.1%, for the years 2010–2013 alone. Calculated overall for employees, for the years 2010–2013 the overall loss is 37.2%, according to the Hellenic Statistical Authority (ELSTAT) and the Labor Institute of the Greek General Confederation of Greece: INE/GSEE-ADEDY, [*The Greek Economy and Employment*]. The difference in the two figures, per capita and the overall of employees, means that the rich maintained their income and perhaps even increased it, while employees and laborers lost more than 1/3 of their income.

18 According to the Annual Report on European small and medium-sized enterprises (SMEs) 2012/2013 (Gagliardi, *A Recovery on the Horizon?*, 39–40), Greece is an exception: "The Greek case is rather exceptional as, between 2008 and 2012, Greek SME employment fell by 33% and Greek SME value added declined by almost 21%. The Greek SME sector comprises mostly micro-enterprises and after five consecutive years of strong GDP decline and austerity measures in place, affecting both the private and the public sectors, the decline in demand is severe".

19 Fouskas and Dimoulas, "The Greek Workshop of Debt and the Failure of the European Project," 24. For a general detailed overview of the figures, Petrakis, *The Greek Economy*. Esp. on poverty, *ibid.*, 228–230.

20 Milios and Sotiropoulos, "Crisis of Greece or crisis of the euro?" 223–239. Fouskas and Dimoulas, ibid., 26.

saving the banks and the bank owners, imposing inhuman and unjust taxation, while at the same time turning a blind eye or even completely erasing the tax obligations and other debts of big enterprises, the mass media and their own political parties. Preserving in every way possible an oligarchy that still rules behind the facade of a meager democracy, providing a huge Private Sector Involvement 'haircut' at the cost of pension funds and small savings investors and burdening the weak in all their policies, they can no longer be considered capable, competent or trustworthy. They cannot handle the amount and depth of public criticism and displeasure; they are no longer resilient. Some have reached the point of political death, yet from the dust new parties emerge that try to renew and prolong the life of what is basically the same system. The political landscape is like moving sand.

Specific mention should be made of Golden Dawn, the extreme right-wing Nazi party, which has emerged out of widespread despair, anger, fear and prejudice that has led part of the population to support this pseudo-anti-establishment opposition to mainstream Greek politics. On the one hand, people seek consolation for the wounds of the present in the glory of the past, in an ethnocentric way of thinking, a nationalistic utopian nostalgia; on the other hand, this trend is nurtured by the resentment spawned by the EU/IMF policies, which are creating defensiveness and atavistic worries. People combine and confuse negative historical experiences with present events and political attitudes, oversimplifying to produce the dangerous idea of 'history repeating itself.' Seeing as they do in affluent, liberal cosmopolitanism a camouflaged strategy set to further amplify a colonial-type enslavement of the peoples in the framework of globalization, people have been huddling together, coalescing into an introspective community marked by strongly anti-German, anti-European undertones, rapidly becoming defensively (yet also aggressively) anti-everything. It is against this backdrop that some turn to extreme right-wing political thinking and practice. In practice, they have deeply internalized the hard core of the EU/IMF policies, namely that the catastrophe of capital should further burden the weakest, and so they seek for strength and deliverance by turning against the yet weaker and more miserable members of society,[21] mainly but not exclusively the foreigners, mostly regarded as 'illegal immigrants'. Dublin II, and the EU policy of closed borders towards the outside world, is actually aggravating and not healing or moderating this

21 The close relation between financial liberalism and the rise of extreme right movements in periods of crisis is a contested issue but strongly supported. E.g. from a historical viewpoint, Blinkhorn, ed., *Fascists and Conservatives*, passim. For an overall view by a political scientist, Hainsworth, *The Extreme Right in Western Europe*, 5–23.

aggressive mentality.[22] The classical trope of the 'external and internal enemy,' the traitor from within, reflects phobic stereotypes deeply rooted in Greek culture and society, not unrelated to Greece's political wounds after the Second World War.[23] Furthermore, the sense of kinship as a means to fight one's way up in life becomes a political metaphor. It turns community belonging into mafia-type familial relations which guarantee patronage, loyalty and support—all in one.

It is a tragic irony: a country that fiercely fought Nazism and suffered immensely because of it currently has more or less 10% of its population who like to believe they are patriots, yet seek refuge in Nazi ideology. The irony is accentuated when we take into consideration the hostility towards immigrants in a country that has intimate knowledge and experience of migration, its inhabitants still migrating by the thousands today. However, given the overall confusion, this may not take us by surprise. Widespread confusion, along with the distortion of fundamental concepts and logical thought patterns, as previously shown, do not facilitate the fight against a disastrous choice—the frightened recourse to the far right which will prove to be the utmost evil, the "last deception" that is worse than the first (see Mt. 27:64). But although one cannot and should not lay the blame on external factors, the despair we have described may well explain historically the present, sad course of events in Greece, even if it can by no means justify it.

Daily life is forcing Greeks to confront these problems. The worry to survive, to pay taxes, to keep one's home, not to get sick, to avoid violence and criminality, to keep one's sanity, to support one's closest. People are sharing the worries of experts in finances, at a cognitive and an experiential level. The political issues have become of existential, life and death importance. The Greek people would be willing to make sacrifices, face sparseness and increase efforts, if these amounted to some solid hope for them and their country. The case not being such, but rather a one-way path leading to a long, torturing and asphyxiating dead-end, people counteract.

---

22 Kirstoglou, "The Dark Ages of the Golden Dawn," 106.

23 A civil war leading to the marginalization of those who fought against fascism and the return to power of *the deep state* was the immediate aftermath. A military dictatorship came later, concluding with a territorial loss of half of Cyprus in 1974.

The Mission of the Orthodox Church in Present Day Greece

Meeting the Basic Concerns

When a house is on fire, we first have to put the fire out. This sense of emergency has been a guide in the Church's activities. Under the inspiration and the lead of the Archbishop of Athens, Ieronymos II, the Church of Greece has concentrated on the work of social *diaconia*, organizing soup kitchens for those in need. The first priority is therefore distribution of food. Since 2010, the portions as well as the distribution points have doubled.[24] Supported by mass media and the vast majority of supermarkets, the Church has been acting as an intermediary. The great advantage of the Church's structure is that it is Pan-Hellenic and politically neutral, welcoming everybody. Besides the distribution of cooked meals, where a great number of voluntary workers are involved, many more families in need are provided with the basics of nutrition.

Along with the provision of free meals, the Church is active in the distribution of new clothing, footwear and other equipment. It provides nurseries to serve the working mother, free medical care for the whole family, hostels for the needy and homeless, free camps for children and teens, student housing and financial aid to students. Besides that, the Church operates traditional institutions: orphanages, nursing homes for the elderly, rehabilitation centers for drug addicts and ex-convicts, as well as homes for the homeless and for women who have experienced violence, and single-parent families, especially single mothers.[25] As an example, the Rev. Father Sophrony Gkoutzinis, Chancellor at the Metropolis of Xanthi, e-mailed us at our request on March 15, 2014 a reliable outline of the diaconical work of a peripheral Metropolis, arising from the new needs emerging in the period of crisis:

> According to data kept by the Holy Metropolis of Xanthi, the Metropolis keeps a General Benevolent Fund and Parish Funds. The General Benevolent Fund responds to requests for special financial assistance, such as those involving health problems. The Parish Funds deal with needs on a smaller scale. At the same time, there is a support agency for the third child in each family, which spends 1 million € annually. There is also a "Table of Love" (soup kitchen, since 1996) which daily feeds 150 families for free (also delivering at home). Another initiative is the Social

---

24 « Διπλασιάζονται από Σήμερα οι Μερίδες Φαγητού » ["Number of Portions Distributed Doubled from Today"].

25 A more detailed picture at the official site of the Church of Greece: http://www.ecclesia.gr/greek/koinonia/koinonia.htm, last accessed October 28, 2014.

> Health Clinic and the Social Pharmacy, started some 18 months ago. This applies to uninsured and unemployed fellow citizens, who may be examined for free and receive free drugs on prescription. During the first year of operation, the Social Pharmacy and Clinic treated 1,200 patients.

This is the picture from an outlying diocese. Thanks to a series of agreements between Church and State,[26] it seems that the way will be open for the Church to undertake as part of her diaconia a large part of the state social services. However, there seems to be a risk, read between the lines in different agreements, that the Church is being called on to substitute for the welfare state, which is meant to shrink to almost nothing.

Second Thoughts and Reflections

Besides the immense effort of the Church and the corresponding negligence of the State, there are also some other important questions. From the viewpoint of the Church administration, the question is crucial: To what extent will the Church need to deliver? For how long? Will the Church structures be able to meet the needs adequately? Are there any signs of fatigue as far as the volunteers are concerned? Is the average parish priest ready, capable and willing to undertake this additional project? Not infrequently, the Church's resources have reached their limit, and assistance from the Greek communities abroad has been called for, at the highest level.

From a more sociopolitical viewpoint one could identify three major issues of concern. First, philanthropy as business: This would refer to the whole spectrum of fundraising and consequent interdependence with European projects, mass media, multinational companies and all possible financial sources. The question of transparency in all transactions is also important, and much progress has been achieved under the auspices of the current Archbishop Ieronymos. However, a past scandal of financial mismanagement in the non-governmental Church-initiated organization Αλληλεγγύη (Solidarity),[27] led the new archbishop to close it down and to start a new organization, called Αποστολή (Mission) on a new basis.[28]

---

26 E.g.: "Αρχιεπίσκοπος και Χατζηδάκης συμφώνησαν να ενισχυθεί το κοινωνικό έργο της Εκκλησίας" [Archbishop and Chatzidakis agreed on enhancing the social work of the Church]. Chatzidakis was the Minister of Development and Competitiveness at the time.

27 On the extent and diversity of the scandal, see: Κατή, « Ιδού το Αμαρτωλό Φαγοπότι » [Kati, "Behold the Sinful Dinner Party"].

28 The official website: http://www.mkoapostoli.gr/, (last accessed November 2, 2014).

The second issue concerns doubts as to the usefulness of the breadth and permanence of the philanthropic effort. More than 30,000 homeless people live in Athens, which is a very high number.[29] The new poor of Greece have lost everything in a very short period of time. Yet, there seems to be no way out, if one considers the unemployment rate. This way of actually trying to feed people, a ceaseless reenactment of the miracle of the multiplication of the loaves and fishes, is not financially viable. Moreover, it is spiritually disastrous as something that further dehumanizes people. Would people die if not for the soup kitchens, or would they rise up to claim their right to live? Charity comes as a solution, and this is an ultimate lie, a lie perpetuating and further entrenching the devastation of the Greek economy.

The philanthropic industry is creating and developing power structures. The Church is bending over the needy, and help comes from high up, still keeping people down. Philanthropy is not a substitute for struggle in life; additionally, rather than being an individual effort, survival requires the creation of brotherly/sisterly solidarity based on grassroots structures. Indeed, in some cases, people have taken the initiative. Instead of waiting for rain to fall from a bureaucratic mechanism, they form solidarity groups, including the parish structures in these mechanisms. One can see in such cases initiatives for barter or commerce without intermediaries. Yet these examples are rare: not only because it is in the nature of such initiatives to come and go, but also because of the lack of experience and tradition. Besides, there seems to be general disapproval and prohibition on the part of the state under various pretexts: referring to public hygiene, questions of preservation of food, suitability of venue, lack of permission, obligation to obtain a professional license and register officially as a business, etc. This has escalated to a general ban on itinerant trade in towns of more than 3,000 inhabitants, introduced recently as a law.[30] The Church for her part is hesitant about trade activities and as an institution is in many a case preserving hierarchy rather than encouraging initiative. Despite all this, active and lively local parishes have hosted such alternative trade events.[31] In other cases, efforts within society were strongly supported by volunteers from the local parish.[32] As an initiative structurally independent

---

29 Vavouyios, "Greek Economic Crisis is Becoming a Humanitarian Crisis."

30 N. 4264/2014 (ΦΕΚ Α 118/15–5–2014): *Άσκηση εμπορικών δραστηριοτήτων εκτός καταστήματος και άλλες διατάξεις* [Exercise of commercial activities outside a store and other provisions], esp. article 25.

31 E.g. in Crete: Μακάκη, «Φτώχεια, εξαθλίωση, αλληλεγγύη» [Makaki, "Poverty, misery, solidarity"].

32 E.g. « Μια Άλλη Κοινωνία » ["A Different Society"].

of the official Church but closely connected with a local parish, we may mention the formation of a cooperative grocery store, which did not last very long because of economic hardship.[33] Nevertheless, many other similar initiatives in society find strong support from Christians on their own personal initiative and in loose connection to the Church's infrastructure. There is also another kind of discussion within society: whether Church-based groups should and can be included in the whole civil solidarity and volunteer network. It seems that ideological questions can sometimes get in the way of people meeting with people. This kind of segmentation is, however, quite often overcome in the face of the difficulties and necessities of life.[34]

As for the Church's verbal witness to the Gospel and its quest for righteousness, a comforting and liberating *kerygma*, there have been some sporadic attempts. Most important among these is the synodal encyclical *To the People*, of November 2010, which exhibits a real call for justice and a plea for change of policy.[35] There was a strong counter-action by circles supporting the government to sabotage and prohibit the actual circulation of the encyclical. Indeed, the print-out of the encyclical did not always reach the parishes it was intended for. However, it was circulated on the internet and extensively and controversially commented upon through the mass media.[36] Weirdly enough, it also created some delayed reaction within the Hierarchy, by a handful of hierarchs well known for their deeply conservative political views.[37] Despite all counter-action, the historic phrase included in the encyclical was widely heard: "We are a country under occupation and execute commands of the sovereign—our lenders. Our country seems to be no longer free, but ruled in fact by our lenders." This encyclical has had a great impact and given much courage to the people, contributing to the river of resistance that matured over time and led to the vast demonstrations of the 'indignados' in Athens from the following Spring to the end of Autumn 2011.

Yet since then, no less due to the strong and continuous reaction from governmental and state circles, most official documents of the Synod have been

---

33 It was called Έλγη [Elgi] and lasted from March 2013 to June 2014 in a suburb of Athens. http://elgisynpe2012.blogspot.gr/ (last accessed November 2, 2014).

34 The whole discussion is reflected in Μπουρίκος, *Κοινωνική Αλληλεγγύη* [Bourikos, Social Solidarity].

35 Ιερά Σύνοδος της Εκκλησίας της Ελλάδος [Holy Synod of the Church of Greece], « Η Εκκλησία Απέναντι στη Σύγχρονη Κρίση ». ["The Church facing the Current Crisis"].

36 E.g. Χριστόπουλος, « "Προς τον Λαό" » [Christopoulos, "'To the People'"].

37 Παπουτσάκη, « Αμετανόητη η Δεξιά του Κυρίου » [Papoutsaki, "The right [hand] of the Lord does not repent"]. The title is indicating the identification of part of the Church with right-wing politics.

aligned with major state choices. This is really depressing, because although the Church claims not to take any part in politics, it is only utilizing a worn-out sophistical argument favoring the status quo.

Something similar used to be the case with the Church's reaction to the Golden Dawn (Chrisi Avgi) Nazi party, until recently. A dozen metropolitans raised their voices soon enough and clearly stated that Nazi ideology is in total contrast to the Christian faith. In the meantime, supporters of the extreme right engaged in massive proselytizing tactics, not without significant success. This has however been strongly resisted by faithful people. Among Orthodox Christians who opposed the fascists individually, worth mentioning are two organized groups who have raised their voices to ask for the Church's official condemnation on solid theological grounds. In response to this lay initiative, high ranking clergy repeatedly indicated to lay theologians dealing with the issue that it is for the latter to teach and preserve what is true to the Gospel, the patristic tradition and Orthodoxy. The placing of such an important responsibility in the hands of lay people would have been a reason to celebrate, had it not been for diplomatic double talk. Happy and honored though we were *to be* in the *vanguard of this battle, we could not help wondering where the* regular army is.[38] For all its activism and philanthropy, the Church of Greece had been largely silent while murderous attacks against immigrants had been taking place for some time; it was not until after the murder of a Greek citizen, the rap singer Killah P [Paulos Fyssas] on September 18th, 2013, that the Standing Holy Synod finally released a vague communiqué, condemning the specific incident and violence from all sides.[39] Yet on August 26, 2014 there was an important development that led to significant and notable progress. The Standing Holy Synod discussed the anti-racism bill officially, in the framework of a general public discussion. It gave the Bill its approval, including in the official press-release a clear and sound anti-racist argumentation based on theological tradition and the practical feed-back from recent experience of the Church's

---

38 I am mainly referring to a small historical Christian Socialist political party (called Christian Democracy, but having nothing to do with the political ideology of that name as known in Europe and the USA), inspired by Christian faith as a liberating faith, that initiated the official request to the Synod, and a group of people supporting the request, organized as a Facebook group called 'christianantirafana', an Initiative of Christians contra racism, fascism and neo-Nazism, http://www.facebook.com/groups/christiananti rafana/, that operates a blog, too: http://antirafana.blogspot.gr/. These are also characteristic examples for a different style of mission, from the grass roots.

39 Τριανταφύλλου, « Η Ιερά Σύνοδος πήρε Θέση για τη Χρυσή Αυγή » [Triantafyllou, "The Holy Synod took a Stand on Golden Dawn"].

activities. The Church spoke up. It was a major step giving great satisfaction, as a clear, theological, ecclesial voice condemned any form of discrimination.[40]

Generally speaking, the Church keeps a low profile, teaching through example and action. It is a pillar of major importance in Greek society, especially in this period of crisis. The Church is in many cases the only refuge for the poor and dispossessed, including immigrants. As to the soup kitchens, the fact that the Church has been assisting people indiscriminately has been a cause of anger and even prompted threats against it as a whole, and against individual priests, by Golden Dawn. One has to admit the vast importance of silent resistance to racist thinking and racist criminal activism. The Church's diaconal activity is really comforting people and moderating things in a peaceful way.

For the most part, the Church has been trying to explain and meet the crisis as a spiritual phenomenon. Yet this approach strikes a lot of people as a luxury. Those who think of the crisis as primarily a spiritual phenomenon have not really been touched by its material financial consequences. The vague call for repentance, omnipresent in encyclical letters and repeated so often in Sunday sermons, unfortunately stands for many as a sign and proof of the Church's privileged status in society. Furthermore, right-wing bishops, who always flatter authority instead of following the path of the cross and who understand themselves mostly as high ranking diplomats, use the Christian notion of repentance in the same way some EU officials have opted to do, as discussed in the first part of this article: namely, as a means of internalizing guilt and submission. Sometimes, the critique leveled against the Church on this score can be very harsh, yet some metropolitans see nothing but the applause of their flock (in the narrow sense), a flock often fashioned in their own image and likeness. In view of this phenomenon, many thinking people find church talk appalling and offensive to their democratic sensibilities.

Spiritual, Social and Political Tools in the Mission of the Greek Orthodox Church

A Holistic, Integral Tradition

The tension between desert and empire goes a long way back in the Eastern part of Europe, the world of the New Rome. It is one of the antinomies of Christian history, as the erudite Father Georges Florovsky called it.[41] This tension also

40 « Η Ιερά Σύνοδος για το Αντιρατσιστικό νομοσχέδιο » ["The Holy Synod on the Anti-Racism Bill"].

41 Florovsky, "Empire and Desert: Antinomies of Christian History," 133–159.

exerts a strong influence upon the missionary work and understanding of the Church.[42] Byzantine philanthropy was to a great extent Church-based.[43] Tight-knit, loving relations within the Christian community, expressed as they were in terms of solidarity and communion in everything (Acts 4: 32) and the fact that "there were no needy persons among them" (Acts 4: 34), were among the most solid non-verbal 'arguments' in the proclamation of the Christian faith. This has been commonly recognized as a major factor in the expansion of Christianity by all relevant scholars, whether missiologists, Church historians, or historians of the Late Antiquity.[44] The importance of the exemplary life of Christians, linking dogma and ethos, faith and its expression in daily life, has been stressed by the Church fathers not only as a natural consequence of the Christian creed, of following in Jesus Christ's steps as His disciples, but also as an important factor in witnessing to the Gospel. John Chrysostom (4th–5th century), developed this aspect, not only within the framework of pastoral care but as a means of serving mission, as part and indeed the foundation of a missiological method.[45] This would bring back the missionary ideal, care and preoccupation to the very core of Christian life, he argued. Feeling deeply rooted in a Church tradition, John Chrysostom understands the question of ethos as primarily a social one. Furthermore, social justice, the critique of the rich, condemnation of wealth and especially of the notion of accumulating wealth, let alone the habit of lending money at interest, are common *loci* in patristic thinking.[46]

Unfortunately, one cannot but notice that in contemporary theology such traditional ideas regarding the social teaching of the Gospel have receded in

---

42 For some background information on this antinomy, sometimes taking the form of a dilemma, but in most cases leading creatively to a synthesis, quite dynamic for the missionary field, see: Βουλγαράκη-Πισίνα, « Μοναχισμός και Ιεραποστολή » [Voulgaraki-Pissina, "Monasticism and Mission"], 39–59. Παπαθανασίου, *Η Εκκλησία γίνεται* [Papathanasiou, The Church comes into being], 95–153.

43 Constantelos, *Byzantine Philanthropy and Social Welfare*, 65ff.

44 Brown, "The Rise and Function of the Holy Man," 80–101. Brown, *The Making of Late Antiquity*, passim. Harnack, *Die Mission und Ausbreitung des Christentums*, vol. 1, ^{4}1924, 115 and 395–397. Frohnes and Knorr (eds.), *Kirchengeschichte als Missionsgeschichte*, vol. 1, passim. Bardy, *La Conversion au Christianisme*, 137 and 146–157. Yannoulatos, Anastasios. "Monks and Mission in the Eastern Church During the Fourth Century," 208–226.

45 Βουλγαράκη-Πισίνα, *Η Προσέγγιση των Εθνικών* [Voulgaraki-Pissina, Approaching the Pagans], 115–163.

46 Holman, *Wealth and Poverty*, 2008, provides us with a broad spectrum of representative ideas and actions of the Eastern Fathers.

favour of a fashionable pious and introspective quietism, which has permeated almost the entire spectrum of Orthodox Christian theology and life. And even when the theology of the more 'socially minded' fathers, as we call them, is called upon, for example, their ideas of solidarity and social justice, their insights are usually not translated in terms of modern conditions. I shall try to elaborate a bit more on these two points.

Building Walls in Theology and Church Life

Our relationship to the West has been ambivalent. It has gone from envious admiration to hatred, from rejection to imitation, back and forth. All these are signs of a civilization repeatedly bruised, kept in chains for historical reasons and feeling at a disadvantage compared to its Western counterpart. They are indicative of a culture regretting its present, while idealizing the past and trying to catch up. The picture is not much different where theological studies are concerned. From the passive imitation of Western academic theology in the past, the pendulum of Orthodox Christian scholarship swung to the rediscovery of its own roots, meaning mostly the renaissance of patristic theology. Starting in Greece in the early '60s, and flourishing till the '80s or mid-'90s at the latest, this 'return to the fathers' suffered a weariness in Greece at the end of the 20th and the beginning of the 21st century.

World-shaking events have not left theology untouched: These include the resurgence of religion worldwide; the regression of human rights—most obvious in but not exclusive to the Near and Middle East; the prevalence of a more conservative thinking; the fall of communism and the large scale disappointment with visionary, ambitious ideologies—let alone the proclaimed end of ideologies;[47] the frequency and permanence of peripheral wars; the increase of the gap between rich and poor; and the *dystopia* of the post-democratic era.

In recent years, theology in Greece has become less open to dialogue and more 'confessionally' attuned to the elements that differentiate it from the West, mistaking them for its genuine, constitutive characteristics. If Western spirituality was mainly of an activist nature, the East focused on hesychastic contemplation instead. Little by little, an important line in our tradition usurped prominence as the main line, if not the only line. Little by little, the meaning of words and theological concepts started to fade or blur. For example, the notion of obedience, originally conceived of as the renunciation of one's own will, as an ultimate path to freedom from egocentrism, became a pretext for imposing an elder's will upon his spiritual charges, a means of

47 Bell, *The End of Ideology*. Compare, Fukuyama, *The End of History*, though the author later moderated his original views.

turning believers into followers, thereby cultivating blind submission in the name of spirituality. Such a flagrant distortion of obedience constitutes, in fact, a heresy within Orthodoxy. Fortunately this problem is nowadays acknowledged and addressed in a subtle, candid way.[48]

It is high time for a self-respecting, more spiritually mature theology (1 Cor. 13: 11), moving away from childish imitation or adolescent-type rejection. We Orthodox Christians owe it to ourselves as much as to our rich tradition. We cannot delay further. Thankfully, not only do people seem ready and eager for dialogue and an engagement with others, for a self-critical reflection, but the times themselves raise urgent and inevitable issues to be dealt with.

Missional Understanding of the Church as a Factor of Change

When back in the '60s the idea of mission deeply motivated the minds and hearts of Anastasios (Yannoulatos), the current archbishop of Albania, and Elias Voulgarakis, the late Missiology professor at Athens, the two of them were thought to be young and foolish. Given how exotic the missional idea appeared in that era in Orthodox circles, one need not wonder at the apologetic tone of the first missiological literature. One had to justify mission, especially external mission. Given the ethnocentricity of most Orthodox churches, still prevalent today,[49] the insistence on mission was a call for openness to the world. The two pioneers had to emphasize the word "external", as a means of encouraging people to cross borders, mainly geographical but ultimately borders of all kinds.[50]

This movement was related to missiological questions discussed at the International Missionary Conferences (especially the third one, held in Tambaram, India, in 1938) and subsequently in the WCC, as well as in the

48 In this direction, John Chryssavgis, "Orthodox Spirituality and Social Activism," 131–138.

49 Fitzgerald, "Ethnic Conflicts and the Orthodox Churches," 139–147. Tsetsis, "Ethnicity, Nationalism and Religion," 148–158. Clapsis, "Ethnicity, Nationalism and Identity," 159–173.

50 Βουλγαράκη-Πισίνα, « Εσωτερική ή Εξωτερική Ιεραποστολή; » [Voulgaraki-Pissina, "External or Internal Mission?"], 8–9. Today, there is a general reservation as to the external, delegating character of mission: Mortensen and Nielsen, "Church and Mission Engaging Plurality," 2. Vähäkangas, "The Future of Missiologies," 217–229. The same overall spirit prevails in Währisch-Oblau and Mwombeki, *Mission Continues* (2010). However, thinking contextually and referring to the "beyond the borders" missions supported by the Church of Greece, one cannot help noting that the financial crisis of today had a big negative effect on them, too. They do not have a very long history and background, and it is not yet time for the mother Church to completely withdraw. However, the lack of financial resources, the increasing needs, and the overall global crisis, are all leading us to new ways in our mission, which may accelerate indigenization and the path to adulthood for young churches all over the world. The crisis may also become an opportunity in this regard.

context of Syndesmos (World Fellowship of Orthodox Youth), and led to the founding of the Inter-Orthodox Centre 'Porefthendes' ('Go ye'), in Greece in 1961. While those missionary pioneers gave the impression of voices crying in the wilderness, slowly and tentatively a first breeze of mission had begun to blow.[51] Yet Elias Voulgarakis was not content with simply importing ideas; he searched for the roots of missionary thinking and action in our own tradition. And it is in the light of this tradition that he set the standards for flexibility and openness, so essential and fundamental for missionary work.[52]

The few Orthodox missionaries emerging in the following decades have not been lazy nor did they use theology, theory and contemplation as an excuse for conveniently refraining from action. Therefore, solidarity and social *diaconia* issues have been raised adequately, and a valuable practical experience has been obtained in missionary fields, on different levels.[53] However, there is still a need not to rest content exclusively with diaconal work. It is also important, from a missiological point of view, not to use charity as a way of chaining people to the church, nor to see it as an end in itself, for that might turn the Church into a mere humanitarian agency; the point, rather, is to see *philanthropy* as a liberating factor in the light of the resurrection, offered but not imposed.

This is a debate taking place at present within church circles in Greece. In some cases, priests feel—justly or unjustly—overloaded and wish to avoid what they perceive as an unbearable burden; other clergymen, however, are expressing a sincere concern regarding the theological and missional value of humanitarian and charitable activities, considering some of them as a worrying sign of the Church's secularization.

In the Greek context, political relevance seems to be becoming a need. This is something new from an Orthodox missionary point of view.[54] In extreme conditions, the emergency that calls for immediate, practical response to people's needs and requirements takes precedence over theoretical contemplation. The need demands creative responses. In this case theory is led by *praxis*, by the very experience obtained on the level of action. This viewpoint may

---

51 Voulgaraki-Pissina, "Mission and Evangelism in Modern Greece," 114–121.

52 Papathanasiou, "Some Key Themes and Figures in Greek Theological Thought," 228. Βουλγαράκη-Πισίνα, «Ηλίας Βουλγαράκης» [Voulgaraki-Pissina, "Elias Voulgarakis"], 273–275.

53 One can select two characteristic examples: *Ο Ιεραπόστολος του Ζαΐρ π. Κοσμάς Γρηγοριάτης* [The Missionary in Zaire Fr. Kosmas Grigoriadis], 46–55. Forest, *The Resurrection of the Church in Albania*, 89 ff.

54 It is new within the Orthodox tradition, but not in the overall missiological experience. Such a paradigm is proposed for Korea by Keum, "Korean War," 109–133.

be somewhat innovative in Orthodox missiology, still fearful of the political element, and the path taken is experimental. Yet Christ was usually to be found near and surrounded by His people, people with real and specific needs. The possibilities offered by democracy, regardless of its true range, become new responsibilities. Church leaders do not only have to convey the wishes of the authorities to their flock, nor are they confined to interceding at a personal level in favor of specific members of their flock or bringing peace and solace to those who mourn and sorrow; they can also be with and work with the people for whom Christ was crucified. When the Church supports the State in suppressing the people, when it uses civil authority in order to impose itself and its views, it has already lapsed into a form of theocracy. When the Church supports and defends the people in the face of authority, on the other hand, it is offering a firm sign that the Church follows in the Lord's steps, thereby avoiding the second temptation of Christ (Luke 4:6–8).

These ideas need to be explored anew from a missiological viewpoint. But they are not new. They were present already in the history and tradition of Orthodox missions before the 20th century. Wherever missionaries chose to fight for the people, faith was deeply rooted in the society in question. This was the paradigm followed by the Orthodox missionaries in Alaska against the brutal exploitation by Russian traders[55] and the example set by St. Nikolai Kassatkin, missionary in Japan, during the Russo-Japanese war (8 February 1904–5 September 1905).[56]

Beyond our own tradition, one can look at the experience of Liberation Theology as a source of inspiration, on the theological academic level and most importantly within the Church's life. This is a difficult question, indeed, and not solely because of our introspective general altitude. Liberation Theology is a contextual theology. It cannot be transferred as such into a different context.[57] Yet the experience obtained in one context can enrich our understanding in another, while at the same time being creatively and eclectically studied.[58] In the light of the Gospel, all theology is liberating. This liberating element represents also the core of the Orthodox tradition, and even more: a 'resurrectional' spirit. A critical cross-cultural encounter can help us translate our basic anthropological and eschatological beliefs into a variety of forms within our current specific situation. This is also the sense of *koinonia*, signifying in Greek both Holy *Communion* and human *society*, the sharing of what is

---

55 Oleksa, *Orthodox Alaska*, 81–93.

56 Stamoolis, *Eastern Orthodox Mission Theology*, 35–40.

57 Codina, "The Poor, the Church and Theology," 63–70.

58 Bouteneff, "Liberation: Challenges to Modern Orthodox Theology," 24–33.

common (*κοινόν*). Beyond theoretical theological issues, a more profound difficulty in the encounter with Liberation Theology is the readiness of people for sacrifice. This is also true for Christian people and applies to the natural leaders of the Orthodox communities, the episcopate and the clergy, as well. One has to recognise that resisting authority might lead to sacrifice, even martyrdom, a possibility not to be excluded in an unstable world. But one has also to consider from a missiological point of view that the lack of such readiness on the part of believers is one reason for the strong atheist tradition within European social movements. An incarnate understanding of liberation might well be an important and valuable lesson taught by the Global South to what is in fact becoming a post-Christian Europe.

Greece is becoming more and more like Latin America, where Milton Friedman's financial theory was applied for the first time through IMF policies.[59] The results of these policies are still apparent today, representing a *dystopia* of our own future. More than within Church structures, in peoples' movements Latin America represents a paradigm of importance on multiple levels. This includes Liberation Theology as source of inspiration for peoples' movements. Yet in the Church's structures, the example of Liberation Theology would mean that much would have to change.[60] Even at a local, parish level it would mean introducing a style of community relations different from current ones, which are quite often characterized by authoritarian clericalism.[61] Today's habits can be bad habits, temptations alienating us from Tradition. It is difficult to change, but it is our continuous calling to take the hard path of *metanoia*. This path would restore Orthodox theology to its true nature: not to build abstract doctrinal and philosophical constructions, but to start out from the deep existential experience of God's presence in history, the personal encounter with Him in the ecclesial community. In taking this path and daring to employ political tools within missionary work, certainly wisdom and caution are required:

- as to the Church being a force for love and unity, not taking partisan sides in the way political parties do by their very nature,
- as to the relativity of all worldly matters and proposals compared to the catholicity of the truth, and the need for apophatism in dealing with them,
- as to the consistency with the fact that Christ's kingdom is not of this world (Jh. 18:36) and
- as to the adequate interpretation of the eternal in terms of the transient.

---

59 Klein, *The Shock Doctrine*, 59–66.

60 Bell, *Liberation Theology after the End of History*, 42–84.

61 Dawson, "The Origins and Character of the Base Ecclesial Community," 109–128.

Epilogue

It is important for the mission of the Church to point to God's kingdom, to mirror it in fact in daily reality. This is the so-called Liturgy after the Liturgy; this is the unity of faith and ethos; this is Logos incarnate in the entirety of the human condition.[62]

Missiologists are here to understand, evaluate and critically support the new, the good news, being always themselves renewed as they open up to the renewing and resurrecting power of our Lord Jesus Christ and the refreshing breeze of the Holy Spirit, the joyful message: the feast at His Kingdom in the light of his resurrection:

> The table is fully laden: let all enjoy it.
> The calf is fatted: let none go away hungry.[63]

Bibliography

Αλεβιζοπούλου, Μαρινίκη, Ντίνα Ιωακειμίδου and Μαρίνα Σπύρου. « "Να έχουμε και Νεκρούς": Αυτοκτονίες στην Ελλάδα της Κρίσης ». [Alevizopoulou, Mariniki, Dina Ioakimidou and Marina Spyrou. "We may as well have Dead": Suicides in Crisis-ridden Greece]. *Unfollow* [monthly political magazine, Athens]. Issue 27 (Mars 2014): 66–75.

« Αρχιεπίσκοπος και Χατζηδάκης συμφώνησαν να ενισχυθεί το κοινωνικό έργο της Εκκλησίας ». *Ρομφαία. Επικαιρότητα. Εκκλησία της Ελλάδος.* [Archbishop and Chatzidakis agreed on enhancing the social work of the Church. Romfea. News. The Church of Greece]. Posted February 7, 2014. Last accessed October 28, 2014. http://www.romfea.gr/epikairotita/22236-2014-02-07-14-01-03.

"Athen muß sein Hausaufgaben machen: Merkel und Schäuble gegen neuen Schuldenschnitt. " *Reinische Post.* Posted July 12, 2013. Last accessed October 18, 2014. http://www.rp-online.de/politik/deutschland/merkel-und-schaeuble-gegen-neuen-schuldenschnitt-aid-1.3532523#comment-list.

Bardy, Gustave. *La Conversion au Christianisme durant les premier sciècles*, Paris: Aubier (Éditions Montaigne) <Théologie, 15>, 1949.

62 For a slightly different, more reserved but fair short outline of the issue, see Clapsis, "Politics and Christian Faith," 221–224, however first published in 1992, quite close in time to the collapse of the Soviet regime and its broad effects on Church and society.

63 St. John Chrysostom's Paschal sermon, http://www.orthodoxchristian.info/pages/sermon.htm, last accessed November 4, 2014.

Bell, Daniel. *The End of Ideology: On the Exhaustion of Political Ideas in the Fifties*, New York: The Free Press, 1960 (^{2}2001).

Bell, Daniel M. *Liberation Theology after the End of History: The Refusal to cease Suffering*. Radical Orthodoxy Series. Routledge: London and New York, 2001.

Blinkhorn, Martin (ed.). *Fascists and Conservatives: The Radical Right and the Establishment in Twentieth-Century Europe*, Oxon: Routledge ^{2}2001 (London: Unwin Hyman, ^{1}1990).

Μπουρίκος, Δημήτρης. *Κοινωνική Αλληλεγγύη στην Ελλάδα της Κρίσης: Νέο Κύμα Ανάδυσης της Κοινωνίας Πολιτών ή Εμπέδωση της Κατακερματισμένης Κοινωνικής Ιδιότητας του Πολίτη; Παρατηρητήριο για την Κρίση. Ερευνητικό κείμενο* No 3/2013. ΕΛΙΑΜΕΠ (Ελληνικό Ίδρυμα Ευρωπαϊκής και Εξωτερικής Πολιτικής). [Bourikos, Dimitris. Social Solidarity in Crisis-ridden Greece: A New Wave in the Emergence of Civil Society or Consolidation of a Fragmented Social Citizenship? Observatory for the Crisis. Research text no 3/2013. ELIAMEP (Hellenic Foundation of European and Foreign Policy)]. Last accessed October 29, 2014. http://crisisobs.gr/wp-content/uploads/2013/04/%CE%95%CF%81%CE%B5%CF%85%CE%BD%CE%B7%CF%84%CE%B9%CE%BA%CF%8C-%CE%9A%CE%B5%CE%AF%CE%BC%CE%B5%CE%BD%CE%BF_3_%CE%94.-%CE%9C%CF%80%CE%BF%CF%85%CF%81%CE%AF%CE%BA%CE%BF%CF%82.pdf.

Bouteneff, Peter C. "Liberation: Challenges to Modern Orthodox Theology from the Contextual Theologies." *Union Seminary Quarterly Review* 63, 3 and 4 (2012): 24–33.

"Bowles: 'Troika's Overall Response to the Crisis has lacked Transparency and at Times Credibility'": *European Parliament. News.* Posted November 4, 2013. Last accessed October 22, 2014. Ref.: 20131104STO23604. http://www.europarl.europa.eu/news/en/news-room/content/20131104STO23604/html/Troika%27s-response-to-crisis-has-lacked-transparency-and-at-times-credibility.

Brink, Gijsbert van den, and Harro Höpfl (eds.). *Calvinism and the Making of the European Mind*. Leiden: Brill <Studies in Reformed Theology, 27>, 2014.

Brown, Peter. "The Rise and Function of the Holy Man in Late Antiquity": *The Journal of Roman Studies* 61 (1971): 80–101.

———. *The Making of Late Antiquity*, Cambridge, MA: Harvard University Press, 1978.

Charrel, Marie. "Errements européens et erreurs de la « troïka » pèsent toujours sur Athènes." *Le Monde*. Posted March 13, 2014. Last accessed October 18, 2014. http://www.lemonde.fr/economie/article/2014/03/13/errements-europeens-et-erreurs-de-la-troika-pesent-toujours-sur-athenes_4382098_3234.html.

Chryssavgis, John. "Orthodox Spirituality and Social Activism: Reclaiming Our Vocabulary—Refocusing our Vision." In: Emmanuel Clapsis (ed.). *The Orthodox Churches in a Pluralistic World: An Ecumenical Conversation*. Geneva: WCC Publications, 2004: 131–138.

Clapsis, Emmanuel. "Politics and Christian Faith." In: Emmanuel Clapsis (ed.). *Orthodoxy in Conversation: Orthodox Ecumenical Engagements*, Geneva: WCC Publications || Brookline, MA: Holy Cross Orthodox Press, 2000: 221–224. Originally published in the *Greek Orthodox Theological Review* 37, 1–2, 1992: 99–103.

———. "Ethnicity, Nationalism and Identity." In: Emmanuel Clapsis (ed.). *The Orthodox Churches in a Pluralistic World: An Ecumenical Conversation*. Geneva: WCC Publications, 2004: 159–173.

Codina, Víctor. "The Poor, the Church and Theology." In: *Getting the Poor down from the Cross: Christology of Liberation*. International Theological Commission of the Ecumenical Association of Third World Theologians (EATWOT). Organized by José María Vigil. Leonardo Boff, prol. Jon Sobrino, epil. N.p.: Second Digital Edition (Version 2.0), 2007: 63–70.

Constantelos, Demetrios J. *Byzantine Philanthropy and Social Welfare*, New Brunswick—New Jersey: Rutgers University Press <Byzantine Series>, 1968.

Dawson, Andrew. "The Origins and Character of the Base Ecclesial Community: A Brazilian Perspective." In: *The Cambridge Companion to Liberation Theology*. Christopher Rowland (ed.). Cambridge: Cambridge University Press, 1999: 109–128.

« Διπλασιάζονται από Σήμερα οι Μερίδες Φαγητού στα Κέντρα Ενοριακής Αγάπης της Ι. Αρχιεπισκοπής Αθηνών » ["Number of Portions Distributed at the Parish Agape Centers of the Archbishopric of Athens Doubled from Today"]. *Amen*. Posted September 9, 2010. Last accessed October 22, 2014. http://www.amen.gr/article3507.

Economou, Marina, Michael Madianos, Christos Theleritis, Lily E. Peppou and Costas N. Stefanis. "Increased Suicidality Amid Economic Crisis in Greece." *The Lancet* 378, 9801 (October 22, 2011): 1459. doi: 10.1016/S0140-6736(11)61638-3.

Fitzgerald, Thomas. "Ethnic Conflicts and the Orthodox Churches: An Introduction." In: Emmanuel Clapsis (ed.). *The Orthodox Churches in a Pluralistic World: An Ecumenical Conversation*. Geneva: WCC Publications, 2004: 139–147.

Florovsky, Georges. "Empire and Desert: Antinomies of Christian History." *The Greek Orthodox Theological Review* 3, 2 (1957): 133–159.

Forest, Jim (ed.). *The Resurrection of the Church in Albania: Voices of Orthodox Christians*, Geneva: WCC Publications, 2002.

Fouskas, Vassilis K. and Constantine Dimoulas. "The Greek Workshop of Debt and the Failure of the European Project: Editorial." *Journal of Balkan and Near Eastern Studies* 14, 1 (2012): 1–31.

Frohnes, H. and Knorr, U.W. (eds.). *Kirchengeschichte als Missionsgeschichte*. Vol 1. Die alte Kirche. Munich: Chr. Kaiser Verlag, 1974.

Fukuyama, Francis. *The End of History and the Last Man*. New York: The Free Press, 1992 (^{2}2006).

Gagliardi, Dimitri, Patrice Muller, Edward Glossop, Cecilia Caliandro, Michael Fritsch, Gabriela Brtkova, Nuray Unlu Bohn, et al. *A Recovery on the Horizon? Annual Report on European SMEs 2012/2013: Final Report.* [Brussels]: European Commission. Accessed October 22, 2014. http://ec.europa.eu/enterprise/policies/sme/facts-figures-analysis/performance-review/index_en.htm.

"Greece: EBU Looking Forward, not Back." EBU: Operating Eurovision and Euroradio. Posted August 20, 2013. Last accessed October 22, 2014. http://www3.ebu.ch/sites/ebu/contents/news/2013/08/greece-ebu-looking-forward-not-b.html.

"Greece: Troika Success Story or a Warning Against too Much Austerity?" *European Parliament. News.* Posted January 29, 2014. Last updated March 13, 2014. Last accessed October 18, 2014. Ref.: 20140129STO34108. http://www.europarl.europa.eu/news/en/news-room/content/20140129STO34108/html/Greece-Troika-success-story-or-a-warning-against-too-much-austerity.

"Greek Officials welcome IMF Report." *The Guardian.* Posted July 5, 2013, at 6:23pm. Last accessed October 22, 2014. http://www.theguardian.com/business/2013/jun/05/eurozone-crisis-china-wine-japan-markets#block-51af7320e4b0ae18e994aff6.

"Griechische Finanzmisere: Merkel begrüßt Athener Sparprogramm." *Spiegel on Line.* Politik. Posted March 3, 2010. Last accessed October 18, 2014. http://www.spiegel.de/politik/ausland/griechische-finanzmisere-merkel-begruesst-athener-sparprogramm-a-681595.html.

Hainsworth, Paul. *The Extreme Right in Western Europe*, Oxon—New York: Routledge, 2008.

Harnack, Adolf von. *Die Mission und Ausbreitung des Christentums in den ersten drei Jahrhunderten.* 2 Vols., Leipzig: J.C. Hinrichs'scheBuchhandlung, ^{4}1924.

Holman, Susan R. (ed.). *Wealth and Poverty in Early Church and Society*, Grand Rapids: Holy Cross <Studies in Patristic Theology and History>, 2008.

« Η Ιερά Σύνοδος για το Αντιρατσιστικό νομοσχέδιο » [The Holy Synod on the Anti-Racism Bill]. *Official Website of the Church of Greece.* Posted August 26, 2014. Last accessed, October 31, 2014. http://www.ecclesia.gr/epikairotita/main_epikairotita_next.asp?id=854.

Ιερά Σύνοδος της Εκκλησίας της Ελλάδος [Holy Synod of the Church of Greece], « Η Εκκλησία Απέναντι στη Σύγχρονη Κρίση ». *Προς τον Λαό* 44 (November 2010). ["The Church in Front of the Current Crisis." To the People]. Last accessed November 2, 2014). http://www.ecclesia.gr/greek/holysynod/anakoinothenta/proslao2010.pdf.

ΙΝΕ/ΓΣΕΕ-ΑΔΕΔΥ. *Η Ελληνική Οικονομία και η Απασχόληση: Ετήσια Έκθεση 2013.* [INE/GSEE-ADEDY. The Greek Economy and Employment: Annual Report 2013]. Posted September 5, 2013. Last accessed October 22, 2014. http://inegsee.gr/ekdosi/etisia-ekthesi-2013-i-elliniki-oikonomia-kai-i-apascholisi.

Κατή, Κατερίνα [Kati, Katerina]. « Ιδού το Αμαρτωλό Φαγοπότι ». *Ελευθεροτυπία*. [Behold the Sinful Dinner Party. Eleytherotypia]. Posted November 27, 2010. Last accessed, November2, 2014. http://www.enet.gr/?i=news.el.article&id=228143.

Keum, Jooseop. "Korean War: The Origine of the Axis of Evil in the Korean Peninsula." In: *Peace and Reconciliation: In Search of Shared Identity*. Kim, Sebastian C.H., Pauline Kollontai and Greg Hoyland (eds.). Aldershot: Ashgate, 2008: 109–133.

——— (ed.). *Together towards Life: Mission and Evangelism in Changing Landscapes—with a Practical Guide*. Geneva: WCC Publications, 2013.

Kirstoglou, Elisabeth. "The Dark Ages of the Golden Dawn: Anthropological Analysis and Responsibility in the Twilight Zone of the Greek Crisis. Forum Anthropology and the Crisis in Greece." *Suomen Aiuropologi: Journal of the Finnish Anthropological Society* 38, no. 1 (Spring 2013): 104–108.

Klein, Naomi. *The Shock Doctrine: The Rise of Disaster Capitalism*. New York: Metropolitan Books, 2008.

Lapavitsas, Costas. "Greece doesn't need yet Another 'Rescue' Package—it needs a Way out." *The Guardian*. Posted August 27, 2013. Last accessed October 18, 2014. http://www.theguardian.com/commentisfree/2013/aug/27/greece-rescue-package.

Locks, Benjamin. "Austerity: A German Prescription for a Greek Tragedy." *Stalemates: Bolognia Center Journal of International Affairs*, vol. 16 (May 7, 2013). Last accessed October 18, 2014. http://bcjournal.org/volume-16/2013/5/7/austerity-a-german-prescription-for-a-greek-tragedy.html.

Μακάκη, Γεωργία. « Φτώχεια, εξαθλίωση, αλληλεγγύη ». *Νέα Κρήτη*. [Makaki, Georgia, "Poverty, misery, solidarity." Nea Criti]. Posted November 10, 2013. Last accessed November 2, 2014. http://www.neakriti.gr/?page=newsdetail&DocID=1088242.

Meyendorff, John. *Byzantine Theology: Historical Trends and Doctrinal Themes*. New York: Fordham University Press, [2]1983.

« Μια Άλλη Κοινωνία είναι Εφικτή Μέσα από Δράσεις και Συλλογικότητες ». *Ανατολή on line*. ["A Different Society is Possible Through Action and Collective Work." Anatoli on line]. Posted January 30, 2012. Last accessed November 2, 2014. http://www.anatolh.com/crete/chania/item/29927.

Milios, John, and Dimitris P. Sotiropoulos. "Crisis of Greece or crisis of the euro? A view from the European 'periphery'." *Journal of Balkan and Near Eastern Studies* 12, 3 (2010): 223–239.

Mortensen, Viggo and Andreas Østerlund Nielsen. "Church and Mission Engaging Plurality: Edinburgh 1910—Aarchus 2010." In: Viggo Mortensen and Andreas Østerlund Nielsen (eds.), *Walk Humbly with the Lord: Church and Mission Engaging Plurality*, Grand Rapids, MI: Eerdmans, 2010: 1–11.

Ο Ιεραπόστολος του Ζαΐρ π. Κοσμάς Γρηγοριάτης, κατά την Αφήγηση του Πατέρα του Δημ. Ασλανίδη και τις Επιστολές του [The Missionary to Zaire Fr. Kosmas Grigoriadis, according to his Father's Account and his Letters], Άγιον Όρος [Mount Athos]: Έκδοσις Ι.Μ. Οσίου Γρηγορίου [publ. Grigoriou Monastery], 1991.

Oleksa, Michael. *Orthodox Alaska: A Theology of Mission*. Crestwood, N.Y.: St. Vladimir's Seminary Press, 1998.

Papathanasiou, Athanasios N. "Some Key Themes and Figures in Greek Theological Thought." In: *Orthodox Christian Theology*. Mary B. Cunningham and Elizabeth Theokritoff (eds.). New York—Cambridge: Cambridge University Press, 2008: 218–231.

Παπαθανασίου, Θανάσης Ν. [Papathanasiou, Thanassis N.]. *Η Εκκλησία γίνεται όταν ανοίγεται: Η Ιεραποστολή ως Ελπίδα και ως Εφιάλτης* [The Church comes into being when it opens up: Mission as Hope and as Nightmare], Athens: Εν Πλω [En Plo], [2]2009.

Παπουτσάκη, Μαρία [Papoutsaki, Maria]. « Αμετανόητη η Δεξιά του Κυρίου » [The right [hand] of the Lord does not repent]. *Ελευθεροτυπία* [*Eleythetotypia*]. Posted December 24, 2010. Last accessed November 2, 2014. http://www.enet.gr/?i=news.el.article&id=235950.

Petrakis, Panagiotis E. *The Greek Economy and the Crisis: Challenges and Responses*. Heidelberg: Springer, 2012.

Pop, Valentina. "Merkel: 'loves' Europe, insists on 'Homework'." *European Union Observer*. Economic Affairs. Posted December 18, 2012. Last accessed October 18, 2014. http://euobserver.com/economic/118555.

Psyllis, Vassili. « Συναίρεση Θανάτου II ». *Άλιος*. ["Contraction of Death II."Alios]. Posted March 13, 2014. Last accessed October 18, 2014. http://vassilip.blogspot.gr/2014/03/2.html.

"Real Adjusted Gross Disposable Income of Households per Capita." Last updated October 16, 2014. Last accessed October 22, 2014. http://epp.eurostat.ec.europa.eu/tgm/table.do?tab=table&plugin=0&language=en&pcode=tec00113.

"Real GDP Growth Rate—Volume: Percentage Change on Previous Year." European Commission. Eurostat. Last updated October 16, 2014. Last accessed October 22, 2014. http://epp.eurostat.ec.europa.eu/tgm/table.do?tab=table&plugin=1&language=en&pcode=tec00115.

Regling, Klaus. "Alternatives to Austerity would be even More Mainful, warns ESM Chief Klaus Regling." *European Parliament. News.* Posted September 25, 2013. Last accessed October 22, 2014. Ref.: 20130923STO20628. http://www.europarl.europa.eu/news/en/news-room/content/20130923STO20628/html/Alternatives-to-austerity-would-be-even-more-painful-warns-ESM-chief-Regling.

Shults, LeRon F. *Reforming Theological Anthropology: After the Philosophical Turn to Relationality*. Grand Rapids: Eerdmans, 2003.

"Schulz: Europe is not a Community of Austerity but of Solidarity." *European Parliament. News.* Posted February 29, 2012. Last accessed October 18, 2014. Ref.: 20120223STO39237. http://www.europarl.europa.eu/news/en/news-room/content/

20120223STO39237/html/Schulz-Europe-is-not-a-community-of-austerity-but-of-solidarity.

Stamoolis, James J. *Easter Orthodox Mission Theology Today*. Maryknoll, N.Y.: Orbis Books <American Society of Missiology Series, No. 10>, 1986.

Τριανταφύλλου, Αντώνης [Triantafyllou, Antonis] "Η Ιερά Σύνοδος πήρε Θέση για τη Χρυσή Αυγή" [The Holy Synod has taken a Stand on Golden Dawn]: *Amen*. Posted October 11, 2013. Last accessed November 3, 1014. http://www.amen.gr/article15558.

"Troika helped to avoid the Worst, but flawed Structure harmed Recovery." *European Parliament. News*. Plenary Session/Press Release. Posted March 13, 2014. Last accessed October 22, 2014. Ref.: 20140307IPR38407. http://www.europarl.europa.eu/news/en/news-room/content/20140307IPR38407/html/Troika-helped-to-avoid-the-worst-but-flawed-structure-harmed-recovery.

Tsetsis, Georges. "Ethnicity, Nationalism and Religion." In: Emmanuel Clapsis (ed.). *The Orthodox Churches in a Pluralistic World: An Ecumenical Conversation*. Geneva: WCC Publications, 2004: 159–173.

"Unemployment statistics." European Commission. Eurostat. Data up to January 2014. (Next planned update October 31, 2014). Last accessed October 22, 2014. http://epp.eurostat.ec.europa.eu/statistics_explained/index.php/Unemployment_statistics.

Vähäkangas, Mika. "The Future of Missiologies." In: Viggo Mortensen and Andreas Østerlund Nielsen (eds.), *Walk Humbly with the Lord: Church and Mission Engaging Plurality*, Grand Rapids, MI: Eerdmans, 2010: 217–229.

Vassiliadis, Petros. "An Orthodox Assessment of the New Mission Statement": *International Review of Mission*, vol. 102, no. 2 (November 2013): 174–178.

Vavouyios, Argyris. "Greek Economic Crisis is Becoming a Humanitarian Crisis." *Demotix. Society*. Posted January 22, 21012. Last accessed November 2, 2014. http://www.demotix.com/news/1568484/greek-economic-crisis-becoming-humanitarian-crisis#media-1568433.

Βουλγαράκη-Πισίνα, Εύη [Voulgaraki-Pissina, Evi]. « Μοναχισμός και Ιεραποστολή: Μια Σχέση Δημιουργικής Έντασης: Μελέτη στο Βίο, την Πολιτεία και τη Διδασκαλία του Αγίου Ιωάννη Χρυσοστόμου » ["Monasticism and Mission: A Relation of Creative Tension: Study in the Life, Times and Teaching of St. John Chrysostom"]. *Σύναξη* 78 (2001): 39–59.

———. *Η Προσέγγιση των Εθνικών κατά τον Άγιο Ιωάννη το Χρυσόστομο* [Approaching the Pagans According to Saint John Chrysostom], Μαΐστρος <Σπουδή των Πατέρων, 1 || Ιεραποστολικές Σπουδές, 2> [Maistros , Study of the Fathers, 1 || Missiological Studies, 2>, 2013.

———. « Εσωτερική ή Εξωτερική Ιεραποστολή; Ξανακοίταγμα ενός Παλιού Διλήμματος » [External or Internal Mission? Reexamining an Old Dilemma]. *Πάντα τα Έθνη* [All Nations] 70 (1999): 8–9.

———. Entry, « ΗλίαςΒουλγαράκης » ["Elias Voulgarakis"]. In: *Μεγάλη Ορθόδοξη Χριστιανική Εγκυκλοπαίδεια* (MOXE) [Great Orthodox Christian Encyclopedia]. Vol. 4, 2011: 273–275.

———. "Mission and Evangelism in Modern Greece. A Selective Guide through Major Missionary Initiatives in the 20th and 21stCentury." *Teologia* 55,2 (2013): 114–121.

Βουλγαράκης, Ηλίας. « Ο Σημερινός Θεολογικός Λόγος για τη Σωτηρία και η Κατανόησή του από Μέρους του Σύγχρονου Ανθρώπου ». In *Σωτηρία: Η Πανανθρώπινη Αγωνία. Εισηγήσεις Γνωριμίας και Επικοινωνίας Ορθοδόξων Νέων (Σπάτα Ηλείας 1987)*, Collect. Athens: Νεανικός Επιμορφωτικός Όμιλος Σύρου, 1988, 109–133. [Voulgarakis, Elias. "Contemporary Theological Soteriology and the Way it is Understood by Contemporary Man," in Salvation: The Agony for All Humanity. Introductory Presentations at an Orthodox Youth Gathering (Spata, Ilia, 1987), Athens 1988: 109–133].

Weaver, David. "The Exegesis of Romans 5:12 Among the Greek Fathers and Its Implications for the Doctrine of Original Sin: The 5th-12th Centuries" [three-part essay]. *St. Vladimir's Seminary Quarterly*, vol. 27, no. 3 (1983), 187–206; vol. 29, nos. 2 and 3 (1985): 133–159 and 231–257.

Weber, Max. *The Protestant Ethic and the Spirit of Capitalism*. Translated by Talcott Parsons. Introduction by Anthony Giddens. London and New York: Routledge Classics, 2001 [Taylor and Francis e-library, 2005 / First published 1930 by Allen and Unwin].

Währisch-Oblau, Claudia, and Fidon Mwombeki (eds.). *Mission Continues: Global Impulses for the 21st Century*. Oxford: Regnum Books International (Oxford Centre for Mission Studies), 2010.

Χριστόπουλος, Δημήτρης [Christopoulos, Dimitris].« "Προς τον Λαό": Να ορθώνει Πολιτικό Λόγο η Εκκλησία; » ["To the People": Should the Church speak up on Political Matters?]. *TVXS*. Posted December 28, 2010. Last modified July 29, 2011. Last accessed, November 2, 2014. http://tvxs.gr/news/%CE%B5%CE%BB%CE%BB%CE%AC%CE%B4%CE%B1/%C2%AB%CF%80%CF%81%CE%BF%CF%82-%CF%84%CE%BF%CE%BD-%CE%BB%CE%B1%CF%8C%C2%BB-%CE%BD%CE%B1-%CE%BF%CF%81%CE%B8%CF%8E%CE%BD%CE%B5%CE%B9-%CF%80%CE%BF%CE%BB%CE%B9%CF%84%CE%B9%CE%BA%CF%8C-%CE%BB%CF%8C%CE%B3%CE%BF-%CE%B7-%CE%B5%CE%BA%CE%BA%CE%BB%CE%B7%CF%83%CE%AF%CE%B1.

Yannoulatos, Anastasios. "Monks and Mission in the Eastern Church During the Fourth Century." *International Review of Mission* 58/230 (1969): 208–226.

CHAPTER 7

Interreligious Liberation Theologies, Money and Just Relations

Ulrich Duchrow

Liberation theologies in the Abrahamic faiths and the liberation philosophy of Engaged Buddhism can be regarded as forceful efforts to retrieve the original resistance of their founders and their scriptures to the emerging imperialist money-civilization in antiquity, the climax of which we are experiencing today.[1] The following article argues four consequences of this fundamental thesis:

- Firstly, the context of our scriptures was shaped by the emerging pre-form of today's imperialist-capitalist civilization built on the notion of money, private property, and economies linked to egocentric individualism, imperial expansion, and oppression. It is in this context that the mission of the people of God must also be seen.
- Secondly, therefore, contemporary liberation theology, in its critique of capitalism and empire, can directly build on the critical and constructive heritage of the scriptures, thereby orienting the mission of the church, and strengthening people's struggles with its strong spiritual support.
- Thirdly, this civilization is necessarily coming to an end because it is leading humanity and the earth to destruction, which means that a new culture of life needs to be developed. If it is true that the pillars of the dominating system are money and private property linked to egocentric individualism,

1 It may sound presumptuous to lump together all major religions under the concept of liberation. The arguments for this approach can be found in Torre, Miguel A. De La (ed.): *The Hope of Liberation in World Religions*, 2008 (here you find Puntarigvivat, Tavivat, on Buddhism, pp. 131–154). See also Ellis, Marc H.: *Toward a Jewish Theology of Liberation*, 1987, for the Jewish, and Esack, Farid: *Qur'an Liberation & Pluralism: An Islamic Perspective of Interreligious Solidarity against Oppression*, 1997, Reprinted 1998, for the Muslim perspective. Biblical theology *must* center around liberation because the biblical God presents Godself as the one liberating from slavery (cf. e.g. Deut 5:6, the Preamble of the Decalogue: "I am the Lord your God, who brought you out of the land of Egypt, out of the house of slavery; 7you shall have no other gods before me.")

 | DOI 10.1163/9789004318496_009

imperial, and patriarchal violence, then it is at these points that the crucial tasks of liberation theologies and the churches' mission lie.

- Fourthly, as the threat to life is global and as our various scriptures deal with the same context from Greece to China, it is necessary and possible to undertake liberation theology inter-religiously and in alliance with all humanistic social movements.

Let us look at these four consequences one by one.

1. Ancient and modern civilization built on money, private property, egocentrism, imperialism, racism and patriarchy

What we are currently experiencing started nearly 3,000 years ago within what is called the Axial Age, commencing in the 8th century BCE and occurring across the whole of Eurasia from Greece to China. At that time, a new economy built on money and private property began to appear in daily life which had tremendous social as well as psychological and spiritual effects; analyzing what happened at that time therefore helps us to understand what is happening today. In addition, it is vital to acknowledge and examine the resistance movements of that time, mostly appearing in the form of peasant movements supported by contemporaneous religions and philosophies, because their texts comprise the basis of liberation theologies today.

The philosopher Karl Jaspers coined the term "Axial Age".[2] According to Jaspers, the experience of violent crises between 800 and 200 BCE might have prompted the parallel efforts of the prophets, Buddha, Confucius, Daoism and even Greek philosophy to seek different foundations for living together. He characterized the new approaches as intellectual and spiritual (*geistig*), looking only marginally at the economic and political context. As far as the socio-historic context of the Axial Age is concerned, an amazing research has been published over the last 10–20 years showing the parallel monetizing of the economies and cultures in Greece and Rome, Judah, India, China and later the Arab Peninsula. The most comprehensive studies we owe to Richard Seaford (*Money and the Early Greek Mind etc.*) and David Graeber (*Debt. The First 5,000 Years*).[3] Combining their insights with my own research on the situation in

---

2 Jaspers, *The Origin and Goal of History*, 2010.

3 Seaford, Richard: *Money and the Early Greek Mind. Homer, Philosophy, Tragedy*, 2004; id.: *Cosmology and the Polis: The Social Construction of Space and Time in the Tragedies of Aeschylus*, 2012. He is about to publish another book on the historical comparison of early Indian with early Greek thought including an analysis of early Buddhist writings. The context of the Buddha is the theme of Chakravarti, Uma: *The Social Dimensions of Early Buddhism in*

Ancient Israel, Judah and the Jesus movement[4] let me summarize how the new economy affected the ancient societies and how religious, philosophical, and social counter-movements responded.

Money as unit of account was used in the palaces and temples of Mesopotamia as early as approximately 3000 BCE, but the ordinary economy of people in daily life functioned via a system of mutual credit. This changed as soldiers and mercenaries became professionals and war-making was raised to previously unknown levels. Military forces had to be paid and the most important sources of wages were the spoils of war. As precious metals could easily be transported, they started to circulate in little pieces as a kind of money. Around 600 BCE authorities in Lydia, India, and China began, almost simultaneously, to coin the metals in order to pay the mercenaries and soldiers. Along with the growth of these practical currencies, local markets accepting monetary exchange also developed to service the daily transactions of ordinary people. Cash and unified Markets are therefore linked from their inception with male, imperial violence.

At the same time, slaves—usually prisoners of war but increasingly also debtors—were becoming a negotiable commodity, thereby increasing the exploitation of workers, including sexual exploitation. Furthermore, the whole system only functions as long as it expands through further conquest so it is no surprise that it is easily wedded to imperialism. Increasingly the empires also request tribute payment in the form of money, a development that finds its first climax in the Hellenistic-Roman empires.

On this basis, the logic of calculated exchange in markets emerged. Goods for daily needs were exchanged with money as the unit of account. Money became the "one" for a variety of commodities; however, at this point, not as a "thing", detached from the social processes in which people recognize its value, as the Buddhist economist Karl-Heinz Brodbeck points out.[5] Nonetheless, the daily use of money is also beginning to change the soul and the thinking of people: besides communicating by speech, that is, using words (*logos*), they

---

India. Delhi: Oxford University Press, 1987. Graeber, *Debt. The First 5,000 Years*. 2011, combines the analysis of several contexts, especially also China.

4 Cf. Duchrow/Hinkelammert, *Property for People, Not for Profit: Alternatives to the Global Tyranny of Capital*, 2004; Duchrow/Hinkelammert, *Transcending Greedy Money: Interreligious Solidarity for Just Relations*, 2012; Duchrow, *Gieriges Geld: Auswege aus der Kapitalismusfalle—Befreiungstheologische Perspektiven*, 2013. The Spanish translation of parts of Transcending Greedy Money also contains my studies on China: *Más allá del dinero y la avaricia. Alternativas para una cultura de la vida*, 2014.

5 Brodbeck, *Die Herrschaft des Geldes. Geschichte und Systematik*, 2012.

were communicating by calculating in money (*ratio*). In so doing, the individual ego gains precedence over community relations, a process furthered by the fact that, in the process of exchange in the market, the money owner has more power than the producer of goods. Money as such offers access to the market while the product has first to be in demand. Coping with this risk is only possible by having as much money as possible. This is the objective base of the phenomenon of greed which emerged and increased during this period. An economy in which money is made a commodity for accumulation's sake is inherently greedy. One of the "Sages of Antiquity", Pittakos of Mytilene (c. 640–586 BCE), underlined this, saying: "Profit is insatiable".[6] He does not say: "The one who makes profit is insatiably greedy." An economy in which money is made a commodity is inherently greedy, which is why, in our new book, Franz Hinkelammert and I speak of "greedy money" and not just of greedy bankers and their agents and associates.[7] This is another word for "capital", as distinct from money, as Karl Marx analyzed it in his *Das Kapital*.[8] Instead of using money as an instrument for the exchange of use value it is invested to create more money (M-C-M^1 or even M-M^1), thereby producing an "objective" base for the greed to accumulate money without limits within certain monetary structures, the first of which was the concept of interest. The other implication of this development is that money begins to provide the right to private property *beyond personal use*. Money, therefore, gives access to the market, cushions the risks, measures the exchange value, and gives access to property rights. Combined with the development of hierarchies and classes in larger societies, money and private property start to attribute added value the economic, social, and political power of people within societies.

As a further effect, private property and money reinforced male domination in the form of *patriarchy* since only men could own property, which was also a way of giving them political power. The housefather (in Greek: *despotes*; in Latin: *dominus*) was seen as the owner of the land, women, children, slaves, and cattle. Consequently, Greek democracy was nothing more nor less than a democracy of property owners. In Roman law, private property even attained the status of an absolute; that is, men were legally allowed to use, misuse, or destroy private property.

Thus the result of introducing money as a commodity, and private property as an absolute, combined with imperial conquest, was increased division in

6 Cf. *Die Fragmente der Vorsokratiker*, 1964.

7 Duchrow and Hinkelammert, *Transcending Greedy Money: Interreligious Solidarity for Just Relations*, 2012.

8 Marx, *Das Kapital. Kritik der politischen Ökonomie*, 1969.

societies between masters and slaves, and men and women; an increasingly precarious situation for small farmers; and, in general, dire impoverishment and suffering for the majority of people. This was not just a structural problem, however, because money also changed people's souls. Besides communicating through speech and cooperation, they start calculating each other's performance in terms of monetary competition. The problem, therefore, was not just structural, but took on a psychological and spiritual dimension, each of which mutually reinforced the other.

Let us briefly analyze how modern capitalist civilization has built on the early idea of a connection between money/private property/the economy, providing it with new dynamics. In early capitalism—from the 13th to 14th centuries CE—the market set out to conquer one sphere of life after another. A fundamental step was the privatization of common land through enclosures, thereby subjecting agriculture to the mercantile coordination of labor. Another new element was the introduction of compound interest. However, the most decisive new introduction was the invention of double-entry bookkeeping that spread through the most prominent Italian trade and banking cities. Here everything was calculated according to debit and credit, costs and return, input and output—with the single goal being to gain maximum profit. This was not just a social technique but also the decisive characteristic of a new worldview in which the world was seen as a functional mechanism for producing profit for oneself. The calculation of utility followed the means-end rationality, the typical way of thinking in European modernity, which came to dominate the whole world. As the economy serves the single purpose of maximizing profits, normal people judge everything according to a single yardstick: "What's in it for me?"

It was Thomas Hobbes and John Locke in the 17th century CE who formulated contemporary Western concepts of the human being and democracy.[9] Hobbes defined the human being as a competitive, atomized individual striving for limitless accumulation of wealth, power, and reputation, all this taking place in the context of the political body—the Leviathan—whose blood is defined as money. Locke understood the human being as a property owner, and democracy as the political order whose only purpose is to protect property—thus laying the ground for subsequent Western constitutions.

Structural, cultural and personal greed thus starts to be seen as *something positive*. Concluding this line of thought, Jeremy Bentham and Adam Smith define greed and egoism as virtues: the economy's decisive motor. The

9 Cf. Duchrow and Hinkelammert, *Property for People, Not for Profit: Alternatives to the Global Tyranny of Capital*. 2004, chapters 2 and 3.

mechanism of continuously re-investing profit in new projects in order to gain higher profits created an obsessive accumulation machine. Money which is constantly re-invested for accumulation purposes is called capital, which is not simply money but money or assets in monetary terms invested in order to procure more money, or frozen to capital in the form of machines serving accumulation. So "greedy money" is an exact description of the nature of capital, of profit which is thirsty for more profit. This is why capitalism is the precise term for the economic system and the mental form of the societies of Western modernity, while "market economy" is a euphemism in order to avoid touching on the taboo. If you want to use this term in a capitalist context, however, you need to say "capitalist market economy" because in the past there were, and in the future there will be, other kinds of market economies. For example, there can be exchange markets that do not make use of money at all, but also markets with money, though not in the form of a commodity geared at accumulation.

Industrial capitalism deepened the division of labor and increased the split between the classes. But its key new feature is the increased transmission of energy and resources for profit's sake, aggravated by the fact that consumerism has to be stimulated for the sake of maximum capital accumulation. The result of this shift is only becoming visible now as we face crises in energy sources and global ecology. Karl Marx was prophetic when he stated: "Capitalist production, therefore, develops technology, and the combining together of various processes into a social whole, only by sapping the original sources of all wealth—the soil and the laborer."[10] His analysis also defined the obsession for accumulation through commodity-money mechanisms as a fetishism that drives people and societies even against reason. The clear implications are that capitalism is more than an economic system: it is a religion—an insight further developed by Walter Benjamin in his essay on capitalism as religion.[11] This is exactly what we are experiencing today as a growth fetishism which is destroying the earth, but which can only prevail because people have internalized the spirituality of calculating money subjects.

Today this fetishism has taken the form of financial capitalism since it has emerged that infinite growth is not possible in a finite world. Within the financial sector the growth obsession has turned to speculation with ballooning financial assets in all kinds of forms. But this is not without a link to the real economy because, when the balloons burst as they did in the years following 2007, neoliberal governments take real money from the working tax payers and throw it into the voracious jaws of the money owners and their agents, the

10 Marx and Engels, *Capital*, vol. 1, org. 1867.

11 Benjamin, *Kapitalismus als Religion*, 1972.

banks. This demonstrates that today our formal democracy is unable to serve the interest of the people. Rather, it is a democracy of the banks, by the banks, for the banks. As this policy increases the debt of the public budgets, big capital is blackmailing the governments to pay ever higher interest rates and curb social benefits. It seems certain that the whole system will one day collapse, thereby increasing the suffering of people even further. Financial capitalism is the ultimate climax of a development starting in the Axial Age.

For me the conclusion is that we are not dealing with this or that singular crisis, but rather that the whole civilization is destruction-bound, not merely the economy. It is only because the majority of people, and to some extent all of us, are imprisoned in the same kind of logic, spirit, and practice, that the system is still able to operate. Are there possibilities for structural and personal transformation in order to find a new culture of life? And what would the role of liberation theologies and the mission of the church be within this project?

2. Liberation theologies on the basis of Axial Age religions

As the dominating civilization of today builds on an earlier form produced in antiquity, so may contemporary liberation theology, in its critique of capitalism and empire, directly draw upon the critical and constructive heritage of the scriptures, thereby providing strong spiritual support for people's struggles.[12] The following are responses, in a nutshell, of Axial Age religions and philosophies concerning the emerging imperial "money/private property/economy" matrix and its effects on people:

- The prophets and the Torah in Israel/Judah respond with the call for justice and legal provisions.
- Buddha stresses overcoming the three poisons of greed, aggressive hatred, and the illusion of the Ego by mindful insight into the mutual interdependency of all beings, the new ways of living together outlined in the Sanghas, and admonition to the rulers.
- Laozi gives priority to gentle over hard in the way of the Dao; Confucius prioritizes the constant rectification involved in fulfilling one's role in an ordered society.
- Socrates places the search for the true behavior of the soul (*arete*) above wealth and reputation; Plato is concerned with justice in the *Politeia*;

12 Of course, as shown, there are clear differences between antiquity and modernity. However, there is also continuity which could be shown by demonstrating how early capitalist actors in the Middle Ages draw upon Roman law, institutions and behavior, while introducing new methods like double-entry bookkeeping.

Aristotle critiques chremastic accumulation of money, the ethics and politics of the natural economy of the house, and exchange without accumulation.
- Jesus calls for a choice between God's justice and the money idol mammon, thereby highlighting the religious character of money.
- Muhammad condemns the illusion of limitless wealth accumulation, prohibits charging interest on loans (on the basis of biblical heritage) and asks for sharing of wealth through taxes (*zakat*) in order to get people out of poverty.

Let me summarize the response of the Jesus movement and the early church on the basis of the Hebrew Bible in further detail. Historically it seems that the prophet Amos in the second part of the 8th century BCE was the first to react to the upcoming money/private property economy in Eurasia. His central theme was the threat to small farmers: they were losing their possessions through seizures, sold into slavery for excessive debts, and women were being abused as debt slaves, among other practices (Amos 2:6–8). To counteract the destruction of human social relations through the mechanisms of money and private property, Amos attributed a central position to justice in order to correct all power asymmetries (cf. 5:24), when he declaims: "Let justice roll down like waters, and righteousness like an ever-flowing stream."

The other prophets of Israel and Judah—Hosea, Micah, Isaiah, Jeremiah—follow the same line: the latter identifies knowledge of God with doing justice to the poor (Jer 22:16). The prophets and their followers were, however, a minority in Israel and Judah. Only King Josiah made a difference in the second part of the 7th century BCE. It was under his rule that the message of the prophets started to be implemented in the form of legal reforms, which eventually led to the Torah. Central to this process is the Book of *Deuteronomy*. Here one finds the Decalogue, presenting God as liberating people from slavery, thereby demanding and protecting just human relations. Only in this way can freedom be secured (Deut 5:6–21). It is not by accident that the last of the Ten Commandments is about greed and accumulation:

> Neither shall you covet your neighbor's wife.
> Neither shall you desire your neighbor's house,
> or field; or male or female slave, or ox, or donkey,
> or anything that belongs to your neighbor.

The socio-economic laws are found in Deut 14–15 and later elaborated in Lev 25. They contain the prohibition of interest, and the regular release of debts and of slaves, among other provisions.

When the political economy of greed and conquest becomes totalitarian in the Hellenistic empires, the Jewish faithful (*chassidim*) react with apocalyptic underground literature characterized by resistance and hope for God's intervention. The classical text for this is the Book of Daniel where, in Chapter 3, we find the story of the three Jewish men who defied the emperor's demand that everybody should fall down and worship the golden statue. In Chapter 7 a vision of Daniel is narrated in which the empires in the shape of greedy predatory animals are overcome by God's new order descending from heaven in the shape of a human being. The message is that the human, in the image of God, will have victory over the beast-like, destructive, imperial order. That is the hope that feeds persistent resistance.

This is the tradition on which Jesus, his movement and the early church are building new messianic communities in the context of the Roman Empire. This I understand to form a second wave of Axial Age faiths and philosophies. (I regard Islam as the third wave, building on the biblical traditions, in the context of Arab merchant society). Jesus proclaims that God's new domination-free order with a human face—what he terms 'Kingdom of God' as announced by Daniel—is beginning with his presence. It is the suffering, the poor, and the outcast who become the first subjects of this new order, which turns the imperial hierarchy upside down. The first will be the last and the last will be the first. He creates a spirituality of trust in God's care to overcome the external and internal rule of mammon, the idol of those collecting treasure in the form of the accumulation of money and property. "Strive first for the kingdom of God and God's justice, and all these things will be given to you as well" (Matt 6:33).

It is important to realize that Jesus does not only liberate the poor in order to change their own lives and build communities of solidarity, but that he also acts politically in relation to existing institutions. One of his key actions in this regard is his confrontation with the Jewish collaborators of the Romans; the priestly elites in the temple were the 'central bank' of the time (Mark 11:15–19). The key text to understanding the identification of God and Jesus with the people impoverished by, and suffering from, economic injustice is found in Matt 25:31ff. Here the victims—the hungry, the thirsty etc.—are portrayed as the yardstick for all people and peoples to be accepted in the final judgment. The judge is the human being referred to in Daniel 7. This text is crucial for interfaith relations and interfaith solidarity in terms of justice. Those judged are not judged according to the criteria of belonging to this or that religion but by the criteria of providing for the basic needs of the most impoverished with whom Jesus identifies.

In the tradition of Isaiah 2, Micah 4, and Deutero-Isaiah Jesus views the new community of the commencing reign of God as God's original intention when calling on Abraham, the Egyptian slaves, and ancient Israel. Here the intention is that they should be a blessing for the nations, a shining example that a different world, one not perverted by sin, is possible, and can be realized through trust in God. For this reason, he terms the new community that lives by the rules of the Sermon on the Mount (in reality the Torah), "Salt of the earth", "City on the mountain", and "Light of the world" (Matt 5:13–16). Only in this way can community be the true Israel, and people true disciples of Jesus. The test of this lie in one's actions towards the "least of these" (Matt 25:31ff). Jesus even goes so far as to say that those who act humanely towards the least of these belong to him and are the true Israel—whether they confess him with their mouth or not. True confession is acting in the spirit of the reign of God and its justice. This is the core of the mission of the church, what I call "mission by attraction". Mission is living together as community contrasting the status quo. This has been an extreme challenge to the church up to the present because it is dangerous.

It is of central importance that Jesus consciously risks his life when he forms communities living in solidarity in confrontation with the Roman Empire and the collaborating Jewish elites. He utilizes prophetical forms of direct non-violent action, such as the cleansing of the temple. He does not condemn attempts at violent uprisings against Rome, but chooses a different strategy, because the former attempts remain locked into the logic of the violence of the empire. The rulers murder him on the cross, however—the punishment for rebels and escaped slaves. By choosing not to act with counter-violence, because he trusts in God and God's order that is free from domination, he breaks the personal and institutional logic of selfish interests and violence, thereby destroying the legitimacy of the powerful, or—following Girard's argument—exposing the lack of legitimacy of those in power. The faith in the resurrection claims that God is faithful to the one who suffers and is murdered for justice. Failure cannot destroy hope. In this spirit, the disciples were encouraged, at the conclusion of Mark's gospel (Mark 16:7), to return to the marginalized territory of Galilee, to grass-roots, and to follow Jesus, thereby healing and liberating the oppressed as Jesus did.

The early Christian communities followed Jesus on this path. The classical text is Acts 4:32–35. The community voluntarily shares property, especially that of those having landed property and houses. This balancing of the relations within the community is portrayed as fulfillment of the Deuteronomy Torah when it states: "There was not a poor person among them" (cf. Deut 15:4). With this, the text claims, "the apostles gave testimony to the resurrection of the Lord Jesus" with great power (Acts 4:33). Living as a solidary community in the midst of, and in contrast to, imperial, money-driven society is their testimony. The whole Roman Empire was to be subverted by this. The society reacted by saying: "Look, how they love one another!" which might be interpreted to mean: "how they live in solidarity" in the midst of an ego-centered society. The reaction of the people shows that this type of mission by attraction is very effective.

Another key witness for this approach is the Apostle Paul. He adds two important insights to the Jesus tradition. The first states that reason can be co-opted by greed. In his First Letter to the Corinthians, he shows that reason is folly when it orientates itself to a form of wisdom in the service of the strong, the rich, and the mighty. (Today this is exemplified when, for example, scientists work in the service of Transnational Corporations to smokescreen the ecological dangers of a product which destroys ecosystems). Thus wisdom is only true wisdom when it orients itself to the criteria of the weak, vulnerable, and despised in order to be truly inclusive. Secondly, Paul shows in the letter to the Romans that the law, meant to serve life in community, can also be co-opted by greed (Romans 6 and 7). In that case it kills. (Today we can see this in the case of debt mechanisms: when the law that debt has to be repaid is made an absolute, it can kill by producing hunger and even death through Structural Adjustment Programs). Therefore, the overarching criteria for law must be love and solidarity. In Roman 8, Paul elaborates that the only way to do justice is by living in the spirit of the Messiah in new messianic communities. They will revolutionize the Roman Empire with this new spirituality. This is the whole purpose of Paul's counter-cultural mission, because it realizes God's justice.

Summarizing the core of the Hebrew Bible and the messianic Second Testament in relation to our topic, we can say that it consists of the identification of the God of Israel and Jesus with impoverished people in order to build a just society from below. Therefore, justice in the hearts and minds of people, and justice in community relations and institutions, are the key contributions of the biblical traditions. This is the mission of the church towards interfaith solidarity for just relations.

Christian liberation theologies today recover this heritage in the context of late imperial capitalism and peoples' struggles against it. This started in different contexts and therefore took different forms. In Latin America and South Korea, for example, the context was the national-security military dictatorships installed by the US, who pushed through the opening of the domestic markets to transnational capital. The key discovery to counter this was the biblical option for the "Minjung" (the poor): looking at history and the present situation from below, and siding with struggling movements for liberation. The US and its collaborators responded with persecution of the liberating churches and movements who followed Jesus. I have documented this phase in the book "Total War against the Poor" including an analysis of secret military, and US Santa Fe documents.[13] Black theology and Kairos theology responded in the context of the struggle against apartheid. Palestinian liberation theology addressed the occupation of Palestinian land by Israel, backed by the USA and Europe. Also important is another type of liberation theology in the South Asian situation: in India it is represented as Dalit theology while in Sri Lanka Aloysius Pieris has addressed the situation of the poor in a multi-religious context from its inception. His thesis is that liberation theology must be inter-religious and work towards "human communities". The particular contribution of Christianity here is that Jesus is "God's defense pact with the poor".[14] The Ecumenical Association of Third World Theologians (EATWOT) has taken up this inter-religious perspective and published a whole series of studies looking at all religions from the perspective of liberation, actually under the name "Colección TIEMPO AXIAL."[15]

It should be noted that this phase of liberating theologies was quite successful. Even the great Latin American political changes taking place in countries like Bolivia, Venezuela, and Ecuador, and to a certain extent in Brazil, Uruguay, and Argentina are due to the alliance between social movements and liberation theology—among other factors. This is a sign that struggles based on the persistent alliance-building of church-related and people's movements is a key to transformation.

3. A new culture of life transforming the money, property, and political order connected with personal and collective conversion

Because it is leading humanity and the earth to destruction, dominating imperial capitalist civilization is necessarily coming to an end, which is why a whole new culture of life needs to be developed, rather than only single elements. If it is true that the pillars of the dominant system are money and private property linked with egocentric individualism, imperial, and patriarchal violence,

---

13 Duchrow, U., Eisenbürger, G., and Hippler, J. (eds.): *Total War against the Poor*, 1990.

14 Cf. Pieris, "A Liberation Christology of Religious Pluralism", pp. 1–20. He clearly shows how in inter-religious solidarity for justice there is a common ground among the religions, but there are also particular contributions each religion has to make. So this mutual solidarity does not mean an amorphous religious cocktail.

15 Ecumenical Association of Third World Theologians (EATWOT), accessed August 15, 2012, http://www.eatwot.org/. See also Torre, *The Hope of Liberation in World Religions*, 2008, and Vigil, *Por los muchos caminos de Dios: Desafíos del pluralismo religioso a la teología de la liberación* (4 vols. Colección TIEMPO AXIAL) 2003–2006.

then it is at these points that liberation theology and the church's mission, if it wants to be true to Jesus, has its crucial tasks today.

The key feature for a new money order is that money must turn from a commodity for accumulation into a public good, democratically managed. It has to be an instrument for exchange and credit, not a goal. This is already practiced at local and regional levels with regional, interest-free parallel currencies and Local Exchange and Trading Systems (LETS). But in the long run it has to be envisaged even at a global level. The most important economist of the 20th century, John Maynard Keynes, proposed this as early as 1944 at the Bretton Woods conference when he suggested a global central bank with the political reserve currency "bancor". The US at that point rejected this proposal because they wanted the dollar to be globally hegemonic. As the present financial system moves from one crisis to the next, however, there may come a moment when Keynes' proposal will have a chance.

The banks in such a new order will only have the role of managers of public money, rather than being the winners through interest and speculation without labor. This is already happening on a small scale with cooperative and democratic banks. A new property order will be built on the commons, on the world as a gift to be used for life, not as a privatized commodity. This starts with land, water, air, and seeds but includes common cultural goods produced by collectives such as the internet. Consequently all basic goods and services, including, for example, transport, education, and health, which satisfy people's basic needs, must be public. This does not mean that all should be transformed into state property, yet public property must and can be organized as near to the affected people as possible. Indeed, there are many legal forms through which this can be performed.[16] The struggles against privatization together with the struggles against empire-serving capital are the main alliance partners for liberation theology and churches, besides initiatives building up such a new order from below.

However, liberation theology also has a crucial role in transforming the egocentric money-spirituality of people by demonstrating how mutual relationships in cooperation, empathy, and solidarity are the basis for a good human life (*buen vivir*). In this regard all original sources of the Axial Age religions radiate an abundant spiritual power.

---

16 Duchrow, Ulrich and Hinkelammert, Franz J., *Property for People, Not for Profit: Alternatives to the Global Tyranny of Capital*, 2004, ch. 7.

4. Inter-religious solidarity for just relations

As the threat to life is global and as the scriptures of Axial Age religions deal with the same global context from Greece to China, it is necessary to conduct liberation theology inter-religiously and in alliance with all humanistic social movements, particularly with indigenous movements and their culture in Latin America, Africa, and Asia. Here A. Pieris' concept of "human communities" is crucial. Local faith communities can and must cooperate with all humanist forces. According to the messianic writings of the New Testament, God identified with the poor human being, not the Christian religious individual.

In Kairos Europa, we have just started an initiative with Kairos congregations for transformation in Germany, Austria, and Switzerland. They side with the marginalized strugglers produced by the present system in their neighborhoods and simultaneously reread the Bible. They make contact with Muslim congregations in their vicinity and ask them to do the same by rereading the Qur'an. Hopefully, in the future they will reread the Bible and Qur'an together.

The Mission of the church universal has a unique possibility here as it is a single body that transcends the local to the global, inspired and directed by the Messiah Jesus. The World Council of Churches, in its 2nd Mission Declaration, accepted at the 10th Assembly in November 2013, adopted exactly the approach presented in this paper. It says:

> We affirm that the economy of God is based on values of love and justice for all and that transformative mission resists idolatry in the free-market economy. Economic globalization has effectively supplanted the God of life with mammon, the god of free-market capitalism that claims the power to save the world through the accumulation of undue wealth and prosperity. Mission in this context needs to be counter-cultural, offering alternatives to such idolatrous visions because mission belongs to the God of life, justice and peace and not to this false god who brings misery and suffering to people and nature. Mission, then, is to denounce the economy of greed and to participate in and practice the divine economy of love, sharing and justice.[17]

The Mission Statement quotes from the document "Christian Witness in a Multi-Religious World: Recommendations for Conduct" confirming the inter-religious perspective that aims to build "relationships with believers of other faiths or no faith to facilitate deeper mutual understanding, reconciliation and cooperation for the common good" (90).

---

17 TTL § 108.

I know that people in Europe are hesitant to reject clearly imperial capitalism because it is claimed we have a so-called social market economy. However, this is a dangerous illusion. The EU has abolished this concept as a political criterion by legalizing "the principle of open market economy with free competition" in the Lisbon treaty. This policy dismantles the remnants of the European Welfare State step by step. Secondly, the post-war social market economy was possible at that specific period of history because of several particular conditions: firstly, there was competition with historic socialism; secondly, unions were powerful because of the Fordist type of economy; thirdly, unbridled growth was still considered possible as the ecological limit was not yet in sight. Unlimited economic growth, however, is now unsustainable as the planet no longer tolerates it. Yet capitalism must grow because capital is defined by growth, by accumulation. Therefore, humankind must find an alternative way of structuring the economy.

In this, the church can and must reread the Bible and the sources of the other religions contextually. If the context is understood in the way I have outlined, the church must be a pioneer for an alternative culture of life that goes beyond mammon-driven capitalist civilization. Driven by reason and scripture, side by side with movements and people of other faiths and no faith, the church might again form a liberating mission in the spirit of Jesus, the messenger of the God of life.

Bibliography

Benjamin, Walter. *Kapitalismus als Religion, in: Gesammelte Schriften, Frankfurt am Main Bd. IV*. Frankfurt am Main: Suhrkamp, 1972.

Brodbeck, Karl-Heinz. *Die Herrschaft des Geldes. Geschichte und Systematik.* Darmstadt: Wissenschaftliche Buchgesellschaft, (2009) 2012.

Chakravarti, Uma: *The Social Dimensions of Early Buddhism in India.* Delhi: Oxford University Press, 1987.

Duchrow, Ulrich. *Gieriges Geld: Auswege aus der Kapitalismusfalle—Befreiungstheologische Perspektiven.* München: Kösel, 2013.

———. *Más allá del dinero y la avaricia. Alternativas para una cultura de la vida.* Bogota: Universidad Distrital Francisco José de Caldas/Jusititia y Vida, 2014.

Duchrow, U., Eisenbürger, G. and Hippler, J. (eds.). *Total War against the Poor: Confidential Documents of the 17th Conference of American Armies, Mar del Plata, Argentina, 1987.* New York: New York CIRCUS Publications, 1990.

Duchrow, Ulrich and Hinkelammert, Franz J. *Property for People, Not for Profit: Alternatives to the Global Tyranny of Capital.* London and Geneva: Zed Books in association with the Catholic Institute for International Relations and the World Council of Churches, 2004 (in German: *Leben ist mehr als Kapital. Alternativen zur globalen Diktatur des Eigentums.* Oberursel: Publik-Forum (2002), 2005 2. Aufl.).

———. *Transcending Greedy Money: Interreligious Solidarity for Just Relations.* New York: Palgrave MacMillan, 2012 (similar, not identical in the German title).

Ellis, Marc H. *Toward a Jewish Theology of Liberation.* Maryknoll: Orbis Books, 1987.

Graeber, David. *Debt. The First 5,000 Years.* New York: Melville House, 2011.

Kranz, Walter. *Die Fragmente der Vorsokratiker.* Zürich/Berlin: Weidmannsche Verlagsbuchhandlung, 1964, vol. I, 64.

Jaspers, Karl. The *Origin and Goal of History.* London: Routledge Revivals, 2010.

Marx, Karl. *Das Kapital. Kritik der politischen Ökonomie, Karl Marx/Friedrich Engels, Werke, Bd. 23.* Berlin: Dietz Verlag, 1969.

Marx, Karl and Friedrich Engels. Capital, vol. 1. (http://www.marxists.org/archive/marx/works/1867-c1/ch15.htm).

Pieres, Aloysius. "A Liberation Christology of Religious Pluralism." In *Nhanduti Editora/Sri Lanka* (2009): 1–20.

Seaford, Richard: *Money and the Early Greek Mind. Homer, Philosophy, Tragedy.* Cambridge: Cambridge University Press, 2004.

———. *Cosmology and the Polis: The Social Construction of Space and Time in the Tragedies of Aeschylus.* Cambridge: Cambridge University Press, 2012.

TTL

Torre, Miguel A. de la (ed.). *The Hope of Liberation in World Religions.* Waco, Texas: Baylor University Press, 2008.

Vigil, Jose Maria et al. *Por los muchos caminos de Dios: Desafíos del pluralismo religioso a la teología de la liberación,* 4 vols. Colección TIEMPO AXIAL (Quito, Ecuador: Centro Biblico Verbo Divino, 2003–2006).

CHAPTER 8

Economic Development and Christian Mission: A Perspective from History of Mission[1]

Jonathan J. Bonk

> *Christianity is not the bloom, but the root; culture is not the root, but the bloom, of Christianity.*[2]
>
> GUSTAV WARNECK (1834–1910)

> *It may not be in harmony with the current naturalistic theories of social evolution, yet it is the open secret of missionary experience that the humble work of missions is a factor in the social progress of the world which it would be intellectual dishonesty to ignore and philosophic treason to deny.*[3]
>
> JAMES S. DENNIS (1842–1914)

---

1 This paper draws heavily on my "Day Associates Lecture", given at the annual meeting of the Yale-Edinburgh History on the History of the Missionary Movement and Non-Western Christianity at Yale Divinity School, July 3–5, 2003. That original version was published as pamphlet No. 17 in the Yale Divinity School Library's *Occasional Publication* series under the title: *"Not the Bloom, but the Root…": Conversion and Its Consequences in Nineteenth-Century Protestant Missionary Discourse* (New Haven, CT: Yale Divinity School Library, 2003). Some of the content also appeared in another lecture to the same group at their meeting in 2004 on the convening theme, Missions, Money and Privilege, at the Centre for the Study of Christianity in the Non-Western World at the University of Edinburgh (July 1–3, 2004). My lecture was titled "'And they marveled…' Mammon as miracle in Western missionary encounter."

2 Gustav Warneck, *Modern Missions and Culture: Their Mutual Relations*. Translated from the German by Thomas Smith (Edinburgh: James Gemmell, 1883), 245. "We plant and promote civilization when we present the Gospel, and we make the nature-peoples human by making them Christians. Christianity is not the bloom but the root; culture is not the root but a bloom of Christianity." Warneck is here arguing against an alternative view held by "even so sound a theologian as priest Gerland" that argued that "The nature-peoples must first be made human, then Christian. They are slowly trained to and through culture, whose highest bloom is Christianity." (p. 242). Gustav Warneck (1834–1910 *BDCM*) was professor of mission at Halle from 1897–1908, the first chair of its kind in Germany. Although he never served as a missionary himself, he pioneered missiology as an academic discipline encompassing both Protestant and Catholic mission through his monthly journal *Allgemeine Missions-Zeitschrift* (1874). His wide ranging publications cover the gamut of mission subjects, from history to theology and praxis.

3 James S. Dennis, *Christian Missions and Social Progress: A Sociological Study of Foreign Missions*. In Three Volumes. Volume I (New York, Chicago, Toronto: Fleming H. Revell Company, 1897), x.

 | DOI 10.1163/9789004318496_010

Take up the White Man's burden—
In patience to abide,
To veil the threat of terror
And check the show of pride;
By open speech and simple,
An hundred times made plain,
To seek another's profit
And work another's gain.

Take up the White Man's burden—
The savage wars of peace—
Fill full the mouth of Famine,
And bid the sickness cease.[4]

RUDYARD KIPLING (1865–1936)

Protestant missions have long identified with the civilizing mission of the West, crediting Christianity in general and Protestant Christianity in particular with the most noble impulses and remarkable accomplishments of Western "civilization." Missionaries have, of course, been critics of certain *aspects* of the civilizing and development agendas and modus operandi of the West. One thinks of their objection to the Opium Wars, or of their efforts to expose the grisly hoax of Leopold's civilizing mission in the Belgium Congo a few decades later. But on the whole, few seem to have escaped the deep seated assumption that one outcome of Christian conversion would be a way of life that would more or less resemble that enjoyed by Western societies, and that on the whole this was a desirable outcome.

Mindful of their sacred Scripture's insistence on proactive care for the weak and needy—an emphasis infusing Sabbatical and Jubilee guidelines in Leviticus and Deuteronomy and reinforced in the parable of the Good Samaritan—it is inevitable that active response to human need was and is integral to the theological DNA of Protestants generally and of Evangelicals particularly.[5] To "pass by on the other side" is not an option (Luke 10:25–37). "Anyone, then, who knows the good he ought to do and doesn't do it, sins"

4 Rudyard Kipling, "The White Man's Burden," 1899.

5 David W. Bebbington's oft cited "quadrilateral" identified the four core orientations characteristic of evangelicals: Biblicism crucicentrism, conversionism, and activism. See his *Evangelicalism in Modern Britain: A History from the 1730s to the 1980s* (Unwin Hyman/Routledge, 1989).

(James 4:17). *"If anyone has material possessions and sees his brother in need but has no pity on him, how can the love of God be in him?"* (1. John 3:17).

The question asked by this paper is whether what missionaries have offered as "civilization" or "development" meets the ethical test of "helping one's neighbor." If so, by whose definition, to what or whose ends, and for how long? If the answer to the first part of this question is "Yes" for one generation, could the passage of time require that the answer evoke a more ambiguous "Maybe" or even an emphatic "No!" a century later?

Social Derivatives of Christian Conversion

I begin with William Carey, whose *Enquiry*[6] is commonly evoked as marking the beginning of the modern era in Western Protestant mission. The *Leicester Herald* for Saturday, May 12, 1792 drew attention to Carey's slim volume with this advertisement:

> This day is published, Price 1S. 6d.
>
> *An Enquiry into the Obligations of Christians*
> *to use means for the*
> *Conversion of the Heathens*
> *in which the religious state of the world, the*
> *success of former undertakings and the*
> *practicability of further undertakings*
> *for that Purpose are considered*[7]
> BY WILLIAM CAREY

Anticipating that his grandiose evangelical proposal might be greeted with skepticism by learned critics, Carey asked, rhetorically:

6 William Carey, *An Enquiry into the Obligations of Christians, to use means for the Conversion of the Heathens. In which the Religious State of the Different Nations of the World, the Success of Former Undertakings, and the Practicability of Further Undertaking, are Considered.* Leicester: Printed and sold by Ann Ireland, and the other Booksellers in Leicester; J. Johnson, St. Paul's Church yard; T. Knott, Lombard Street; R. Dilly, in the Poultry, London; and Smith, at Sheffield. [Price One Shilling and Six-pence.] MDCCXCII.

7 From Ernest A. Payne's *Introduction* to the 1961 new facsimile edition published in London by the Carey Kingsgate Press, p. v. Leicester: Printed and sold by A. Ireland, and the other booksellers: sold also by J. Johnson in St. Paul's Churchyard; Dilly In the Poultry; Knott, Lombard Street, London, and Smith, Sheffield.

> Can we as men, or as Christians, hear that a great part of our fellow creatures, whose souls are as immortal as ours, and who are as capable as ourselves, of adorning the gospel, and contributing by their preaching, writings, or practices to the glory of our Redeemer's name, and the good of his church, are enveloped in ignorance and barbarism? Can we hear that they are without the gospel, without government, without laws, and without arts, and sciences; and not exert ourselves to introduce amongst them the sentiments of men, and of Christians? *Would not the spread of the gospel be the most effectual means of their civilization* [italics mine]?[8]

Among those who responded negatively to Carey's proposal was Canon Sidney Smith (1771–1845). He took Carey and his "nest of consecrated cobblers and their perilous heap of trash" severely to task in a series of articles appearing in the *Edinburgh Review* in 1808. "It is scarcely possible to reduce the drunken declamations of Methodism to a point, to grasp the wriggling lubricity of these cunning animals, and to fix them in one position," he wrote. Not only would evangelical efforts to convert Hindus fail to elevate them to civilization, but—he predicted—their activities would have catastrophic effects on British imperial interests. Missionary efforts to convert "a few degraded wretches," Smith prophesied, "... would infallibly produce the massacre of every European in India; the loss of [British] settlements, and consequently of the chance of that slow, solid and temperate introduction of Christianity, which the superiority of European character may ultimately effect in the Eastern world."[9]

His caustic wit could not stop what soon swelled into the historical phenomenon popularly known as the modern missionary movement. By the end of the nineteenth century, an impressive volume of documentation had appeared, vindicating William Carey's hypothesis that "the spread of the gospel [*was*] the most effectual means of [human] civilization." In the words of David Jonathan East no one could "become a Christian in the true sense of the term, however savage [they] may have been before, without becoming ... civilised."[10] In his

8 Carey, *An Enquiry*, 69–70.

9 Sydney Smith, "Indian Missions," *Edinburgh Review* (April 1809): 40, 42, 50. Smith had entered the debate over whether East India Company regulations limiting missionary activity on the Indian sub-continent should be relaxed in the February 1808 issue of the *Edinburgh Review*, but in the end, neither his wit nor his wisdom prevailed. In 1813—the year of the founding of the Methodist Missionary Society—the charter of the East India Company was revised by Parliament, granting legal recognition to missionary work in India.

10 David Jonathon East, *Western Africa: Its Condition, And Christianity the Means of its Recovery* (London: Houlston & Stoneman, 1844): 243.

Preface he writes: "While the writer fully admits the importance of all subordinate agencies which may be employed for the benefit of Africa, he aims to show that Christianity is the only sufficient means of its recovery."[11]

Publications lauding Christian missions for their demonstrably key role in the social, economic, and political transformation of peoples and nations became increasingly common toward the end of the nineteenth century. Most notable among these—in chronological order—were William Warren's *These for Those. Our Indebtedness to Foreign Missions: or, What we Get for What we Give*;[12] Thomas Laurie's *The Ely Volume; or, The Contributions of our Foreign Missions to Science and Human Well-Being*;[13] and John Liggins' *The Great Value and Success of Foreign Missions. Proved by Distinguished Witnesses: Being the Testimony of Diplomatic Ministers, Consuls, Naval Officers, and Scientific and Other Travelers in Heathen and Mohammedan Countries; together with that of English Viceroys, Governors, and Military Officers in India and in the British Colonies: Also Leading Facts and Late Statistics of the Missions.*[14]

But the genre reached its apogee with the publication, over a span of nine years, of James Dennis's encyclopedic three volume work, *Christian Missions and Social Progress: A Sociological Study of Foreign Missions.*[15]

James Dennis [1842–1914 *BDCM*] was born and raised in Newark, New Jersey. Following graduation from Princeton Theological Seminary and ordination by the Presbyterian Church, U.S.A., between 1868 and 1871 Dennis served with the ABCFM in Syria. Following a brief furlough and marriage to Mary Elizabeth Pinneo, he returned to Syria under the auspices of the PCUSA to serve as principal and professor of theology at Beirut Theological Seminary. Returning to the

---

11 Ibid., vi.

12 William Warren, *These for Those. Our Indebtedness to Foreign Missions: or, What we Get for What we Give* (Portland, Maine: Hout, Fogg and Breed, 1870).

13 Thomas Laurie, *The Ely Volume; or, The Contributions of our Foreign Missions to Science and Human Well-Being* (Boston: American Board of Commissioners for Foreign Missions, Congregational House, 1881). The book's peculiar title derives from the wishes of the book's patron, "The Hon. Alfred B. Ely, Newton, Mass., who made provision for the publication of this volume" in memory of his father, the Rev. Alfred Ely, D.D., Monson, Mass.

14 John Liggins, *The Great Value and Success of Foreign Missions. Proved by Distinguished Witnesses: Being the Testimony of Diplomatic Ministers, Consuls, Naval Officers, and Scientific and Other Travelers in Heathen and Mohammedan Countries; together with that of English Viceroys, Governors, and Military Officers in India and in the British Colonies: Also Leading Facts and Late Statistics of the Missions* (London: James Nisbet & Co., 1889).

15 James S. Dennis, *Christian Missions and Social Progress: A Sociological Study of Foreign Missions.* 3 Volumes (New York, Chicago, Toronto: Fleming H. Revell Company, 1897, 1899, 1906).

United States in 1891, Dennis began to indulge his passion for world missionary statistics, lecturing and publishing widely on missiological themes.[16]

Dennis inaugurated the newly established Students' Lectureship on Missions at Princeton Theological Seminary by giving six lectures in the spring of 1893, published in the fall of that year in his 368-page volume, *Foreign Missions after a Century*.[17]

Still in its infancy as a discipline, sociology was widely and understandably regarded as the domain of irreligious skeptics and atheists. But to Dennis, the fledgling discipline held immense promise as a complement to missionary endeavor. A joint invitation by Princeton's Sociological Institute and Missionary Society brought Dennis back to Princeton in 1896 to lecture on "The Sociological Aspects of Foreign Missions."[18] His intention, he said, was to demonstrate that while "Christianity as yet touches the age-encrusted and unyielding surfaces of heathen society only in spots.... It is sufficiently apparent... that a new force of transcendent energy has entered the gateway of the nations and has planted itself with a quiet persistency and staying power in the very centers of the social life of the people."[19] "It may not be in harmony with the current naturalistic theories of social evolution," he admitted, "yet it is the open secret of missionary experience that the humble work of missions is a factor in the social progress of the world which it would be intellectual dishonesty to ignore and philosophic treason to deny."[20]

Among those attending Dennis's lectures was Malbone Graham, who preserved his recollection of the lectures in an unpublished manuscript entitled "Origin of a Great Missionary Book."[21] The "book"—four large volumes

---

16 "The very smell of a statistic," Andrew Walls writes, "can send Dennis into an orgy of calculation." See *The Cross-Cultural Process in Christian History* (Maryknoll, N.Y.: Orbis Books, 2002): 52.

17 James S. Dennis, *Foreign Missions A Century* (New York, Chicago, Toronto: Fleming H. Revell, 1893).

18 Dennis, *Christian Missions and Social Progress*, Vol. 1, vii.

19 Dennis, *Christian Missions and Social Progress*, Vol. 1, ix.

20 Dennis, *Christian Missions and Social Progress*, Vol. 1, x. Dennis made a distinction between Christian sociology and Christian socialism, making clear that his book was an illustration of the former, not the latter. See his chapter, "The Sociological Scope of Christian Missions," Vol. I, 21–59.

21 The manuscript, by Malbone Watson Graham of Berkeley, California, had been evidently sent to Delavan L. Pierson, editor of *The Missionary Review of the World*. The manuscript, accompanied by a letter from Pierson, dated April 18, 1916, was sent to Charles H. Fahs of New York (who, with Harlan Beach, would co-edit the 1925 *World Missionary Atlas*), indicating that while the *MRW* could not make use of it, perhaps it might be of interest to

published between 1897 and 1906, comprising a total of 2034 pages replete with illustrations, 307 in all, illustrating the tangible challenges, means and results of missionary endeavor[22]—was by any measure an outstanding accomplishment, easily rivaling the prodigies of our own twentieth-century, computer-assisted missiometrician, David Barrett.[23]

The table of contents alone, totaling some 40 pages, is both daunting and illuminating to read. Dennis, while anticipating reader fatigue, makes no apology for the mass of information. "If any reader is inclined to think that the author has trespassed upon his patience," he writes in his Preface to the third volume, "... it would be well for him to recall that very large and significant claims on behalf of missions which have been advanced in the previous lectures ought to be made good by ample and sufficing evidence."[24]

One reviewer, acknowledging the commonly held view that "Christian missions in foreign lands and sociological theories have nothing in common,"

James Dennis himself. The MSS and the letter are found in folder 55, Box 1, of the James Dennis Papers in the Union Theological Seminary (New York) archives.

22 James S. Dennis, *Christian Missions and Social Progress: A Sociological Study of Foreign Missions*. 3 Volumes (New York, Chicago, Toronto: Fleming H. Revell Company, 1897, 1899, 1906); *Centennial Survey of Foreign Missions: A Statistical Supplement to "Christian Missions and Social Progress," being a Conspectus of the Achievements and Results of Evangelical Missions in all Lands at the Close of the Nineteenth Century* (New York, Chicago, Toronto: Fleming H. Revell Company, 1902). So popular were his 1896 (February 9–14) Princeton lectures that Dennis delivered them as The Morgan Lectureship at Auburn Theological Seminary in New York a week later (February 19–27, as Lane Theological Seminary's "Lectures on Missions" in Cincinnati two weeks later (March 4–10), and as The Elliott Lectureship at Western Theological Seminary in Cincinnati a week after that (March 12–18)! Although I was not able to locate Dennis's letters requesting photographs from missionaries all over the world, the James Sheppard Dennis Papers in the archives of the Union Theological Seminary in New York do contain 51 personal letters from all over the world, all dated in 1905, from his respondents. In all instances, they are responding to his request for photographs to include in the third volume of *Christian Missions and Social Progress*. This gives some intimation of the prodigious correspondence that Dennis must have carried on with missionary correspondents around the world. I am assuming that most of his papers are held in the Speer Library at Princeton Theological Seminary.

23 David B. Barrett is editor of the 1010-page *World Christian Encyclopedia: A Comprehensive Survey of Churches and Religions in the Modern World, AD 1900–2000* (Nairobi, Oxford, New York: Oxford University Press, 1982). The second edition of his encyclopedia, co-edited by George T. Kurian and Todd M. Johnson, was published in 2001. Two volumes were published by Oxford University Press, while a third companion volume, *World Christian Trends AD 30–AD 2200: Interpreting the annual Christian Megacensus*, was published by William Carey Library. The total number of pages in the three volumes is 2633.

24 Dennis, *Christian Missions and Social Progress*, Vol. 3, v.

echoed Dennis's argument that in the "Christian scheme" not only does society play a direct role in the extent to which an individual might actualize his full divinely given human potential, but that remarkable individuals exert a significant influence on the health and transformation of society. This being the case, the reviewer went on, Christian missions and sociology shared considerable common ground.[25] As Benjamin Kidd acknowledged, religion—especially the Christian religion—was an elemental force in human social evolution. "... In the eyes of the evolutionist," Kidd explained, "... the Christian religion has tended to raise the peoples affected by it to the commanding place they have come to occupy in the world."[26]

"Christian missions are a social force," Dennis argued,

> because if they change the religious and moral character of the man, they put him immediately into a new attitude toward the domestic, civil, economic, and ethical aspects of society. They introduce also new institutions into social life; not only new ecclesiastical organizations, but new educational and philanthropic movements. Plant germs of new political and industrial ideals, open a new realm of intellectual and religious thought, stir a new conception of liberty and a nobler, purer social life.[27]

Dennis devoted more than half of the first volume to his second lecture, "The Social Evils of the Non-Christian World."[28] The table of contents for Lecture II constitutes a dense, five-page, tiered synopsis of social evils. Individuals in the non-Christianized world, he said, were prone to a sorry litany of behaviors guaranteeing their social and economic dysfunction.[29]

---

25 J.C. Calhoun Newton, "The Contribution of Christian Missions to Sociology," *The Methodist Review: A Bimonthly Journal Devoted to Religion and Philosophy, Science and Literature* (May–June, 1898), pp. 239–245.

26 Benjamin Kidd, *Social Evolution* (London and New York: Macmillan and Co., 1895), 165–166.

27 Dennis, *Christian Missions and Social Progress*, Vol. I, 43.

28 Dennis, *Christian Missions and Social Progress*, Vol. I, 71–352.

29 These included intemperance, drug addiction, gambling, immorality, self-torture, suicide, idleness, improvidence, excessive pride, and dishonesty; evils affecting families included the degradation of women, polygamy and concubinage, adultery and divorce, child marriage and widowhood, defective family training, and infanticide; tribal groups to various degrees suffered from the traffic in human flesh, slavery, cannibalism, human sacrifice, cruel ordeals, punishments and torture, brutality in war, blood feuds, and lawlessness; social relationships among non-Christians were distorted by ignorance, quackery, witchcraft, neglect of the poor and sick, cruel customs, insanitary conditions, lack of public

Attempts at reform had proven to be consistently ineffectual and would continue to fail (Lecture III). Nations required a supernatural remedy, and Christianity—as a moral force that provided a philosophy of progress, a solution for sin, a true estimation of humankind, and a stimulus to philanthropy—was the only social hope of the nations (Lecture IV).[30]

"Christian missions enter this socially disorganized environment with its varying aspects of degeneracy," Dennis observed,

> from the higher civilization of the Orient to that of barbarous races, and in most cases without the aid of legal enactments, engage in a moral struggle with old traditions and immemorial customs which have long held sway in society. They deal with a religious consciousness almost painfully immature in spiritual things, so that the splendid task of Christian missions is to take by the hand this childhood of heart and mind, put it to school, and lead it by the shortest path into the largeness of vision and ripeness of culture which have come to us all too slowly and painfully.... And yet, slowly and surely change comes. It comes through the secret and majestic power of moral guidance and social transformation which seems to inhere in that gospel which Christian missions teach.[31]

It is in Dennis's contribution to one of the greatest of all missionary gatherings, the New York 1900 Ecumenical Missionary Conference,[32] that we find the most succinct summary of his apologia. The list of delegates to the New York Ecumenical Missionary Conference of 1900 suggests that Christian missions had reached a level of public acceptance never before, or since, achieved. Representing approximately 15,000 Protestant missionaries serving with 400 societies all over the world, some 2500 delegates—including internationally

---

spirit, mutual suspicion, poverty, tyrannical customs, and caste; nationally, the shortcomings included civil tyranny, oppressive taxation, subversion of legal rights, corruption and bribery, massacre and pillage; commercially, a lack of business confidence, together with deceit, fraud, financial irregularities, and primitive methodologies frustrated advance; and as for religion, the well-spring of everything else, the non-Christian world suffered from degrading conceptions of nature, idolatry, superstition, religious tyranny and persecution, and scandalously immoral leaders. See the Table of Contents in Dennis, *Christian Missions and Social Progress*, Vol. I, 9–16.

30 Dennis, *Christian Missions and Social Progress*, Vol. I, 10–16.

31 Dennis, *Christian Missions and Social Progress*, Vol. I, 45.

32 *Ecumenical Missionary Conference New York, 1900. Report of the Ecumenical Conference on Foreign Missions, held in Carnegie Hall and Neighboring Churches, April 21 to May 1.* 2 Volumes (London: Religious Tract Society; and New York: American Tract Society, 1900).

acclaimed Christian leaders and missionary heroes—mingled with dignitaries, politicians, and national celebrities.

On opening night (Saturday, April 21, 1900), a wave of emotion swept through the 2500 attendees as, directed by Ira D. Sankey himself, they rose to sing "Jesus Shall Reign."[33] Theodore Roosevelt, John G. Paton, Bishop Thoburn, Hudson Taylor, and Robert Laws were among the luminaries seated in the front row on the platform. In his capacity as honorary chairman, former president of the United States Benjamin Harrison gave the opening address. He was followed by the President of the United States, William McKinley. As he made his way to the platform on the arm of Morris K. Jessup, chair of the New York Chamber of Commerce, there was a spontaneous outburst of cheering. Acknowledging the convergence of Christian missionary activities and the ideals of Western civilization, McKinley said:

> I am glad of the opportunity to offer without stint my tribute of praise and respect to the missionary effort which has wrought such wonderful triumphs for civilization. The story of Christian missions is one of thrilling interest and marvelous results....
>
> Wielding the sword of the Spirit, they have conquered ignorance and prejudice. They have been among the pioneers of civilization....
>
> Who can estimate their value to the progress of nations? Their contribution to the onward and upward march of humanity is beyond all calculation. They have inculcated industry and taught the various trades. They have promoted concord and amity, and brought nations and races closer together. They have made men better. They have increased the regard for home; have strengthened the sacred ties of family; have made the community well ordered, and their work has been a potent influence in the development of law and the establishing of government.[34]

Dennis played a key role in the conference, serving as Chairman of the Committee on Statistics "appointed to present a paper."[35] Having already published two volumes of his three-volume *Christian Mission and Social Progress*,

---

33 See Thomas Askew, "The New York 1900 Ecumenical Missionary Conference: A Centennial Reflection," *International Bulletin of Missionary Research*, Vol. 24, No. 4 (October 2000), 146–154.

34 *New York 1900*, Vol. 1, 38–40.

35 James S. Dennis, *Centennial Statistics: Paper Prepared for the Ecumenical Conference on Foreign Missions. New York City, April 21–May 1, 1900* (New York: Committee on Statistics, 1900), vii.

Dennis had amassed data for a volume that was to serve as their statistical complement.[36] The distillation of this 400+ pages volume was printed and distributed to conference attendees, subsequently appearing as an appendix in the official two-volume report of the conference.[37]

The nine categories beneath which the data were arranged provide insight into the expected outcomes of conversion to Christianity. First and most extensively treated among the categories was "Evangelistic," providing detailed statistics on the "income, staff, and evangelistic returns of missionary societies."[38] This was followed by detailed statistical information on educational, literary, medical, philanthropic and reformatory, and cultural dimensions of missionary endeavor. One cannot but be impressed by even a cursory overview of the scope of missionary work at the time.

Education statistics (section II of the summary) included information on 93 universities and colleges, 358 theological and training schools, 858 boarding and high schools and seminaries, 167 industrial training institutions, 63 medical schools, 127 kindergartens, and 18,742 elementary or village day schools. Over one million students were enrolled, nearly one third of these women, in 20,407 institutions.[39]

Section III of the summary, under the heading "Literary," provided statistics on 427 Bible translations and more than ten million pieces of general literature published by 148 mission publishing houses on every continent; some 366 periodicals with a combined circulation of nearly 300,000 reinforced missionary evangelistic and educational efforts.[40]

Medical statistics (section IV of the summary) tabulated 355 hospitals—including 10 in Palestine, 40 in Africa, 106 in India, and 124 in China—and 753 dispensaries, registering treatment of some 2.5 million patients the previous

---

36 This data was published in 1902 in his book, *Centennial Survey of Foreign Missions. A Statistical Supplement to "Christian Missions and Social Progress," being a Conspectus of the Achievements and Results of Evangelical Missions in all Lands at the Close of the Nineteenth Century* (New York, Chicago, Toronto: Fleming H. Revell Company, 1902). The volume, including table of contents and tables of abbreviation and maps, runs to 430 pages.

37 James S. Dennis, "Statistical Summary of Foreign Missions Throughout the World," in *Ecumenical Missionary Conference New York, 1900*, Vol. II, 419–434. In compiling the statistics, Dennis benefited from an incredible 90% response to his questionnaire, with most of the missing 10% accounted for by the Boer War in South Africa.

38 *New York 1900*, Vol. II, 424. Interestingly, the U.S. dollar—British pound sterling exchange rate was calculated at $4.90 to the pound.

39 *New York 1900*, Vol. II, 428–429.

40 *New York 1900*, Vol. II, 430–431.

year.[41] The Philanthropic and Reformatory section of the report provided "statistics of institutions and societies for relief and rescue" including 213 orphanages, 90 leper hospitals and asylums, and 30 schools and homes for the blind and the deaf. This section also included mention of the work of some 280 temperance societies, "rescue work" through the aegis of 154 homes for converts, widows, homeless women, and rescued slaves, and 126 societies established "for the promotion of purity, prison reform, abolishment of foot-binding, and work for soldiers, sailors, and prisoners."[42]

The sixth section of the summary, labeled "Cultural," included "the reproduction abroad of many well-known agencies at home."[43] Dennis concludes his summary with statistics on fifty-four "Native organizations for extension of knowledge and the furtherance of national, social, moral, and religious reform" (Section VII), eighty-seven "missionary training institutions and agencies in Christian lands" (Section VIII), and sixty-seven "Mission steamers and ships used in evangelistic, medical, and other departments of mission service in the foreign field" (Section IX).[44]

Edinburgh 1910 World Missionary Conference

At the Edinburgh 1910 World Missionary Conference ten years later, Dennis once again rendered service as one of eighteen vice-chairmen of the commission responsible for producing the *Statistical Atlas of Christian Missions*.[45] The categories are familiar, and the information marshaled impressive. Twenty maps, in color, locate all known mission stations, with nineteen maps for Protestant missions, and a single map for Roman Catholic and Greek Catholic

41 *New York 1900*, Vol. II, 432.

42 *New York 1900*, Vol. II, 433.

43 *New York 1900*, Vol. II, 434. Included in this list of well-known agencies are: the United Society of Christian Endeavor, the Methodist Church (North), the Methodist Church (South), the Brotherhood of St. Andrew, the Order of the Daughters of the King, YMCA, YWCA, World's Student Christian Federation, Student Volunteer Movement in Mission Lands, Children's Scripture Unions, Boys Brigades, Gleaners Unions, and Sowers' Bands.

44 *New York 1900*, Vol. II, 434.

45 *Statistical Atlas of Christian Missions. Containing a Directory of Mission Societies, A Classified Summary of Statistics, an Index of Mission Stations, and a Series of Specially Prepared Maps of Mission Fields.* Compiled by Sub-Committees of Commission I, "On Carrying the Gospel to All the Non-Christian World," As an Integral Part of its Report to the World Missionary Conference, Edinburgh, June 14–23, 1910 (Edinburgh: World Missionary Conference, 1910).

missions.[46] The Committee estimated the "total fruitage of modern Christian missions [Protestant, Roman Catholic and Russian Orthodox] of the past century, represented by living converts Christianized from non-Christian peoples, as approaching 21,000,000."[47] Educational summary tables tallied 81 universities, 489 theological schools, 1594 boarding schools, 284 industrial training schools, 28,901 elementary schools, and 113 kindergartens.[48] 550 hospitals, 1024 dispensaries, and 111 medical schools represented missionary medical activities, to which benevolences could be added 265 orphanages, 88 leper hospitals, 25 institutions for the blind, and 21 rescue homes.[49]

Missionaries were not the exclusive beneficiaries of government, transportation, and communication systems around the world imposed and tightly monitored by colonial Western powers, however. Islam may have been "Christianity's most formidable enemy,"[50] but a more sinister threat was posed by "the deadly gift" of Western civilization itself, with its "habits of luxury and self-indulgence,"[51] and its myriad corrupting influences. It was important that missionary activity pre-empt the building of African and Asian railways, for example, since "the advent of railways [would] bring a large influx of ungodly men, who [would] make the task of evangelisation much more difficult. [For it had] always been true that while men slept the enemy came and sowed tares."[52]

"There are but a few primitive races or peoples left in the world, and the opportunity afforded the Christian Church to reach them under most favorable conditions can last but a brief season," the Commission warned...

> The present opportunity will pass away. Every year will bring new and powerful counter attractions within easy reach of the natives. The wise and experienced missionary workers show convincingly that it is much easier to bring the Gospel to bear on the heathen in his natural state than it is upon the man who has become familiar with the worst side of so-called civilisation.[53]

---

46 These maps were the work of Professor Harlan P. Beach of Yale University.

47 *SACM*, 61.

48 *SACM*, 63.

49 *SACM*, 64.

50 *Edinburgh 1910–1*, 20.

51 *Edinburgh 1910–1*, 22.

52 *Edinburgh 1910–1*, 23.

53 *Edinburgh 1910–1*, 22–24. The themes and concerns identified in the Edinburgh 1910 conference continued to be promoted through the aegis of its Continuation Committee and its scholarly quarterly, the *International Review of Missions*. The disbanding of the Continuation Committee at the conclusion of the Great War did not mean that

Missionaries, while not uncritical of Western civilization, were nevertheless animated by the belief that its core principles were traceable directly to Christianity. In a required textbook written by their professor, students at the Disciples of Christ Bible College of Missouri read that

> It is in its social message that Christianity outruns the other missionary religions in its permanent power to uplift.... It becomes a civilizer through its implanting of humane social principles and social ideals in the hearts of its converts, and they leaven the whole of the life about them.... It is... our implanting of the life of Christ, with all it means to our civilization in higher ideals, purer thinking, better homes, greater equality, more value on life as such, a higher standard of living, and more of the spirit of service, that brings the world to him.[54]

Among the plates included in the book is one featuring a group of students posing in front of a large American flag. The caption beneath it reads: "Advanced Class in Urumia College, Persia. Moslems, Jews, and Christians are here drawn together, and ancient hates are lost under missionary instruction."[55]

It was the two great wars, waged by ostensibly "civilized" "Christian" nations that would undermine the till-then-unquestioned notion that Christianity was the bedrock upon which all that was good and worthy of emulation in Western societies was built.

The First [Christian] "World" War 1914–1918

The assassination of Austrian Archduke Franz Ferdinand by teenage members of Black Hand plunged "Christian" Europe and its colonies into the bloodiest

mission organizations had abandoned their interests in global mission. With the formal establishment in 1921 of the permanent, international, co-operative agency known as the International Missionary Council, the nation building and development agendas of Christian mission continued to absorb the attention of conciliar Protestants as evidenced in the three great ecumenical assemblies convened in Jerusalem (1928), Oxford (1937), and Tambaram (1938–39). All three conferences dealt hopefully and extensively with nation building.

54 Alva W. Taylor, *The Social Work of Christian Missions* (Cincinnati: The Foreign Christian Missionary Society, 1914): 15. Taylor was Professor of Social Service and Christian Mission in the Bible College of Missiouri (Disciples of Christ). His textbook, published in 1911, was enjoying its third printing by 1914.

55 Taylor, *The Social Work of Christian Missions*, bottom plate facing p. 172.

and quite possibly the most meaningless conflagration in human history. It also marked the end of innocence for missionary apologists, who, until then, had held up their own societies as evidence of the vitality and virtue of Christian influence.

In his admirable book on the subject, Hew Strachan points out that this European war became known as the First World War because people from all over the world came to fight in the civilized nations' cause. Britain mobilized more than three million troops from her colonies (two million of these from Africa), while France mobilized half-a-million from hers. The war's ultimately pointless savagery sent a shudder through the terra firma on which confidence in the moral, social and political superiority of Western societies was based.[56] Missionaries who had confidently proclaimed European civilization to be the natural and inevitable result of a society permeated by Christian values were likewise shaken to their ideological foundations by the war and its aftermath.[57] Commenting on the decline of Chinese interest in mission school education, the Hocking Commission observed that while "By 1920 it had become 'almost the fashion to become a Christian'; since 1922 the tide [had] turned," due, understandably, to "... the disillusionment of the World War and the widespread impression it left that the West did not really believe the Christianity it taught."[58]

The Second [Christian] "World" War 1939–1945

Tony Judt sketches the breathtaking scale of the second great European slaughter in *Postwar: A History of Europe Since 1945*.[59] "The European war that began with Hitler's invasion of Poland in September 1939 and ended with Germany's unconditional surrender in May 1945"—he reminds those of us too young to

---

56 Hew Strachan, *The First World War*, Volume I, *To Arms* (London: Oxford University Press, 2002). Reviewed by Niall Ferguson in the February 13, 2003, issue of the *New York Review of Books*, 21–23. See also Donovan Webster, *Aftermath: The Remnants of War* (New York: Random House, 1996).

57 William Pfaff, *The Wrath of Nations: Civilization and the Furies of Nationalism* (New York: Simon & Schuster, 1993). "The Great War was the most important event of the twentieth century. It was a decisive historical event, a marker" (232–233).

58 William Ernest Hocking, *Re-thinking Missions: A Laymen's Inquiry After One Hundred Years* (New York and London: Harper & Brothers, Publishers, 1932): 154–155.

59 Tony Judt, *Postwar: A History of Europe Since 1945* (New York: Penguin, 2005).

remember, too naïve to imagine, and perhaps too idealistic to admit—"was a total war. It embraced civilians as well as soldiers."[60]

In Europe and the USSR alone, more than 19 million non-combatant civilians were slaughtered, victims of deliberate mass exterminations, death camps, killing fields, slave labor camps, carpet shelling and bombing of cities, and strafing of refugee columns. It is estimated that between 1939 and 1945, around 36.5 million Europeans died of war-related causes. This figure does not include death from natural causes, such as old age. Nor do these figures include Japanese, American, and other non-European dead. "No other conflict in recorded history killed so many people in so short a time," Judt observes in the first chapter of his deeply poignant lamentation.[61]

Material destruction was correspondingly horrific and indiscriminate in scale. This was a war waged by the armies of societies that were among the most "Christian" in the world. This tragic story of human destruction of life and property has iterated and reiterated around the world and across the millennia, affirming the veracity of Reinhold Neibuhr's conclusion that the intrinsic incompatibility of individual morality and collective life make conflict inevitable.[62] Any collective, it seems—ethnic, religious, political, or ideological—is susceptible to claiming idolatrous metaphysical status, demanding one's all.

After these wars, missionary triumphalist talk of "civilization" through Christian conversion gradually gave way to programs of "development"

60 Ibid., 13.

61 Ibid., 1–40, passim. See also Jonathan Glover, *Humanity: A Moral History of the Twentieth Century* (New Haven: Yale University Press, 1999).

62 Two deeply persuasive Christian intellectuals offer contrasting views on how this is to be understood and what the implications of that understanding would be: In *Moral Man, Immoral Society: A Study in Ethics and Politics* (Westminster John Knox Press, 2013), first published in 1932, Reinhold Niebuhr [1892–1971] offers a deeply tragic view of human nature and history, arguing that the intrinsic incompatibility of *individual morality* and *collective life* make social and political conflict inevitable. Human collectives, no matter how well intentioned, end up being brutal. How individual morality can mitigate the persistence of social immorality is the question that Niebuhr explores. Similarly, in *The Politics of Jesus* (Eerdmans 1994), first published in 1972, John Howard Yoder [1927–1997] offers a vigorous and persuasive dissent from the commonly touted view that Jesus was unconcerned with political issues, and that he taught his followers to be apolitical. Utilizing a careful reading of the New Testament, Yoder critiques this traditional view and shows the profound impact of Jesus' life, work, and teachings on his disciples' social behavior. He argues that the thinking and teaching of Jesus bear directly and consequentially on social, political, and moral issues.

through Western education, finance, and political rearrangement. The modus operandi of Western mission continued to function much as before, since it was embedded in the very warp and woof of Christian missionary identity. But the confident, breezy, and at times patronizing tone of nineteenth-century missionary apologists migrated into the language and agendas of contemporary non-religious organizations such as the United Nations, the World Bank, and the International Monetary Fund.

Of course, the "Christian" West—especially the United States—continues to wage war against or on behalf of weaker peoples for ethically dubious reasons and with decidedly ambiguous outcomes. Missionary confidence in the efficacy of Christianity as the foundation of all genuine development continues to be undermined by facts on the ground. Take the continent of Africa, for example. The Pew Forum on Religion & Public Life survey made public on August 15, 2010, showed that Africa is the most religious continent in the world. The share of Africans who described religion as "very important" in their lives ranged from 98% in Senegal to 69% in Botswana. That compares with 57% of Americans, 25% of Germans and 8% of Swedes. The study also reported that the number of Christians in sub-Saharan Africa grew faster than the number of Muslims, from 7 million in 1900 to 470 million in 2010. Today, one in five Christians lives in sub-Saharan Africa.[63]

Yet this most polyglot of all continents—home to no fewer than 2,100 "mother tongues"—is notorious for its "vampire" states, savage civil wars, overwhelming pandemics, predatory politicians, rickety infrastructures, and intractable poverty. While the intersecting legacies of slavery, colonialism, and globalization tell part of the story, many of Africa's wounds are self-inflicted. Africa—in the words of Robert Guest, Africa editor of the *Economist* magazine—is *The Shackled Continent* (Smithsonian Books 2004). Despite decades of prodigious "development" efforts fueled by close to $600 billion in aid since the 1960s, living conditions across the continent have steadily declined. Of the 44 countries at the bottom of the World Bank's 186-nation human development index (HDI), 36 are African, with an estimated income per person less than 2 per cent that of Americans.[64]

63 http://pewforum.org/Press-Room/Pew-Forum-in-the-News/Survey-finds-Africa-is-most-religious-part-of-world.aspx (Accessed November 11, 2010).

64 http://hdr.undp.org/sites/default/files/reports/14/hdr2013_en_complete.pdf, accessed March 27, 2014.

Missions, Civilization, Economic Development and Ethical Uncertainties

Today, the West's "civilizing" mission continues, but now in the guise of the global "development" industry. The legitimacy of 'civilizational' or 'developmental' thinking is widely questioned today by, for example, the *Degrowth* movement, which is posited on the belief that overconsumption lies at the root of most of the planet's environmental and social crises and increasing auguries of a grim future.

The impressive sweep of nineteenth-century missionary accomplishments is not surprising. Protestant missionaries trod in the tradition of evangelical nonconformists, who were better known for their social work than for their theology.[65] Missionaries were acutely aware that "faith without works is dead" (James 2:26), and that faith was much more than mere mental assent to theologically correct propositions about God and related questions. Love of God without love of neighbor was tantamount to heresy. And the only authentic way to love a neighbor was to do for him or her what one would personally want were circumstances reversed. Just what this meant was understood in largely Western terms. The lost needed finding; the ignorant needed educating; the illiterate needed illuminating; the destitute needed nurturing; the benighted society needed transforming. Theological justification combined with a sense of civilizational pride to animate, justify and sustain missionary economic development exertions.

That centuries of economic, political, and military domination should foster within a missionary citizenry self-confidence, assertiveness, and illusions of superior virtue is not surprising. As Galbraith wryly observed, "nothing so gives the illusion of intelligence as association with large sums of money."[66] Similarly delusional thinking is to be expected in those whose nations boast overwhelming economic and military power. We human beings are, after all, comparative creatures, constantly, subconsciously measuring and defining ourselves in reference to those around us.

When James Dennis wrote his books, Europe dominated all of Africa, the entire Middle East except for Turkey, and most of the Asian subcontinent. The 35 percent of the earth's surface controlled by Europeans when Carey set sail

---

65 See Kathleen Heasman, *Evangelicals in Action: An Appraisal of their Social Work* (Letchworth: Geoffrey Bles Ltd., 1962); John Briggs and Ian Sellers, eds., *Victorian Nonconformity* (London: Edward Arnold, 1973); and Norris Magnuson, *Salvation in the Slums: Evangelical Social Work 1865–1920* (Grand Rapids: Baker Book House, 1977).

66 John Kenneth Galbraith, "The 1929 Parallel," *Atlantic Monthly*, 259, No. 1 (January, 1987): 62.

for Serampore in 1793 had grown to 84 percent by 1914. The British Empire, incorporating 20 million subjects spread over 1.5 million square miles in 1800, encompassed 390 million people inhabiting 11 million square miles one century later.[67] For many missionaries, such ascendency was an inevitable outcome of the religion they propagated.

It is clear that Western missionaries generally regarded the entire continuum of human betterment as a direct, intended, and positive outcome of successful Christian mission, with their own Western nations as "exhibit A."[68] The deeply ethical ambiguities swirling around the concept of "development" today were not part of missionary discourse then. The three-way debate between advocates of productivist consumerism, sustainable growth, and degrowth economics would emerge much later.[69]

Voices of intellectuals such as E.F. Schumacher, Ivan Illich, Bob Goudzwaard or Andrew M. Greeley, questioning the legitimacy of "civilizational" or "developmental" thinking, have been drowned out by the deafening cacophony of "development" literature and its concomitant institutions and schemes,

---

67 Samuel P. Huntington, *The Clash of Civilizations and the Remaking of World Order* (New York: Simon & Schuster, 1996): 51. Huntington cites D.K. Fieldhouse, *Economics and Empire, 1830–1914* (London: Macmillan, 1984): 3, and F.J.C. Hearnshaw, *Sea Power and Empire* (London: George Harrap and Co., 1940): 179.

68 This was my argument in *"'And they marveled...' Mammon as miracle in Western missionary encounter"*, a paper presented at a conference on "Missions, Money and Privilege", convened at the Centre for the Study of Christianity in the Non-Western World at the University of Edinburgh on July 1–3, 2004. The occasion was the annual meeting of the Yale-Edinburgh Group on the History of the Missionary Movement and Non-Western Christianity. In the paper I argue that the material and social culture of Western missionaries served as a miraculous sign, utilized to prove that missionary religion was right and other religions were wrong. There was little need for spectacular displays of tongues, healings, resurrections, and the like. Gospel credibility was seemingly assured by the missionaries' perceived intimate association with the marvelous—houses, clothing, vehicles, boats, labor-saving devices, money, modern medicine, the presumed backing of powerful governments and organizations (and even the novelty of skin and hair color), all of which added illustriousness and weight to the missionaries' worldwide conversion enterprise. Missionaries frequently declared their way of life to be the logical and inevitable result of personal and national life regulated over the generations by Christian principles. The Holy Spirit so imbued the institutions and material culture of Western society as to make missionary recourse to the paranormal redundant and unnecessary.

69 See Franck-Dominique Vivien, "Sustainable development: An overview of economic proposals", on the SAPIENS website: http://sapiens.revues.org/227. The acronym stands for Surveys and Perspectives Integrating Environment and Society.

secular and religious.[70] Questions about the long term viability of a planet whose burgeoning human populations make strenuous efforts to replicate Western levels of steadily escalating consumption and perpetual economic growth do not appear in the earlier literature. It is only in retrospect that one can question the big picture ethics of the kind of development generated and lauded by missionaries of yesteryear. The inspiration from economic movements such as *Degrowth*, has not yet, to my knowledge, become a significant part of missiological discourse, training, or modus operandi.[71]

Furthermore, one does not need to travel to Africa to observe failed "development" plans. There are significant shortcomings much closer to home. "Facts on the ground" include those marshaled by Richard Wilkinson and Kate Pickett in their groundbreaking study, published as *The Spirit Level*.[72] There are still many in the United States who are convinced that the Christian religion is essential to any society's optimal well-being. Whether or not this is so is a moot point. The fact is that powerful personal, social, and political impulses are at play, subverting or annulling the lofty ideals of the country's dominant religion.

Thus, to some paradoxically, this most "Christian" of twenty-three Western nations comes in dead last on 25 measures, including rates of homicide, incarceration, suicide, infant mortality, life expectancy, gonorrhea, syphilis, abortion, teen pregnancies, marriage duration, divorce, alcohol consumption, life satisfaction, corruption, income inequality, levels of unemployment, and scale of poverty.[73]

This was Paul Gregory's conclusion in a paper published in the July 2009 issue of the online journal *Evolutionary Psychology*.[74] As Gregory explains,

---

70 E.F. Schumacher, *Small is Beautiful: Economics as if People Mattered* (Blond & Briggs 1973); Bob Goudzwaard, *Aid for the Overdeveloped* West (Wedge Publishing 1975); Ivan Illich, *The Church, Change and Development* (Urban Training Center Press 1970); Andrew M. Greeley, *No Bigger Than Necessary: An Alternative to Socialism, Capitalism, and Anarchism* (Meridian 1977).

71 See http://en.demagazine.eu/sharing-ideas/what-economic-degrowth. The degrowth economics school was anticipated by E.F. Schumacher in his *Small is Beautiful: Economics as if People Mattered* (New York, NY: Jar[er & Row, 1973).

72 Richard Wilkinson and Kate Pickett, *The Spirit Level: Why Greater Equality Makes Societies Stronger* (New York, NY: Bloomsbury Press, 2009)... a compellingly documented study of the nature and impact of inequity on the health—social, economic, and physical of societies.

73 Ibid., Appendices C, D, E, F, G, 437–441.

74 "The Chronic Dependence of Popular Religiosity upon Dysfunctional Psychosociological Conditions," in *Evolutionary Psychology*, Vol. 7, No. 3 (July 2009), pp. 398–441. See www.epjournal.net (accessed April 12, 2013).

> As a member of the 1st world the U.S. is an anomalous outlier not only in its religiosity, but in social, economic and political policies as well. Provided with comparatively low levels of government support and protection in favor of less restrained capitalism, members of the middle class are at serious risk of financial and personal ruin if they lose their job or private health insurance; around a million go bankrupt in a year, about half due in part to often overwhelming medical bills. The need to acquire wealth as a protective buffer encourages an intense competitive race to the top, which contributes to income inequality. The latter leaves a cohort mired in poverty. Levels of societal pathology are correspondingly high.[75]

Probably the most troubling outcome of the kind of "development" modeled and advocated by the West, including Western missionaries, since the Industrial Revolution is climate change. According to the most recent report issued by the Intergovernmental Panel on Climate Change, a United Nations group charged with periodically summarizing climate science, "ice caps are melting, sea ice in the Arctic is collapsing, water supplies are coming under stress, heat waves and heavy rains are intensifying, coral reefs are dying, and fish and many other creatures are migrating toward the poles or in some cases going extinct... and the worst is yet to come...."[76]

One of the most credible and accessible current critics of the Western development mentality and its concomitant NGO industry is William Easterly. Professor Easterly's relentlessly scathing indictment of the West's "development" or "civilizing" mission is all the more credible because the author, one of the world's best-known development economists, was a World Bank research economist for sixteen years. He was fired when his earlier book—*The Elusive Quest for Growth*—drew attention to the utter uselessness and, indeed, disastrous effects of most Western schemes for the alleviation of global poverty.

With the highest percentage of its citizens "absolutely believing in God" (63%), believing the Bible to be literally true (30%), participating in religious services regularly (39%), and engaging in prayer (60%), it achieved the lowest International Social Survey Score (ISSP) of 0 out of a possible 10. By way of contrast, Sweden, Denmark, and Germany achieved scores of 9.7, 9.1 and 10, respectively.

75 Ibid., 421.

76 Justin Gillis, "Panel's Warning on Climate Risk: Worst is Yet to Come," *NY Times*, Monday, March 31, 2014 http://www.nytimes.com/2014/03/31/science/earth/panels-warning-on-climate-risk-worst-is-yet-to-come.html?emc=edit_th_20140331&nl=todaysheadlines&nlid=19194742&_r=0 For the full draft of the report, go to http://ipcc-wg2.gov/AR5/report/final-drafts/.

Now a professor of economics at New York University, Easterly is unsparing his depiction of the vast gulf between lofty intentions and actual accomplishments, and questions the industry of well-intended Western development aid.[77] To drive home the point, Easterly points out that "the West spent $2.3 trillion in foreign aid over the last five decades and still had not managed to get 12 cent medicines to children to prevent half of all malaria deaths. The West spent $2.3 trillion and still had not managed to get $4 bed nets to poor families. The West spent $2.3 trillion and still had not managed to get $3 to each new mother to prevent five million child deaths."[78]

Easterly's assessment? The big plan goals of Western governments, banks and non-profit organizations to end poverty are tantamount to an equestrian program setting as its goal a Kentucky Derby-winning cow.[79] These big plans are often demeaning to the people they are ostensibly designed to help, and they simply do not work. In contrast, more modest, feet-on-the-ground local initiatives that meaningfully involve real people in real places in real time in the process of defining and implementing life-and-community improvement goals almost always yield positive results. When missionary efforts at human betterment on a people's own terms have worked—and they have—it is because of this incarnational principle at the heart of their Gospel.

Abbreviations

ABCFM American Board of Commissioners for Foreign Missions.

ACAB Wilson, James Grant and John Fiske (eds.). *Appleton's Cyclopaedia of American Biography*. Revised edition. New York: D. Appleton and Company, 1999.

BDCM Anderson, Gerald H (ed.). *Biographical Dictionary of Christian Missions.* New York: Macmillan Reference USA, Simon & Schuster Macmillan, 1997.

CMSP Dennis, James Shepard. *Christian Missions and Social Progress: A Sociological Study of Foreign Missions*, vol. 1–3. New York: Fleming H. Revell, 1897–1906.

---

77 William Easterly, *The Elusive Quest for Growth: Economists' Adventures and Misadventures in the Tropics* (Boston, MA: MIT Press, 2002).

78 William Easterly, *The White Man's Burden: Why the West's Efforts to Aid the Rest Have Done So Much Ill and So Little Good* (New York, NY: Penguin, 2010): 4. See also his more recent *The Tyranny of Experts: Economists, Dictators, and the Forgotten Rights of the Poor* (New York, NY: Basic 2014).

79 Ibid., 11.

CSFM Dennis, James Shepard. *Centennial Survey of Foreign Missions: A Statistical Supplement to "Christian Missions and Social Progress".* New York: Fleming H. Revell, 1902.

Dennis Papers
James Shepard Dennis Papers, compiled by Paul A. Byrnes, Spring 1977. Union Theological Seminary Archives, New York.

Edinburgh 1910–I
World Missionary Conference, 1910, *Report of Commission I: Carrying the Gospel to all the Non-Christian World.* Edinburgh and London: Oliphant, Anderson & Ferrier, 1910.

New York 1900
Ecumenical Missionary Conference, New York, 1900, *Report of the Ecumenical Conference on Foreign Missions, Held in Carnegie Hall and Neighboring Churches.* London: Religious Tract Society, 1900.

SACM *Statistical Atlas of Christian Missions: Containing a Directory of Mission Societies, a Classified Summary of Statistics, an Index of Mission Stations, and a Series of Specially Prepared Maps of Mission Fields.* Compiled by Sub-Committees of Commission I, "On Carrying the Gospel to All the Non-Christian World," As an Integral Part of its Report to the World Missionary Conference, Edinburgh, June 14–23, 1910. Edinburgh: World Missionary Conference, 1910.

TFT Warren, William. *These for Those. Our Indebtedness to Foreign Missions; or, What We Get for What We Give.* Portland, Maine: Hout, Fogg and Breed, 1870.

Bibliography

Askew, Thomas. "The New York 1900 Ecumenical Missionary Conference: A Centennial Reflection," *International Bulletin of Missionary Research*, Vol. 24, No. 4 (October 2000): 146–154.

Bebbington, David W. *Evangelicalism in Modern Britain: A History from the 1730s to the 1980s* (Unwin Hyman/Routledge, 1989).

Bonk, Jonathan J. *"Not the Bloom, but the Root . . .": Conversion and Its Consequences in Nineteenth-Century Protestant Missionary Discourse.* New Haven, CT: Yale Divinity School Library, 2003.

———. "'And they marveled . . .' Mammon as miracle in Western missionary encounter." A paper presented at the annual meeting of the Yale-Edinburgh History on the History of the Missionary Movement and Non-Western Christianity, convened at the Centre for the Study of Christianity in the Non-Western World at the University of Edinburgh (July 1–3, 2004).

Briggs, John and Ian Sellers (eds.). *Victorian Nonconformity*. London: Edward Arnold, 1973.

Carey, William. *An Enquiry into the Obligations of Christians, to use means for the Conversion of the Heathens. In which the Religious State of the Different Nations of the World, the Success of Former Undertakings, and the Practicability of Further Undertaking, are Considered.* Leicester: Printed and sold by Ann Ireland, and the other Booksellers in Leicester; J. Johnson, St. Paul's Church yard; T. Knott, Lombard Street; R. Dilly, in the Poultry, London; and Smith, at Sheffield. [Price One Shilling and Six-pence.] MDCCXCII. (New facsimile edition published by the Carey Kingsgate Press, 1961).

Dennis, James S. *Centennial Survey of Foreign Missions: A Statistical Supplement to "Christian Missions and Social Progress," being a Conspectus of the Achievements and Results of Evangelical Missions in all Lands at the Close of the Nineteenth Century.* New York, Chicago, Toronto: Fleming H. Revell Company, 1902.

———. *Christian Missions and Social Progress: A Sociological Study of Foreign Missions*. 3 Volumes. New York, Chicago, Toronto: Fleming H. Revell Company, 1897, 1899, 1906.

———. *Foreign Missions A Century*. New York, Chicago, Toronto: Fleming H. Revell, 1893.

East, David Jonathan. *Western Africa: Its Condition, And Christianity the Means of its Recovery.* London: Houlston & Stoneman, 1844.

Easterly, William. *The Elusive Quest for Growth: Economists' Adventures and Misadventures in the Tropics*. Boston, MA: MIT Press, 2002.

———. *The Tyranny of Experts: Economists, Dictators, and the Forgotten Rights of the Poor*. New York, NY: Basic 2014.

———. *The White Man's Burden: Why the West's Efforts to Aid the Rest Have Done So Much Ill and So Little Good*. New York, NY: Penguin, 2010.

Ecumenical Missionary Conference New York, 1900. Report of the Ecumenical Conference on Foreign Missions, held in Carnegie Hall and Neighboring Churches, April 21 to May 1. 2 Volumes. London: Religious Tract Society; and New York: American Tract Society, 1900.

Galbraith, John Kenneth. "The 1929 Parallel," *Atlantic Monthly*, 259, No. 1 (January, 1987): 62.

Gillis, Justin. "Panel's Warning on Climate Risk: Worst is Yet to Come," *NY Times* (Monday, March 31, 2014).

Glover, Jonathan. *Humanity: A Moral History of the Twentieth Century*. New Haven: Yale University Press, 1999.

Goudzwaard, Bob. *Aid for the Overdeveloped West.* JordanStation: Wedge Publishing Foundation, 1975.

Greeley, Andrew M. *No Bigger Than Necessary: An Alternative to Socialism, Capitalism, and Anarchism.* Meridian Book. New York: New American Library, 1977.

Gregory, Paul. "The Chronic Dependence of Popular Religiosity upon Dysfunctional Psychosociological Conditions." *Evolutionary Psychology*, Vol. 7, No. 3 (July 2009): 398–441.

Heasman, Kathleen. *Evangelicals in Action: An Appraisal of their Social Work.* Letchworth: Geoffrey Bles Ltd., 1962.

Hocking, William Ernest. *Re-thinking Missions: A Laymen's Inquiry after One Hundred Years.* New York and London: Harper & Brothers, Publishers, 1932.

Huntington, Samuel P. *The Clash of Civilizations and the Remaking of World Order.* New York: Simon & Schuster, 1996.

Illich, Ivan. *The Church, Change and Development.* Chicago: Urban Training Center Press, 1970.

Judt, Tony. *Postwar: A History of Europe Since 1945.* New York: Penguin, 2005.

Kidd, Benjamin. *Social Evolution.* London and New York: Macmillan and Co., 1895.

Laurie, Thomas. *The Ely Volume; or, The Contributions of our Foreign Missions to Science and Human Well-Being.* Boston: American Board of Commissioners for Foreign Missions, Congregational House, 1881.

Magnuson, Norris. *Salvation in the Slums: Evangelical Social Work 1865–1920.* Grand Rapids: Baker Book House, 1977.

Newton, J.C. Calhoun. "The Contribution of Christian Missions to Sociology," *The Methodist Review: A Bimonthly Journal Devoted to Religion and Philosophy, Science and Literature* (May–June, 1898): 239–245.

Niebuhr, Reinhold. *Moral Man, Immoral Society: A Study in Ethics and Politics.* Luisville: Westminster John Knox Press, 2013.

Pfaff, William. *The Wrath of Nations: Civilization and the Furies of Nationalism.* New York: Simon & Schuster, 1993.

Schumacher, E.F. *Small is Beautiful: Economics as if People Mattered.* London: Blond & Briggs, 1973.

Smith, Sydney. "Indian Missions," *Edinburgh Review* (April 1809): 40, 42, 50.

Statistical Atlas of Christian Missions. Containing a Directory of Mission Societies, A Classified Summary of Statistics, an Index of Mission Stations, and a Series of Specially Prepared Maps of Mission Fields. Compiled by Sub-Committees of Commission I, "On Carrying the Gospel to All the Non-Christian World," As an Integral Part of its Report to the World Missionary Conference, Edinburgh, June 14–23, 1910. Edinburgh: World Missionary Conference, 1910.

Strachan, Hew. *The First World War.* Volume I. *To Arms.* London: Oxford University Press, 2002.

Taylor, Alva W. *The Social Work of Christian Missions.* Cincinnati: The Foreign Christian Missionary Society, 1914.

Walls, Andrew F. *The Cross-Cultural Process in Christian History.* Maryknoll, N.Y.: Orbis Books, 2002.

Warneck, Gustav. *Modern Missions and Culture: Their Mutual Relations*. Translated from the German by Thomas Smith. Edinburgh: James Gemmell, 1883.

Warren, William. *These for Those. Our Indebtedness to Foreign Missions: or, What we Get for What we Give.* Portland, Maine: Hout, Fogg and Breed, 1870.

Webster, Donovan. *Aftermath: The Remnants of War.* New York: Random House, 1996.

Wilkinson, Richard and Kate Pickett. *The Spirit Level: Why Greater Equality Makes Societies Stronger*. New York, NY: Bloomsbury Press, 2009.

Yoder, John Howard. *The Politics of Jesus*. Grand Rapids, Michigan: Eerdmans, 1994.

PART 3

CHAPTER 9

Mission and Money in Two Recent Mission Documents: The WCC's *Together towards Life* and Pope Francis's *Evangelii Gaudium*

Stephen Bevans

What I'd like to do in this short presentation is to briefly compare the reflection on issues around Mission, Money, and the Global Economy in two very recently issued documents on Mission: one the one hand, there is the statement *Together towards Life: Mission and Evangelism in Changing Landscapes*, promulgated at the Tenth Assembly of the World Council of Churches in Busan, Korea in late October of 2013; on the other there is *Evangelii Gaudium*—"The Joy of the Gospel," the Apostolic Exhortation published by Pope Francis in late November of the same year.[1] In the area of Mission, Money, and the Global Economy they are quite similar, and both are very challenging.

Together towards Life

Together towards Life (TTL) is the product of a long drafting and consulting process that had gone on since the Ninth WCC Assembly in Porto Alegre, Brazil in 2006. It is a document that locates Mission in the heart of the Triune God, and is developed in particular from the perspective of Pneumatology. It is an attempt to re-envision the church's Mission as led by the work of the Holy Spirit, always present in the midst of the world, calling the church to care for creation, and to be attentive to God's presence in people and places that the world's powerful have marginalized.

In the WCC Mission Statement, there are five particular places where the topic of Mission, Money and the Global Economy are dealt with.

---

1 World Council of Churches, *Together towards Life: Mission and Evangelism in Changing Landscapes*, http://www.menighetogmisjon.no/wp-content/uploads/2012/11/Mission_statement_approved_KV_2012l.pdf; Pope Francis, *Evangelii Gaudium*, http://www.vatican.va/holy_father/francesco/apost_exhortations/documents/papa-francesco_esortazione-ap_20131124_evangelii-gaudium_en.html.

 | DOI 10.1163/9789004318496_011

The first is in paragraph 7, part of the introductory section of the document that anticipates much of its content. "We are living in a world in which faith in mammon threatens the gospel." This paragraph depicts the Market Economy almost in terms of another religion that offers salvation through unlimited growth, but which in fact is set to destroy not only people's economic life, but their spiritual life as well. The great challenge, the paragraph argues, is how to win over the market, and prevent "economic and ecological injustice on a global scale."

In some ways, paragraphs 30 and 31 echo paragraph 7. Located in the first chapter that speaks of the life-giving mission of the Spirit, they fall under the subsection entitled "Transformative Spirituality." Mission is lived out of a spirituality that transforms people's lives and their world, and one of the great inhibitors of such spirituality is "the policy of unlimited growth through the domination of the global free market" that "is an ideology that claims to be without alternative." The life-giving work of the Spirit is never on the side of a status-quo that exists to maintain the privileges of the powerful. Jesus was clear that we "cannot serve God and mammon" (Matt 6:24). The service of an economy that only benefits one group of people at the expense of others is totally opposed to the Reign of God that God's Mission and the church's Mission serves.

Paragraph 108 is in the final section of the document that consists of a number of affirmations, summing up its main points. It basically repeats the previous three paragraphs that I have cited, emphasizing once again the contention that the service of Mammon in the free market global economy offers a false salvation that can only be a threat to the real life that the gospel promises. "Mission, then, is to denounce the economy of greed and to participate in and practice the divine economy of love, sharing, and justice."

In paragraph 48 the document speaks of Mission and Money, but from another perspective, quite akin to Jonathan Bonk's perspective in his classic book.[2] The passage appears in the second chapter of the document, which talks about Mission's radical commitment to justice by its attention to the places where the Spirit is unmistakably at work: among the world's marginalized. While Mission at its best "testifies to the reign of God at work in the world" (paragraph 47) it recognizes that missionaries are often allied with the privileged and the powerful in a particular situation, "more concerned with being in the centres of power, eating with the rich, and lobbying for money to maintain ecclesial bureaucracy." Bonk's call for the missionary to be one of the

2 Jonathan J. Bonk, *Missions and Money*, Revised and Expanded Edition (Maryknoll, NY: Orbis Books, 2006).

"righteous rich" is a particular challenge in these situations in which expatriate missionaries are inextricably bound, despite their best intentions, with powers that are agents of values at odds with the gospel they preach.[3]

Yet another danger of allying with the free market economy is mentioned in paragraph 62, which is located in the third chapter of the document on community, and in particular in a set of paragraphs reflecting on the bond between Mission and Christian Unity. The competition fostered in the market, the document observes, often translates into a kind of competition among churches and para-churches "to seek to be 'winners' over others." This kind of attitude is nothing but an aggressive proselytism that is fueled by the "profits" of numerical growth and greater power—something unworthy of the gospel to which missionaries witness.

These five locations in the document deal specifically with the issue of Missions and Money, and the corruption of power that obsession with money brings. However, as alluded to above, one of the major themes of the document—"the defining perspective" according to one of the document's principle authors,[4] is the theme of "Mission from the Margins." Rather than conceive Mission in terms of a powerful center moving toward a powerless periphery, the document wants to reverse this movement completely. Where real power is—the power of the Spirit—is among people, places, and situations that have been marginalized. In particular, marginalized people are graced with a particular power that manifests itself in weakness: "People on the margins have agency, and can often see what, from the centre, is out of view. People on the margins, living in vulnerable positions, often know what exclusionary forces are threatening their survival and can best discern the urgency of their struggles; people in positions of privilege have much to learn from the daily struggles of people living in marginal situations" (38). People on the margins have resources that have been under-utilized "reservoirs of active hope, collective resistance, and perseverance that are needed to remain faithful to the promised reign of God" (39). These victims of the global economy tell us that we must be very wary of any collusion with money, which despite its undeniable usefulness in Mission can very quickly reveal itself as "the root of all evil" (1.Tim 6:10).

3 Bonk, *Missions and Money*, 158–88.

4 Metropolitan Geevarghese Coorilos, "God of Life, Lead Us to Justice and Peace: Some Missiological Perspectives," *International Review of Mission* 102, 1 (396) (April, 2013): 5–16, at 9.

Evangelii Gaudium

Pope Francis's Apostolic Exhortation *Evangelii Gaudium* or "The Joy of the Gospel," was written as the Pope's reflections on the 2012 Synod of Bishops on the theme of what has come to be called the "New Evangelization," a phrase coined by Pope John Paul II to address the need to preach the gospel in the context of Western secularism and unbelief. At the Synod itself, and in this remarkable document, however, the term "New Evangelization" is interpreted more as a new way for the church to be in mission—to be a church with its doors always open (46), a community that exudes mercy and welcome (114), a community of irrepressible joy (10).

One of the main concerns of the document, however, to which the Pope devotes an entire, rather lengthy, chapter to the social dimension of evangelization, the relationship of Mission, in other words, to Money. It was this chapter in particular that incurred both the wrath of U.S. ultraconservative radio commentator Rush Limbaugh—who disparagingly said that the Pope was preaching "pure Marxism"[5]—to U.S. President Barack Obama, who openly admired the Pope's perspective.[6] In any case, the Pope is clear, there can be no adequate understanding of evangelization or Mission if there is no consideration of its economic dimensions (176). Catholic economist Jeffrey D. Sachs wrote that in terms of the issues facing global poverty and economic inequality, "we face a moral crisis much more than a financial crisis." Pope Francis, he says, "has lovingly reminded us that our highest aspirations are really within our grasp."[7]

Earlier in the document (53–54), Francis condemns the development of a "disposable culture" that is the emergence of something new. At its root, the pope contends, is a trickle-down theory of economics which promises much (see TLL 7, 30, and 31) but "which has never been confirmed by the facts." This new culture sees people not as society's underside, at society's margins, or merely disenfranchised, but as no longer as even a part of it. "The excluded are not the 'exploited' but the outcast, the 'leftovers'" (53). The market is a system that anaesthetizes those who have money and power against feeling any compassion, listening to the cry of the poor, or seeing people's need. "The culture of prosperity deadens us" (54).

5 "Rush Limbaugh: Pope is preaching 'pure Marxism,' http://religion.blogs.cnn.com/2013/12/02/rush-limbaugh-vs-the-pope/comment-page-169/.

6 "Barack Obama and Pope Francis: Unlikely Comrades?" http://www.cnn.com/2014/01/28/world/obama-pope-comrades/.

7 Jeffrey D. Sachs, "Market Reformer: An Economist considers Pope Francis' Critique of Capitalism," *America* 210, 10 (March 24, 2014): 18–20.

Taking a tack that is consistent with the rich body of Catholic Social Teaching, Pope Francis insists that economic development should serve the common good of society rather than simply privilege a few at the expense of the many. He emphasizes the virtue and practice of solidarity, which recognizes that "the social function of property and the universal destination of goods are realities that come before private property" (189). While human beings have a right to own property, ownership is justified, he says, only "by the need to protect and increase them [the goods people own] so that they can better serve the common good" (189). Solidarity is nothing less than a "decision to restore to the poor what belongs to them." He calls for access for all to education, health care, and employment with a just wage, so that they can "have adequate access to all the other goods which are destined for our common use" (191).

In a phrase that he repeated several times before the document was issued, Francis calls for a church "which is poor and for the poor" (198). Reminiscent of TTL's call for a mission from the margins, Francis insists that those who are not poor need to be evangelized by them. "The New Evangelization is an invitation to acknowledge the saving power at work in their lives and to put them at the center of the Church's pilgrim way" (198). Christians should "embrace the mysterious wisdom which God wishes to share with us through them" (198).

Although Francis is clearly against an overwhelming commitment to a Free Market, Neo-Liberal economy, as we have seen, he does—unlike TTL—have a kind word for Business, if only a small one. He speaks of Business as a "vocation, and a noble vocation" (203), but this nobility is achieved only if those who engage in it "see themselves challenged by a greater meaning in life," and so are able to commit themselves to "serve the common good" (203). In what is perhaps a broad reference to Capitalism, he urges those in Business to "increase the goods of this world," but only in order "to make them available to all" (203).[8]

Conclusion

In an earlier essay on *Together towards Life* I have critiqued the document's somewhat naïve approach to economics, suggesting that rather than undertake the almost Quixotic quest of converting the market economy, the church work to instill a greater ethical consciousness in women and men engaged in business in capitalist economies like those in the United States and Western

---

8 See the interesting reflections of Joseph J. Dunn, "Noble Vocations: A Definese of Business Education in Catholic Schools," *America* 210, 10 (March 24, 2014): 13–16.

Europe.[9] This perspective is also the one of my friend and mentor Gene Ahner in his important 2007 work on business ethics.[10] Pope Francis comes closer to this perspective, even though he, too, comes down rather hard on many aspects of Western capitalism. Nevertheless, in the same way that Francis speaks of a "logic of the incarnation" that moves Christianity into the cultivation and encouragement of cultural diversity (117), such a logic also points to the truth of the dignity of all creatures—the physical world, animals, human beings—that cannot be reduced to what they *have* or what they can *make*, but who they are. Creation is not a commodity to be bought, but a gift to be shared and cultivated. Money cannot buy the gift of creation; Mission needs to witness to this important, transforming Truth.

Bibliography

Ahner, Gene. *Business Ethics: Making a Life, Not Just a Living.* Maryknoll, NY: Orbis Books, 2007.

"Barack Obama and Pope Francis: Unlikely Comrades?" http://www.cnn.com/2014/01/28/world/obama-pope-comrades/ accessed in April 2014.

Bevans, Stephen. "*Together Towards Life*": Reflections on the Proposed WCC Mission Statement," *CMSM Forum*, August, 2013. http://www.cmsm.org/forum/forum_fall13_WCC_Statement.html accessed in April 2014.

Bonk, Jonathan J. *Missions and Money*, Revised and Expanded Edition. Maryknoll, NY: Orbis Books, 2006.

Coriilos, Geevarghese. "God of Life, Lead Us to Justice and Peace: Some Missiological Perspectives," *International Review of Mission* 102, 1 (396) (April, 2013): 5–16.

Dunn, Joseph J. "Noble Vocations: A Definese of Business Education in Catholic Schools," *America* 210, 10 (March 24, 2014): 13–16.

Francis, Pope. *Evangelii Gaudium.* http://www.vatican.va/holy_father/francesco/apost_exhortations/documents/papa-francesco_esortazione-ap_20131124_evangelii-gaudium_en.html accessed in April 2014.

9 Stephen Bevans, "*Together Towards Life*": Reflections on the Proposed WCC Mission Statement," *CMSM Forum*, August, 2013. http://www.cmsm.org/forum/forum_fall13_WCC_Statement.html. This essay was originally delivered at a Mission Training Course at the Finnish Evangelical Lutheran Mission, Helsinki, Finland, in August, 2013. 210, 10 (March 24, 2014): 20.

10 Gene Ahner, *Business Ethics: Making a Life, Not Just a Living* (Maryknoll, NY: Orbis Books, 2007).

"Rush Limbaugh: Pope is preaching 'pure Marxism,' http://religion.blogs.cnn.com/2013/12/02/rush-limbaugh-vs-the-pope/comment-page-169/ accessed in April 2014.

Sachs, Jeffrey D. "Market Reformer: An Economist considers Pope Francis' Critique of Capitalism," *America* 210, 10 (March 24, 2014): 18–20.

World Council of Churches, *Together towards Life: Mission and Evangelism in Changing Landscapes*, http://www.menighetogmisjon.no/wp-content/uploads/2012/11/Mission_statement_approved_KV_2012l.pdf accessed in April 2014.

CHAPTER 10

Mission and Money—Mapping the Field

Mika Vähäkangas

Today, any responsible talk concerning the economy and ethics should inevitably contain a discussion about the ethical dimensions of the capitalist system, either globally or locally, an issue which is even more important when the global capitalist system is approached in relation to Christian mission. This article responds to some of the underlying philosophical and theological issues raised by the rest of the contributors to this volume.[1]

Money and Power

It is common in contemporary Western mission movements to engage in self-flagellation concerning mission history which, indeed, provides many dimensions of which one should be less than proud. One of the questions often discussed is the economic imbalance between the sending and receiving countries: money and power are seen to have been on the side, and in the hands, of the missionary whereas the non-Christian population is often regarded as having been disenfranchised. However, this view is not sufficiently detailed and can therefore present us with a distorted picture. For example, at the time that the Finnish Missionary Society was established in Helsinki in 1859, periodical crop failures and man-made catastrophes like wars were causing starvation, displacement and death in Finland, and this actually continued to be the case over the following sixty years.[2] Not all sending countries were affluent. Therefore, Jon Bonk's approach, building on detailed archive materials, is able to provide us with more accurate glimpses of how the relationship between the trinity of Christianity, Western cultures and capitalism expressed itself.

Taking examples from the Protestant Western missionary movement, Bonk underlines how Christianization and civilization were seen to proceed hand in hand, noting that the progress of Western missions often went hand in hand with the progress of Western cultural hegemony. There have been, however,

1 This chapter is an expanded version of my comment on Kärkkäinen, Kanniainen, Wilfred and Bonk.

2 See Remes 1976.

 | DOI 10.1163/9789004318496_012

cases of missionaries geared towards different types of inculturation throughout the whole of Western mission history from, for example, Matteo Ricci,[3] through Bruno Gutmann,[4] to Vincent Donovan.[5] Furthermore, one may query whether even a radical mode of inculturation necessarily includes a cultural imperialistic dimension. If one considers all attempts to convert non-Christians to Christianity to be a form of cultural imperialism, then all conversion-oriented mission is bound to be categorized as cultural imperialism as it is impossible to delete all cultural background from the transmission of any kind of message; whenever one attempts to communicate something across the cultural boundaries, one tends to communicate at least some dimensions of the disseminating culture as well. This is due to the fact that there is no pure Gospel, no pure communication and therefore any attempt to influence a person of another culture can be labelled cultural imperialism. The message of the Western missionary movement was thus a Western reflection of the earlier versions of the Christian message(s) as there could not have been any other way of conveying the message(s) than through the missionary's culture.[6] Quite another question is, however, whether and to what extent Western missionaries were willing to tolerate local reinterpretations of Christianity.

Unless one subscribes to a nihilist or relativist position where there either is no truth or the truth is so subjective that anything goes, one can maintain that the person holding something to be true has the responsibility to share this truth with others. Let us imagine that a large tree has fallen across a biking route at a sharp corner. Would it not be your responsibility to warn other cyclists approaching the invisible danger rather than ignoring this responsibility on the grounds that they may have a different epistemology which either renders the tree non-existent or allows them to gain foresight of it before the actual visibility zone?[7] However, this right or even responsibility to share one's truth is always related to power. By considering that I know the truth better than the other with whom I want to share it, I propose placing myself in a position of power. Inasmuch as the others accept my truth claim as their new faith, they accept my proposed position. Only when this truth has genuinely become the other's property as their truth can this particular asymmetry be left behind. The fact that mission in the form of proclamation of Christian truth(s) always

3 Bevans & Schroeder 2004, 187–189.

4 Jaeschke 1985.

5 Donovan 2011.

6 For more on this see Vähäkangas 2010.

7 For a highly analytical discussion on the relationship between the ethical responsibility to respect the other and the responsibility of sharing the truth see Fridlund 2012.

involves a power dimension does not, by itself, render it immoral, however. Power relations are always there, no matter whether we accept or perceive them or not.[8] The issue is rather for what purposes that power is used, and how.

Naïve and simplistic faith in one's truth combined with power can be a fatal combination, a fact proved by many terrorist groups and repressive systems which have been backed by a genuine ideology and not simply search for personal or group gain.[9] Unfortunately, often Christian mission of the past, and sometimes even today, can serve as an example of naïve ethnocentric bigotry combined with economic and cultural or, especially during the colonial times, even political and military power. The inequality in power relations cannot be wished away, while different ways of attempting to share power are only actions that reduce the harm of inequality. The fact that someone in a position of power decides to share that power with someone else only reduces but does not terminate the power imbalance because, after all, the power sharing is a voluntary act on the part of the powerful. In addition to various attempts to share power an increased level of self-criticism or humility is absolutely necessary in order not to misuse a position of power. These qualities sprout from the insight that what I hold to be true is not and cannot be self-evidently true for all others who can likewise have good reasons for their faith.[10] This almost inevitably also leads me to doubt my own truth. The outcome of this process, if it does not lead to my abandonment of my truth, is what Paul Ricoeur calls "the second naïveté".[11] In this manner, the power relation is not decimated but its negative effects are reduced.

Thus, following the Lund philosopher of religion, Fridlund, the urge to convert the other to my truth can be ethical, at least in some instances. Yet, in order that it may be so, it must also be in line with other ethical demands, such as respect for the other.[12] Positions of power, like Western economic hegemony (that in due time may disappear), cannot be escaped and, consequently, the question should be how to use those positions in a responsible manner. There is also another issue of note which relates to the global capital order: are

8 Michel Foucault points out that all knowledge presupposes power (Foucault 1979, 27). Therefore, power and power relations are always there. A human society needs to produce knowledge in order to exist.

9 See e.g. Meyer 2008, 13 discussing the concept of duty as seen through the Kantian categorical imperative combined with trust/faith in a totalitarian system resulting in gross human rights violations.

10 Bevans, forthcoming.

11 Ricoeur 1969, 348–353.

12 Fridlund 2012. On the ethical minimum requirements see WCC, Pontificial Council for Interreligious Dialogue & WEA 2011.

globalization and capitalism results of Christianity having an intrinsic relation to it?

Christianity, Globalization and Capitalism

I have argued elsewhere that Christianity can be seen as one dimension of, and an inspiration to, globalization. Christian universalistic ideas, not least the vision to take the message to the whole world, and ideas of interethnic communality, reflect an early genuinely global thought pattern. Of course, this did not appear spontaneously because Judaism already had such tendencies. While representative of globalization (although not all globalization is Christianity), Christianity also includes several different modes of the phenomenon. For example, Christian ideas of mission, coupled with the European formation of national states, contributed to the emergence of European colonialism which can be seen as one decisive step towards the intensification of a global economy and therefore a decisive step towards the formation of global capitalism.[13]

Thus it seems undeniable that Christianity has a strong link to globalization, or at least to some forms of it. Simultaneously, it must be noted that Christianity has also served as a strong impetus to the development of local cultures and identities, among which may be counted European, Ethiopian, Coptic, Assyrian, Armenian and Filipino Catholic examples. However, these local identities are linked with global identities and visions in a manner that reflects the notion of glocalization.[14] In Christian theology and discourse, this global dimension is not seen as problematic, rather the contrary. Therefore, to speak of Christian global identities and visions is usually considered unproblematic whereas globalization more generally has a much more ambiguous reputation due to its interlinking with capitalism. Therefore, even if the global nature of Christianity often involves culturally imperialist traits that can be considered ethically problematic, it seems that more serious ethical problems related to the global dimensions of Christianity are related to the global economic imbalances that are interwoven with power relations in Christian missions.[15] And, indeed, as Gerrie ter Haar argues in this book, inadequate ways of dealing with these inequalities among the mission partners can lead to a reinforcement of inequality. An unacceptable state of affairs like material

13 For a more detailed discussion on Christianity as globalization see Vähäkangas, forthcoming.

14 Vähäkangas, forthcoming.

15 See Helander & Niwagila 1996; Vähäkangas 2003.

inequality can be a thorn in the flesh which leaves the partners no peace, but any solution that seemingly removes the inequality while leaving the power structures intact, albeit hidden, misleads the partners into ignoring the underlying problems.

Judaism and Christianity have been involved with monetary systems for millennia, Christianity having been formed in the context of an early or pre-capitalist monetary and colonial system, as pointed out by Ulrich Duchrow in this book. Yet this marriage is an uneasy one. One needs to ask whether the relationship between Christianity and capitalism is intrinsic or extrinsic: can capitalism be understood without Christianity and vice versa? The renowned Weberian theory creates a connection between Protestantism, work ethos and accumulation of capitals,[16] and one may wonder whether the relation is accidental or intrinsic; that is, whether capitalism emerged in Western Europe at a certain historical period marked by Protestantism by chance or whether Protestant faith at least, if not Christianity in general, was a sine qua non for this process. On the other hand, it is clear from later experience that once this virulent economic order was established, it has been able to thrive in many non-Christian settings like Japan and China.

Is capitalism a logical conclusion of Christian faith and theology? That several of Jesus' parables make use of early capitalist economic structures (e.g. investing the talents in Matt 25:14–30 & Luke 19:11–27; renting a vineyard Mark 12:1–12 & synoptic parallels; the dishonest steward Luke 16:1–9) can either be taken as a proof of such intrinsic connection or merely as an indication of Jesus' contextual approach that took into account the economic realities of a society burdened by Roman occupation and taxation. In my eyes, the second alternative appears more likely. However, there are also profoundly anti-wealth dimensions to the Bible, both in the Old Testament prophetic literature as well as in the New Testament (camel through eye of a needle Mark 10:25 & synoptic parallels; Lukan beatitudes Luke 6:20–26; Magnificat Luke 1:46–55; not being able to serve both God and Mammon Matt 6:24 & Luke 16:13; socialist traits in the Acts). Should Biblical and later theological criticism of debts, interest and blatant differences in standards of living be understood as Christian self-criticism or rather as something external to Christianity being castigated? The Biblical witness looks very ambiguous. On the one hand, not only Protestantism is linked with capitalism; the Catholic Church has also been an ardent defender of private ownership and there have been and still are numerous links between (the spread of) capitalism, mission and Christianity. On the other hand, countless Christian utopian movements have built on

16 Weber 2000.

egalitarianism and common ownership, and there are still missions which are ardently opposed to capitalist modes of production, one example being presented by Tinyiko Maluleke in this book. Ulrich Duchrow's contribution is also an example of a Christian voice strongly dissociating capitalism from basic Christian values. Based on these varying views one can maintain that disputes over the ethics of ownership are bound to be partly in-house Christian business even if the rest of the world cannot remain outside. It is little wonder that there are tensions and paradoxes as well as a great deal of Christian hypocrisy surrounding economics. Christian churches are interested partners in discussions of the ethics of the economy on the basis of their complicity in creating the present world order, and also as critics and stakeholders—one should not forget that many churches have been notable owners of land and other means of production throughout history.

Due to this ambiguous history, and the variety of ways in which Christians have responded to the ethical challenge of poverty and prosperity, it is not a fruitful approach to suggest that the Christian position offers a single view of this question. Rather, one needs to acknowledge the plurality of voices and engage in theological debate with them, for example with the many forms of prosperity Gospel. In spite of the fact that I may not subscribe to any form of Prosperity Gospel, I have to agree that its versions offer possible interpretations of the Bible, approaching and assessing them with an open mind.[17] The result may still be that I find some or all of them incompatible with my Biblical interpretation, that is, theologically false, or even ethically unacceptable due to the social and economic consequences of their doctrines. In that case, it would be my responsibility to attempt to convert my interlocutors to a position I consider more ethical or theologically correct. In this discussion, different cultural, social and psychological analyses are of great help; without them a proper ethical assessment is not possible.[18]

What seems clear is that emerging capitalism and Western colonialism were intrinsically connected. Portuguese colonialism was first launched in the form of global exploration in order to secure better connections in international trade; soon the colonies became means of acquiring raw materials and slaves, and eventually they became markets for industrial commodities. Was Christian mission a random passenger on the colonialist and capitalist ships to the ends of the earth or is it impossible to separate it from the colonialist-capitalist twins?

---

17 This is what I have attempted to do with one case of the Prosperity Gospel in Vähäkangas 2015.

18 E.g. Hasu 2012.

Considering that money is a Biblical topic and that it is an important, if not the most important, political topic of today, it is surprising how little money is referred to in theological work. Veli-Matti Kärkkäinen even goes so far as to say that theologians avoid talking economy. One may wonder whether this is a form of hypocrisy in which one avoids looking at the foundational problems in oneself.

Economic Systems and Mission

Theological discourse on economic systems tends to use a moral, sometimes even moralistic, language. There, the emphasis is often on ideals and ideas and attempts to change the whole economic system, as Steve Bevans points out in this book. According to the critics of such discourse, it often fails to consider concrete approaches, which easily leads to a blame game against the actors in the economic sphere. This is perhaps the weakest dimension of the otherwise excellent World Council of Churches' mission document *Together towards Life*. The point of departure is thus not always fair towards real life actors in the sense that one is comparing ideals with realities on the ground,[19] although naturally, when such criticism is made in a constructive manner, this need not be a problem. Bevans' solution to this moralist's dilemma of approaching reality via comparison with ideals is to "instill a greater ethical consciousness in women and men engaged in business in capitalist economies" (p. 177 in this book). This appears to me to be a realistic compromise between useless moralism and the even more common laissez-faire attitude in theology towards economic issues.

Economistic references to economic systems, in their turn, tend to use the language of natural laws: the way economic systems function is perceived as given.[20] Thus the state or individuals can influence the economy by choosing modes in which to act vis-à-vis the system, which will then respond according to its laws. The system itself, however, cannot be changed or challenged. The view is thus relatively deterministic and limits the ethical responsibility of a person to reacting and responding to the functions of the system. Therefore, one may pose a number of questions to Professor Kanniainen concerning the

---

19 This is how e.g. the Finnish Lutheran bishops' statement on fair society was criticized by the economists. The statement: Kohti yhteistä hyvää, 1999. On the discussion around the statement as well as references to similar ecclesiastical statements elsewhere see Parviainen 1999.

20 See Hallamaa 1999, 206–208.

extent to which one can actually steer the economy. How much of the economy is predestined and how much of it can be changed? How strict and encompassing are its laws? Who has the power to steer the economy—if anyone? Is it even ethical to tamper with the economy if it functions with such regularity?

One of the central dimensions of capitalist or so-called free market economies is incentive. In theological thought, avarice is traditionally considered a mortal sin whereas in capitalist theory-building it is a human's natural response to economic realities. In a sense it is even a virtue because it leads to economic activity.[21] However, when capitalism, the system of plenty, is not functioning in a world of limitless resources, economic activity is no longer necessarily only a positive thing that lifts humans out of hunger and misery. Avarice leads humankind to overspend the earth's resources, the earth's commons in particular: clean, natural air and water, not (usually) owned by individuals or even states, turn into the free objects of merciless exploitation. As the result, contemporary generations are now savouring the bread of those to follow.[22]

The standard economistic answer to this problem would be to point out that it does not lie with the free market but rather that the earth's commons have not been priced. Were they priced it would no longer be profitable to waste them. However, who is to put a price tag on clean air which blows where it wills? Would it be possible to put a fair price on such a commodity? And who should receive the payments as owner, and what kind of likelihood would there be to force the whole world to pay for it?

To go a bit further in argumentation—considering the way economic disparities cause deaths, making the life of, for example, a Bangladeshi textile mill worker worth just a couple of coins—one should also consider whether a human life should have a price tag and whether that price tag should be the same for everyone. In the economic sphere of insurance, costs and profits it seems obvious that our lives have different values.[23] How much for a Chinese or South African miner or a Bangladeshi industrial worker? Or a British engineer, American truck driver or Brazilian professor?

In practice human life in the poorest countries seems to function very much in the way of the earth's commons. Yet setting a price tag on a human life comes questionably close to human trafficking and slave trade. Modern medicine has led governments into a situation where similar decisions need to be made in

---

21 See Parviainen 1999, 360.

22 This has been a concern since the Club of Rome's famous report *The Limits to Growth* (Meadows et al. 1972).

23 On humans' varying value to the economic system see Hallamaa 1999, 214–215. For her, however, all values are not based merely on market value (p. 216).

somewhat softer forms when prioritizing between various forms of health care or between health care and other expenses. Naturally, the most cost efficient way of saving human lives would be to drop expenditure on advanced medicine in rich countries and use the funds for basic medical services for the poor countries instead. Yet we hide behind the idea that human life is priceless. And so it is: my life and those of my nearest and dearest are such that no sacrifice is too great, whereas the lives of the distant poor are, in the eyes of many of us, priceless in the sense of worthless. The global free market values everything in terms of money. Things not having a price tag are not of any value and emotional value seems, mostly, only to adhere to those nearest to us. Who should be setting the price tags on humans and on what grounds?

These grotesque questions force us to admit that our interpretations of economics are based on philosophical anthropology. What is a human being? How is she, basically: *iustus* (just), or *peccator* (sinner); or *simul iustus et peccator* (both just and sinner)? How should a human being be? Is that all there should be? Or is humanity on the way to somewhere? Are there ulterior goals to our human existence?[24]

Another major moral and practical issue that concerns the so-called free market economy is pointed out by Professor Wilfred. He reminds us that crooks prosper, thus bringing the dark side of competition into view. One may wonder whether this is a matter of a malfunction in the system or an inherent part of capitalism. In many countries of today, much of the great capital has been accumulated in ways that are ethically condemnable or questionable. Land grabbing from indigenous populations, corruption, colonialism, slavery and other forms of ruthless exploitation are behind many forms of both older (e.g. USA, Brazil, Belgium, UK) and newer capital (e.g. Russia and many other post-Communist countries, many majority world countries). It is problematic whether one could find a country that could serve as an example of ethically sound capitalism founded on economic theories. There are, no doubt, companies that have been able to navigate between moral hazards, but national economies where fair play has formed the basis of organization since the compilation of capital are fewer on the ground.

All this may suggest demanding increased government regulation. This, however, can lead to ridiculous results like the Vietnamese rats referred to by Professor Kanniainen in this volume. Central regulation also tends to produce systems that are globally weak in performance, and in some cases blatantly irresponsible towards nature or even the needs of the people. The Soviet Union, with its huge central regulatory system, was a major ecological

---

24 See Hallamaa 1999.

catastrophe as well as a system that collapsed largely due to its inefficiency and lack of consideration for the needs of its own people. In such a system, avarice is expressed rather through bureaucracy than the market. The so-called free market economy, on the other hand, is also wasteful and leads to huge inequalities. Only tight government regulation has been able to curb the environmental damage caused by capitalism—something which the free market has not been able to do. Discussion of Piketty's theory on the relationship between work and capital in the formation and accumulation of wealth has also brought the question of inequality back to the limelight.[25] So, basically, what we have in front of us is a frying pan and a fire.

Conclusion: Theologians and the Global Third Way?

There are many who do not wish to encounter either alternative, leading to the search for a third way. It is possible to maintain ideological faith in capitalism or socialism by arguing that there has never been a true capitalist or socialist system, rather that the ideologies have always been imperfectly implemented. However, if humans are basically sinners, then one may conclude that there is no point in hankering after the perfect capitalist or socialist system. The third way could thus be an improved version of either of the basic models, taking into account the human condition.

Today, national economies, environmental hazards and cultural exchanges have become so global that insular solutions à la North Korea are hardly plausible. Consequently, there is a major need to seek out global common ground for the way we see human nature, the worth of human life, modes of global ecological survival and common security. We are, therefore, back to square one—philosophical anthropology—only this time with the further twist of a global and intercultural/interreligious dimension. This may be one of the keys to the survival of our children and grandchildren.

The responsibility of theologians in this situation is not to avoid discussion of the economy but to join it, contributing critical and constructive views on the values behind the economic debate. Additionally, all Christian theology, even here, needs to see itself as a voice among those of several religions and to search for a deepened and widened interreligious sharing. In this, missiologists as theologians concentrating on interreligious encounters have a special role to play.

---

25 Piketty 2014.

Bibliography

Bevans, Stephen B. "Fair or Foul? Contextual Theology and Criteria for Orthodoxy" in Patrik Fridlund & Mika Vähäkangas (eds.). *Philosophical and Theological Responses to Syncretism*, forthcoming.

Bevans, Stephen B. & Roger P. Schroeder. *Constants in Context: A Theology of Mission for Today.* Maryknoll, NY: Orbis Books, 2004.

Donovan, Vincent. *The Missionary Letters of Vincent Donovan 1957–1973.* Ed. John P. Bowen. Eugene, OR: Pickwick, 2011.

Foucault, Michel. *Discipline and Punish: The Birth of the Prison.* Harmondsworth, Middlesex: Penguin/Peregrine Books, 1979.

Fridlund, Patrik. "I See that from Both Sides Now: On the Intricate Relation between Dialogue and Conversion" in *Australian Religious Studies Review* 25/3 (2012): 254–272.

Hallamaa, Jaana. "Kristinuskon kertomus ja eurooppalainen sosiaalietiikka" in Jaana Hallamaa (ed.), *Rahan teologia ja Euroopan kirkot: Lopun ajan sosiaalietiikka*, 139–225. Jyväskylä: Atena, 1999.

Hasu, Päivi. "Prosperity Gospels and Enchated World Views—Two Responses to Socio-economic Transformations in Tanzanian Pentecostal-charismatic Christianity." in *Pentecostalism and Development: Churches, NGOs and Social Change in Africa.* Ed. Dena Freeman. Basingstoke: Palgrave Macmillan, 2012, 67–86.

Helander, Eila & Niwagila, Wilson. *Partnership and Power: A Quest for Reconstruction in Mission.* Makumira Publications 7. Erlangen: Verlag der ev.-luth. Mission, 2003.

Jaeschkeä, Ernst. *Bruno Gutmann: His Life, His Thoughts and His Works: An Early Attempt at a Theology in an African Context.* Erlangen: Verlag der ev.-luth. Mission, 1985.

Kohti yhteistä hyvää. Suomen evankelis-luterilaisen kirkon piispojen puheenvuoro hyvinvointiyhteiskunnan tulevaisuudesta, 1999. http://evl.fi/EVLMateriaalit.nsf/Documents/9FD845C60C0C1703C22570B9004E93EF/$File/kohtiyhteistahyvaa.pdf?openElement Accessed 2014–06–13.

Meadows, Donella H. et al. *The Limits to Growth: A Report for the Club of Rome's Project on the Predicament of Mankind.* New York: Universe Books, 1972.

Meyer, Michel, *Petite métaphysique de la différence: Religion, art et société.* Paris: Presses universitaires de France, 2008.

Parvianen, Seija. "Piispojen luterilainen sosiaalietiikka globaalitalouden paineessa" in *Kansantaloudellinen aikakauskirja* 95/2 (1999): 353–372.

Piketty, Thomas. *Capital in the Twenty-First Century.* Cambridge, Mass. & London: The Belknap Press of Harvard University Press, 2014.

Remes, Viljo. *Lähetysharrastus Suomessa 1835–1858.* Sata vuotta suomalaista lähetystyötä 1859–1959 vol. 1. Helsinki: Suomen Lähetysseura, 1976.

Ricoeur, Paul. *The Symbolism of Evil*. Boston: Beacon Press, 1969.

Vähäkangas, Mika. "Christian Partnership as an Ideal in Inter-Church Cooperation" in *The Role of Mission in the Future of Lutheran Theology,* Viggo Mortensen (ed.), 163–202. Occasional Papers 6. Aarhus: Centre for Multireligious Studies, University of Aarhus, 2003.

———. "Modelling Contextualization in Theology", in *Swedish Missiological Themes* 98/3 (2010): 279–306.

———. "The Prosperity Gospel in the African Diaspora: Unethical Theology or Gospel in Context?" in *Exchange* 44/4 (2015): 353–380.

———. "Christianity as Globalization", in *Orizonturi teologice* forthcoming.

WCC (World Council of Churches), Pontificial Council for Interreligious Dialogue & WEA (World Evangelical Alliance). *Christian Witness in a Multi-Religious World: Recommendations for Conduct*, 2011. Available at https://www.oikoumene.org/en/resources/documents/wcc-programmes/interreligious-dialogue-and-cooperation/christian-identity-in-pluralistic-societies/christian-witness-in-a-multi-religious-world Accessed 2015-10-15.

Weber, Max. *Die Protestantische Ethik und der "Geist" des Kapitalismus.*3e Auflage. Klaus Lichtblan and Johannes Weiß (eds.). Weinheim: Beltz Athenäum, 2000.

Index